Excel 5.0 Slick Tricks

Excel 5.0
Slick Tricks

• • • • • • • • • • • • • •

Joan Bannan

RANDOM HOUSE
ELECTRONIC PUBLISHING

New York

Excel 5.0 Slick Tricks

Copyright © 1994 by Joan Bannan

Composed and produced by Parker-Fields Typesetters Ltd.

Published in the United States by Random House, Inc., New York, and simultaneously in Canada by Random House of Canada, Limited.

Manufactured in the United States of America

First Edition

0   9   8   7   6   5   4   3   2   1

ISBN 0-679-79176-0

Trademarks

New York   Toronto   London   Sydney   Auckland

Contents

Acknowledgments **ix**

Introduction **xi**

1 New Features 1

Files and File Management **1**

New Features for Editing **4**

On-Screen Help Features **6**

New Features for Creating Formulas **7**

New Workspace Operations and Options **9**

Additional New Features **11**

2 Basic Slick Tricks 13

Workbooks **13**

Workbook Features **14**

Opening Files **19**

Windows and Panes **22**

Exiting **25**

Printing **25**

Saving Your Work **26**

Help Features **29**

3 Worksheet Editing 33

Slick Tricks for Selecting 33
Entering and Deleting Data 36
Entering Dates and Times 42
Editing 44
Moving and Copying 48

4 Worksheet Formatting 57

Rows and Columns 61
Text 62
Alignment 63
Borders 64
Numbers 66
AutoFormats 70
Styles 71

5 Toolbars and Workspace Options 75

The Workspace 75
Toolbars 78

6 Views, Outlining, and Printing 87

Views 87
Outlines 93
Printing 95

7 Slick Tricks for Formulas 103

References 104
Apply Names 109
Formula Toolbar Buttons 111
Functions 116
Auditing 120
Locating Problems in Formulas 123

8 Lists, Tables, and Databases 129

Use a Dataform **130**
Sorting **133**
Automatic Subtotals **137**
Filtering **141**
Importing and Consolidating Data **147**

9 Analyzing Data 151

Getting Results **151**
Scenario Manager **156**
Solver **159**

10 Pivot Tables 163

11 Creating Charts 177

What Is a Chart? **177**
Creating Charts with Templates **178**
Choosing Chart Data **180**
The ChartWizard **181**
Chart Parts **186**
Chart Types **188**
Adding Titles, Labels, and Other Chart Items **189**
AutoFormats **193**
Add Objects to Charts **194**

12 Editing Charts 195

Changing the Chart **195**
Sizing **206**
Formatting Tricks **207**

13 Graphics and Object Linking 209

Creating Graphics **211**
Editing and Formatting Graphics **221**
Importing and Exporting **225**

14 Visual Basic and Macros 231

Basic Macro Recording **231**
A Choice of Language **232**
Attached Macros **240**
VBA Help **243**

15 Top-Ten Slick Tricks 245

Most Frequently Used General Shortcuts **250**
Most Frequently Used Shortcuts When Writing Formulas **250**

Appendix 253

Index 265

To the king,
eternal, immortal, invisible,
the only wise God.

Acknowledgments

A special thanks to everyone, professionally and personally, who helped get this book written, tested, edited, and typeset with incredible speed.

To Belinda Catalona and Carole McClendon, my agents at Waterside Productions.

To Tracy Smith, Random House Senior Editor.

To Kim Fryer, Random House Editor.

To Kay Yarborough Nelson, Slick Trick series editor.

To Michael Aquilante, Project Editor.

To Neal Bratchun, the genius in Tulsa, for great suggestions and for scrutinizing the formula and programming chapters.

To Alan Mangini, for existing Excel spreadsheets and chart examples.

To Judy Whittle, fellow author, who made her Macintosh available for testing.

To Lora Banks, for waking me from the confusion caused by the convergence of data tables, add-in functions, and an around-the-clock writing schedule.

To Tina Fikejs, who took Peter when my choice was to miss my deadline or give my three-year-old away temporarily.

To Ella Larsen, for more than once preparing dinner so that I could work until late and still enjoy a wonderful, nutritious meal.

To my children, Charley, Tina, Jennifer, Tony, Debra, and Peter; and grandchildren, Ryan, Beeper (Alan), and Timothy for support and prayer (especially Beeper, who now owns a fictitious airline).

Introduction

This *Slick Tricks* series is based on a simple idea: You don't have to know a lot about a program to get some real power from it! All of the software you buy today is incredibly rich in features, but most of us will use only a few of them because we don't want to wade through the manual or spend hours working through exercises.

But beyond the programs' intimidating interfaces lies a wealth of tricks that you can master easily—without taking a complex tutorial on a program's whole feature set, or thumbing through a huge doorstop-sized tome. You can flip through the pages of this *Slick Tricks* book, find a topic that's related to what you're working on, and see how to do a trick or use a shortcut that will make your work a lot easier.

Why Slick Tricks?

Most of these tricks are just that: tricks, short statements about how to use a keyboard shortcut to do something faster, or how to go through a back door to get a complicated sequence done quickly. We're not starting from ground zero and teaching you the program's basics, though. To get the most from a *Slick Tricks* book, you'll at least need to be familiar with the program's absolute basics, such as selecting with a mouse (if you're in a Windows or Macintosh book) or reading a prompt (if you're in a DOS book).

Using a *Slick Tricks* Book

You can think of a *Slick Tricks* book as a cookbook—browse its pages and try out a "recipe" or two. But these are fairly "right-brained" books, so you may need to browse until you find the recipe you need. These books offer basic tricks—the ones you'll use all the time—and include tricks for customizing, printing, managing your documents, and any special features of the programs. These short, friendly books can't possibly cover *all* the features of a program or system, but neither would you want them to.

Trick

You'll see different icons in a *Slick Tricks* book. The professor indicates a hands-on procedure or trick, showing you how to do something. A "Tip" gives you a helpful, general hint about how to approach a task or work out a solution to your problem. "Traps" tell you procedures to avoid, and "sidebars" provide background material for a particular topic. These *Slick Tricks* books won't always take you step by step through every possibility and every detail, but programs today have incredibly good Help systems, and you can use them to get details about a specific topic. So, do that.

Tip

Trap

Each *Slick Tricks* book follows the general conventions of the program or system it's about. You'll find the keys you need to press in boldface type and what you actually need to type in sans serif type, like this: Press **F12** and type weekly report. In all of these, if you need to press two keys at once, you'll see them with a plus sign between them, like this: Press **Ctrl+Z**.

Sidebar

Excel 5.0 Slick Tricks addresses both the Windows and Macintosh versions of the program, so it uses a different set of conventions. If you're using the Windows version, you access the menu bar by using the Alt key. On a Mac, you use the forward slash (/) key. To simplify the text, when keystrokes are given, the first one is the combined Windows/Macintosh code: Alt/. For example, if you need to choose the Open command from the File menu, you'll see:

Alt/, F, O

You'll see lots of keyboard shortcuts like this, because using the keyboard is often much faster than choosing from menus.

In all other cases, if there's a difference in keystrokes:

Ⓦ will precede the Windows command.

Ⓜ will precede the Macintosh command.

Macintosh users: When you see the **Enter** key, you can use the Return key on your keyboard. When you see the **Esc** key, that's your Command+period. Both Windows and Macintosh users will see **Shift+click** as the instruction for holding down the Shift key and clicking with the mouse, and **Ctrl+click** as the instruction for holding down the **Ctrl** (Control) key and clicking.

You're on Your Way

· ·

That's it! You can figure out the rest as you go along. For example, if you see any instructions that talk about screen color, just ignore them if you have a monochrome monitor. You may see tips and tricks repeated in different chapters, but that's to keep you from jumping back and forth in the book. Have fun with these books and amaze your friends with what you can do!

Excel 5.0 Slick Tricks

Chapter 1

· ·

New Features

THIS CHAPTER IS FOR THOSE OF YOU who are familiar with former versions of Excel, and who can't wait to read this whole book to find out what is new in Excel 5.0. If you are not familiar with former versions, skip this chapter. These new features are scattered throughout the book in their appropriate chapters.

Files and File Management

· ·

Workbooks—A New File Format The biggest change from version 4.0 is the way Excel now saves files as workbooks. In version 4.0, workbooks were optional. When you save a worksheet in 5.0 format, you are saving a workbook with a worksheet contained in it. The same is true for templates, charts, and macrosheets. For instance, when you save a chart, you save a workbook with a chart contained in it.

You can save related worksheets, charts, and macro sheets in the same workbook or save them in individual workbooks.

When you name a cell or cell range within a workbook, it will remain unique. (See page 7 in this chapter for more new features affecting names.) Add-ins and workspace files are still saved as independent files.

Moving within Workbooks

The good news is that it is very easy to move around in these new workbooks because they contain tabs. These nifty tabs are also included in some of the 5.0 dialog boxes.

To move from sheet to sheet in a workbook:

♦ Use the scroll buttons to the left of the tabs to view the tabs. (See Figure 1.1.)

♦ Click on the tab of the sheet you want to activate.

To move to the next tab to the left, press Ⓦ Ctrl+Page Up or Ⓜ Command+Page Up (or Ⓜ Option+Left arrow).

To move to the next tab to the right, press Ⓦ Ctrl+Page Down or Ⓜ Command+Page Down (or Ⓜ Option+Left arrow).

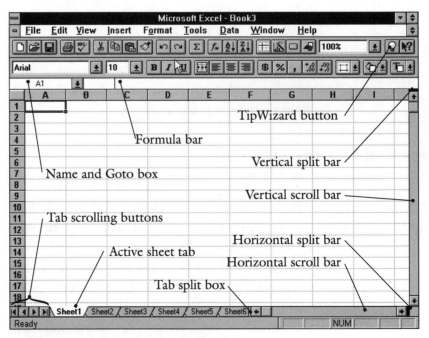

Figure 1.1 **Excel 5.0 Workbook with tabs**

To switch workbook windows:

♦ Press Ⓦ Ctrl+Tab (Ⓜ look for a comparable command—Macintosh Excel 5.0 was not available at the date of this printing) to switch to the next workbook.

♦ Press Ⓦ Ctrl+Shift+Tab (Ⓜ look for a comparable command—Macintosh Excel 5.0 was not available at the date of this printing) to switch to the previous workbook window. (If there are only two workbooks open, you do not need to use the Shift key.)

To cycle through the tabs in a dialog box, press Ⓦ Ctrl+Tab, or Ctrl+Shift+Tab (Ⓜ look for a comparable command—Macintosh Excel 5.0 was not available at the date of this printing).

For more about using workbooks, see Chapter 2, "Basic Slick Tricks."

The New Find File Feature

To access Find File, choose File, Find File (**Alt/**, **F**, **F**) or choose the Find File button in the File, Open dialog box (**Alt/**, **F**, **O**).

The advantage of using Find File over File Manager is that it can search through Excel Summary Information, which you can create each time you save a file for the first time. It can also preview the document when it finds it. It works in a very logical way, but if you have any questions, open the Find File dialog box and then choose the Help button for step-by-step instructions.

Menus

Menus and commands have been reorganized and enhanced in Excel 5.0. If you use other Microsoft applications, such as Word for Windows, you will appreciate the changes. Excel and Word now share many of the same icons and shortcut keys. If you like the way these were in Excel 4.0, you can switch to the old menu format, but you will lose some of the new choices available in 5.0.

To Switch to 4.0 Menus

Choose Tools, Options (**Alt/**, **T**, **O**), choose the General tab, and then turn on the Microsoft Excel 4.0 Menus check box.

To Switch Back to 5.0 Menus

Choose Options, New Menus (**Alt/, O, N**).

What You Will Miss

If you work in the 4.0 menus in version 5.0, you will not have access to several commands, including some 4.0 commands, such as Add-ins and Analysis Tools. Some of the new commands which will not be available are:

Command	Menu	See Chapter
Find File	File	2
Pivot Table	Data	10
Text to Columns	Data	8
Solver	Tools	9

Changing the Command Options on the File and Edit Menus

Some things are still the same as they were in Excel 4.0, such as using the Shift key to change the command options on the File and Edit Menus.

- ♦ Hold down the Shift key as you click on the File menu (**Alt/, F**). The Close command changes to Close All.
- ♦ Hold down the Shift key as you click on the Edit menu (**Alt/, E**). The Copy and Paste commands change to Copy Picture and Paste Picture.

New Features for Editing

• •

New Enter Key Action

There is a new enter key action: When you press Enter, the cell below the active cell becomes the new active cell.

Typing and Editing Tips

♦ To enter data directly into the active cell rather than in the Formula bar, click on the cell and start typing.

♦ To edit a cell, double-click on the cell or select the cell, press F2, then place the cursor where you want it, using the mouse or the Home or Arrow keys.

♦ To type in the Formula bar, select a cell, then click in the Formula bar.

When you are editing a formula, you will see the formula in the Formula bar and the results in the cell (unless you press Ⓦ Ctrl+' Ⓜ Command+'). When the active cell contains data other than formulas, you may prefer to type in the Formula bar if the window has been zoomed out or the font is small.

New Delete Key Action and New Delete Button

When you press Del, formulas and data are removed without presenting the familiar little dialog box which prompts you to select what you want to delete, such as Formulas, All, Formats, etc. If you prefer, you can click the Clear Contents button 🖉 instead of pressing Del.

Custom List to Use with AutoFill

You can now create your own custom list to use with AutoFill. In version 4.0 you could continue a series, such as Jan, Feb, Mar, or 1, 5, 10. In version 5.0 you can also create your own list to automatically fill, such as a list of product or department names. For more about this feature, see Chapter 3.

Scrolling Long Distances

You can now hold down the Shift key as you drag the scroll box to scroll long distances. Watch the name box in the Formula bar to see your destination. (See Figure 1.2.)

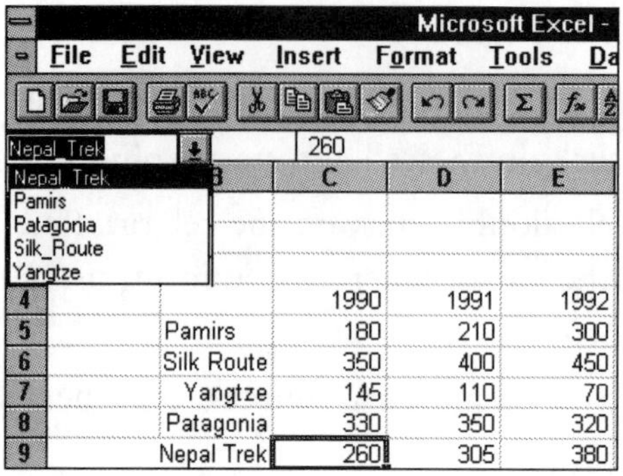

Figure 1.2 The Name and Go To Box

On-Screen Help Features

There are two new features in Windows (and one for the Macintosh) that are like having a friend looking over your shoulder, just waiting to tutor you when you ask a question.

TipWizard

Each time you perform an action, the TipWizard is analyzing and deciding if the task could have been done more simply. If it thinks so, the little light bulb will light up (turn yellow). The light bulb will turn "off" when you click the scroll arrows in the TipWizard box.

Reading TipWizard Tips

You can read the tips from the TipWizard immediately or keep them hidden, let them accumulate, and read them later. You can also customize your workspace to make the toolbar buttons TipWizard suggests available immediately. For more about TipWizard, see Chapter 2. For more about customizing your workspace, see Chapter 5.

ToolTips

In Windows, the second "friend" waiting to help you is **ToolTips**. ToolTips is a tiny bubble with information about button images, which appears when your mouse "hangs out" with toolbars.

Turning ToolTips On or Off

1 Right-click on a toolbar and choose Toolbars; or choose View, Toolbars (**Alt/**, **V**, **T**).

2 Click the Show ToolTips check box.

To Read a Description of a Button Image

When you place the mouse cursor above a button image, a small text box will appear with a description.

A similar, but more complete description than the tiny bubble also appears in the status bar. If you turn off ToolTips, you only turn off the small text box—not the description in the status bar.

New Features for Creating Formulas

Naming a Cell

To name a cell or range, type the name into the box to the left of the Formula bar (see Figure 1.2).

Go To a Named Cell or Named Range

Type the name you want to Go To into the name area to the left of the Formula bar; or, to display a list of all the names in the workbook:

1 Click on the drop down arrow next to the name box to the left of the Formula bar.

2 Select the name you want from the list.

These names will stay unique throughout the workbook. For instance, if you give the name Tina to cell A1 in Sheet1, then you move to Sheet2 and type Tina, it will take you to (Go To) A1 in Sheet1. It will not let you create the name Tina again in the same workbook.

Don't Double-Click

When you use the Go To drop-down list to select a name, only click once.

Function Wizard

This latest, greatest wizard helps you step through the process of writing formulas in a worksheet, just as the ChartWizard helps you step through the process of creating a chart.

Three Ways to Use the Function Wizard

♦ Press Shift+F3.

♦ Click on the Function Wizard button on the Standard toolbar (see Figure 1.3).

♦ Press F2 to activate the Formula bar, then click on the Function Wizard button on the Formula bar.

Formula Features

3-D Formulas and 3-D Names—Within the new workbook file format it is now possible to create formula references and names that pick up information from more than one worksheet. For more about these possibilities, see Chapter 7.

Automatic Totals—You can now automatically create subtotals and grand totals using the Subtotal command. For more about automatic subtotals, see Chapter 8.

The smart AutoSum button is even smarter than it used to be. If you click on it and it finds subtotals in the logical direction of its search, it will ignore the other values and assume that you want to total the subtotals. For more about the AutoSum button, see Chapter 7.

Locate Problems in Formulas—It's now possible to display precedent, dependent, and error tracers directly on your worksheet. The new Auditing toolbar makes it easy to place tracer arrows which indicate the direction of data flow on your worksheets. For more about using these, see Chapter 7.

New Formatting Capabilities—It is now possible to format individual characters within cells. There are also three new font formats—single and double underline, and strikethrough. New buttons on

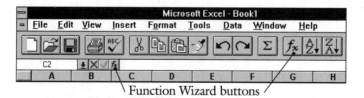

Function Wizard buttons

Figure 1.3 Function Wizard button on the Formula bar and Standard toolbar

the formatting toolbar combine features from Word for Windows or the Macintosh and from Excel 4.0, to make text formatting possible with the click of your mouse. Added to these features is the hottest new format feature of all: Format Painter.

Copying Formats with Format Painter

The Format Painter button on the Standard toolbar is used to copy formats from one cell to another. You may want to move or copy the button to the Formatting toolbar, or keep it handy on a toolbar of its own. For ways to do this, see Chapter 5.

To copy the format of a cell (or object) to other cells (or objects):

1 Click on the cell which has the format you want to copy.

2 Click the Format Painter button. (If you change your mind, click the button again or press Esc).

3 Click on the cell, or paint the cells, where you want the format copied to.

To copy the format to more than one place:

1 Click on the cell that has the format you want to copy.

2 Double-click on the Format Painter button.

3 Click where you want the format copied to.

4 Continue to click wherever you want the format copied.

5 Click on the Format Painter button or press **Esc** to turn it off.

For more worksheet formatting tricks, see Chapter 4.

New Workspace Operations and Options

· ·

Enter completes an edit then moves to the cell beneath the active cell. To complete an action and stay in the same cell, click the check mark on the Formula bar.

Two new terms appearing on menus and in the TipWizard are **Button Image** and **Tear-off palette**. Button image refers to what Excel 4.0 called a Toolface. The Tear-off palette is described below.

Tear-Off Palettes

You can now place a palette of borders, colors, patterns, and font colors that you want to use right at your mousetips:

1 Click on any of the button images which have drop-down arrows.

2 Drag the palette off the button image onto your workspace.

Once you tear off a palette, you can use it like a visible toolbar (see Figure 1.4).

Enlarging the Work Area on Your Screen

Excel 5.0 makes it easy to switch to a full screen. In doing so, you eliminate everything on the screen except the worksheet area and menus. It's just as easy to switch back, placing all the convenient toolbars, the title bar, and the status bar back into view.

To switch to Full Screen using the Main menu, choose View, Full Screen (**Alt/, V, U**). Your screen will switch to full screen and the **Full** toolbar (left) will become visible. To switch back, all you have to do is click on the toolbar.

To switch to Full Screen using the Toolbar button:

1 Ⓦ Right-click or Ⓜ Control+click a toolbar.

2 Choose Toolbars.

3 Turn on the Full Screen check box.

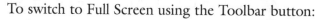
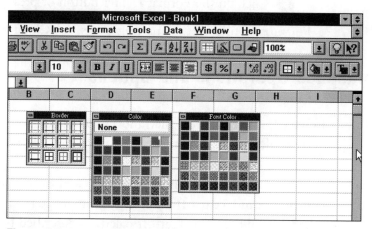

Figure 1.4 Torn-off palettes

The Full toolbar will stay on your screen in both modes so that you can click to switch back and forth.

Making Toolbar Buttons Larger

Toolbar buttons are often hard to read. The Large Button feature makes it much easier to see them—even for those fortunate enough to have excellent eyesight. To make the buttons larger:

1 Ⓦ Right-click Ⓜ Control+click a toolbar.

2 Choose Toolbars.

3 Turn on the Large Buttons check box.

You can also easily change the images on toolbar buttons. For more about this and other ways to customize toolbars, see Chapter 5.

Graphics Can Slow Down Your System

The more graphics you are using, the slower your system will run. If your system runs fast enough for you, no matter what features and applications you are running, you can ignore this advice—but if you are running Graphic User Interface (GUI) software like Excel, displaying graphics may slow down operations. To minimize this, you may want to familiarize yourself with the buttons when they are large, then switch them back to the smaller size. You may even want to remove the color from the button images using the same Toolbars dialog box used in the Slick Trick above.

Additional New Features

Printing Names —You now have a larger selection of built-in headers and footers.

Databases—Use the following new features, described in Chapter 8, for organizing and managing lists and database information:

♦ AutoFilter to hide data that does not meet certain criteria

♦ Sort by column labels

♦ Create custom sort orders, such as High, Med, and Low

♦ Automatically add subtotals and grand totals

♦ Use TextWizard to parse data files when you import them

Analyzing Data—Use the New Scenario Manager to create, manage, protect, merge, and track changes in scenarios. (See Chapter 9.)

Use the PivotTable Wizard to cross-tabulate, summarize, rearrange, and recalculate data. (See Chapter 10.)

Charts—The following new features, which are designed to make charting easier, are described in Chapter 12.

♦ Draw graphics directly onto charts

♦ Use new Chart AutoFormats

♦ Drag data directly onto a chart to add a data series or data points

♦ Scale more easily

♦ Position chart items anywhere easily

♦ Add treadlines and error bars to your data series

Linking, Importing, and Exporting—Use the following new features, described in Chapter 13, to link, import, and export data:

♦ Activate and edit embedded objects without leaving Excel

♦ Drag and drop data between applications to cut, copy, and paste

Programming and Application Development—Though it is not the focus of this book to teach programming, some tricks for the Excel programmer are included in Chapter 14. Three new programming features—the first is a major makeover—are available for those of you who want to write applications that use the Excel interface, or who want to write powerful macros. They are:

♦ Visual Basic programming system, Applications Edition

♦ New functions, listed on-line, that enhance the Excel 4.0 Macro Language

♦ Dialog Sheets to create custom dialog boxes

Note that the Excel macro recorder now records in Visual Basic or the Excel 4.0 macro language.

Chapter 2

. . . .

Basic Slick Tricks

THIS CHAPTER ESTABLISHES THE FOUNDATION for the book. It illustrates new terms, such as Tab workbooks and Tab dialog boxes, and gives slick tricks for the basics of menu and window operations, toolbars, opening, saving, and printing.

Workbooks

. . . .

Excel 5.0 saves files in a workbook format. Workbooks contain sheets, such as worksheets, chart sheets, Visual Basic modules, or Excel 4.0 macro sheets. Each sheet is identified with a tab and contains what was previously an individual file. For instance, when you save a chart, you save a workbook with a chart contained in it. Sheets are easy to rearrange, rename, move, copy, and delete. Moving and copying is just as easy to accomplish between workbooks as within. All of the tasks that used to require saving and retrieving to disk are simplified. Add-ins and workspace files are still saved as independent files.

You can save related worksheets, charts, and macro sheets in the same workbook, or save them in individual workbooks.

Cell or cell range names within a workbook remain unique. For more about naming cells and cell ranges, see Chapter 7, "Slick Tricks with Formulas."

Figure 2.1 shows some of the familiar features brought forward from former versions and some of the new workbook features in Excel 5.0.

Workbook Features

Sheets, Sheet Names, and the Active Sheet

When a new workbook opens, it contains 16 worksheets. The names for the sheets are Sheet1, Sheet2, etc. You can have worksheets, chart sheets, Visual Basic modules, dialog sheets, and Excel 4.0 macro sheets (including international) contained in a workbook. The active sheet tab has the appearance of being connected to the sheet. It appears white, as opposed to shaded, and the name on the tab appears in bold print. If more than one sheet is selected, all selected sheets will be white, but

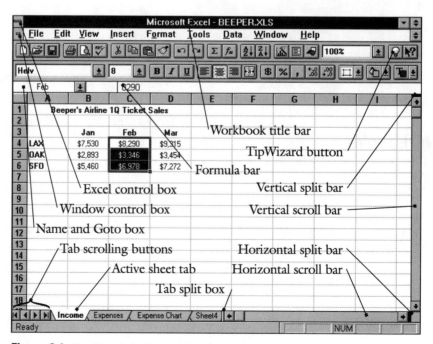

Figure 2.1 An Excel 5.0 workbook

only the active sheet will have bold print. The active sheet in Figure 2.1 is *Income*. The first three sheets in Figure 2.1 have been renamed. The fourth sheet, Sheet4, still has the name it had when the new workbook was opened.

If 16 sheets seem like a lot to open, see the trick, "Changing the Default Number of Sheets in a New Workbook," later in this chapter.

Renaming a Sheet

If you are familiar with former versions of Excel and are used to thinking of a sheet as a file, one of the first tricks you will want to learn is how to give a sheet a meaningful name.

To rename a sheet:

1 Double-click on the tab you want to rename.

2 Type the new name into the dialog box, and choose OK.

Alternatively:

1 Ⓦ Right-click Ⓜ Control+click the tab, and choose Rename.

2 Type the new name into the dialog box and choose OK.

Grouping Sheets

You can group sheets together to edit and format them simultaneously. Each change you make to the active sheet will affect the rest of the sheets in an identical manner. This is very handy if you need to update several cloned worksheets.

♦ To select all sheet tabs, Ⓦ right-click Ⓜ Control+click one of the sheet tabs and choose select All Sheets.

♦ To select contiguous sheets, Shift+click on the first tab and the last tab in the selection.

♦ To select noncontiguous tabs, Ⓦ Ctrl+click Ⓜ Command+click on each tab you want to select.

You can also click on the first tab and scroll to bring the last tab into view, then Shift+click on it; or you can select all visible tabs, then continue to Shift+click on each partially visible tab. Excel will add that tab to the selection and scroll to bring another into view.

Ungrouping Sheets

To ungroup sheets, Shift+click the active sheet tab or:

1   Ⓦ Right-click   Ⓜ Control+click on the tab you want to be active after you ungroup.

2   Choose Ungroup Sheets.

Tab Scrolling Buttons and the Tab Split Box

The Tab Scrolling Buttons scroll through the tabs without changing the active sheet. Slide the Tab Split box to the left if you want to have more of the horizontal scroll bar in your workbook window, and to the right if you want to see more tabs.

Moving from Tab to Tab

Because they contain tabs, it is now very easy to move around in these new workbooks.

♦ To move to the next tab to the left, press Ⓦ Ctrl+Page Up or Ⓜ Command+Page Up (or Ⓜ Option+Left arrow).

♦ To move to the next tab to the right, press Ⓦ Ctrl+Page Down or Ⓜ Command+Page Down (or Ⓜ Option+Left arrow).

♦ To move through tabs in a dialog box, click on the tab you want to activate or press Ctrl+Tab to cycle through the tabs. Ctrl+Shift+Tab reverses direction.

To move from sheet to sheet in a workbook, use the tab scroll buttons to the left of the tabs to bring the tab you need into view, then click on the tab of the sheet you want to activate.

What if You Can't See the Tabs?

If for some reason, the tabs are not visible, you can make them visible. To do this:

1   Choose Tools, Options (**Alt/, T, O**), and choose the View tab.

2   Turn on the Sheet tabs check box and choose OK.

If this option is already activated, try maximizing your window; it may be that the tabs are out of view.

Use the Sheet Tab Shortcut Menu to Insert, Copy, and Delete Sheets

All of the commands in the Tab Sheet Shortcut menu (with the exception of Select All Sheets) bring up a dialog box to carry out the action. If you need step-by-step instructions, click on Help in the dialog box.

Each of the commands in the Tab Sheet Shortcut menu—Delete, Rename, Move, Copy, Select All Sheets—can also be accomplished with other slick tricks as well, such as the Rename trick above and the three following tricks.

To use the Tab Sheet shortcut menu:

1 Select the tab or tabs you want to insert, delete, copy, or move.

2 Ⓦ Right-click Ⓜ Control+click on one of the selected tabs.

3 Choose the command you want.

4 Make your selections in the dialog box and choose OK.

Inserting Sheet(s)

You can insert one sheet or several sheets at a time. Inserting sheets is like inserting rows and columns: If you have selected four sheets, four new sheets will be inserted to the left of the active tab.

♦ To insert one worksheet, press Shift+F11, which is the shortcut for Insert, Worksheet (**Alt/, I, W**). The new sheet will be inserted to the left of the active sheet. If a workbook is not open, a new workbook with one worksheet will open.

♦ To insert more than one worksheet, Shift+click to select the number of sheets you want to insert, then press Shift+F11.

♦ To insert a chart sheet, press F11. A new chart sheet opens, and the floating Chart toolbar appears. When you switch to a sheet other than a chart sheet, the Chart toolbar will hide until you return.

♦ To insert an Excel 4.0 macro sheet, press Ctrl+F11.

Moving and Copying Sheets

You can move or copy a sheet by dragging it with the mouse. If you press the Ⓦ Ctrl key or Ⓜ Option key as you drag, you will copy instead of move.

To move or copy a sheet:

1 Click on the tab of the sheet you want to move and hold down the mouse button; if you want to copy, hold down the Ⓦ Ctrl or Ⓜ Option key as you drag.

2 Drag the tab until the black triangle points to the location where you want the sheet inserted.

Moving More than One Sheet

To move or copy more than one sheet, Shift+click or Ctrl+click to select more than one tab before you start to drag.

Moving between Workbooks

Use the same methods as above to move or copy between workbooks. Make sure the tabs for both workbooks are visible before you start. To create a new workbook, drag tabs into the Excel Workspace.

Use the Title Shortcut menu (Ⓦ right-click Ⓜ Control+click on the menu or title bar) and the Arrange command to see all open windows.

Deleting Sheets

To delete sheets:

1 Select the sheet(s) you want to delete.

2 Choose Edit, Delete Sheet (**Alt/**, **E**, **L**).

Changing the Default Number of Sheets in a New Workbook

When Excel opens, the default number of sheets in a workbook is 16. The number was most likely determined by some hexadecimal genius buried deep within the Microsoft programming team. You can change this number using the General tab in the Options dialog box.

1 Choose Tools, Options, and the General tab.

2 Change the number in the Sheets in a New Workbook box, then choose OK.

Scrolling with the Mouse

When you scroll through a sheet with the mouse and scroll bars or scroll arrows, you change the view of the sheet on your screen without changing the active cell or object.

To:	Do this:
Scroll one row or column	Click on one of the scroll arrows.
Scroll one window	Click on the bar on the side of one of the scroll boxes in the direction you want to move.
Scroll to a specific row or column	Drag a scroll box and watch the name area to the left of the Formula bar to see the new destination.

Scrolling Long Distances

You can hold down the Shift key as you drag the scroll box to scroll long distances. Watch the name area in the Formula bar (see Figure 2.2) to see your destination. To scroll to the last used row in a worksheet, hold down the Ctrl key as you scroll the vertical scroll bar down.

Opening Files

Open a New Workbook

To open a new workbook, press Ctrl+N, which is the same as File, New (**Alt/**, **F**, **N**); or click on the New Workbook button on the Standard toolbar ⬜.

Opening Existing Files

When you open a worksheet from a former version of Excel or a spreadsheet from another program, you can work with it in Excel 5.0 and save it back into it's former format. However, you may lose some of the cool things you did in Excel 5.0. Keep a few things in mind:

In Excel 4.0 (Windows):

♦ The filename extension for worksheets was XLS.

♦ The filename extension for workbooks was XLW.

In Excel 5.0:

♦ The filename extension for workbooks is XLS.

♦ The filename extension for a workspace is XLW.

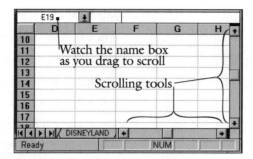

Figure 2.2 Scrolling Tools

Opening an Existing Worksheet from a Former Version

If you open a former version XLS, it will open as a workbook containing a single worksheet. They will both have the same name, but the workbook will have the filename extension. For instance, if the worksheet you opened was named TINA.XLS, the title bar on your worksheet will read TINA.XLS and the name on the sheet tab will read TINA.

Opening an Existing Workbook from a Former Version

When you open a former version XLW, you won't see it immediately; you will need to unhide it using the Unhide command on the Window menu. It will keep the former version filenames until you save it as an Excel 5.0 document.

See the trick, "Saving the Workspace," later in this chapter for more information.

Open a File

To open a file, regardless of what format it is in:

1 Press Ctrl+O or click on the Open button 📖.

2 Select the file and choose OK.

Bypass the File, Open Dialog Box

The last four files you had open are listed at the bottom of the file menu. You can bypass the Open dialog box if you want to open one of the listed files:

1 Click on File (**Alt/**, **F**).

2 Click (once) on the name of the file you want to open, or type the number in front of it.

Opening Several Files at the Same Time

To open several files at once from the Open dialog box:

1 Ctrl+click on each file you want to open, or Shift+click the first file and the last file to select all contiguous files in between them.

2 Choose OK.

The New Find File Feature

The new Find File feature is like having a mini-File Manager or mini-Finder within Excel.

To access Find File, choose File, Find File (**Alt/**, **F**, **F**), or choose the Find File button in the File, Open dialog box (**Alt/**, **F**, **O**).

Opening a Workbook or Template When You Start Excel

There are two ways to open a file as you start an Excel session. One way is to double-click on the workbook file in Ⓦ File Manager Ⓜ Finder. The other is to place the file in the Ⓦ XLSTART subdirectory Ⓜ EXCEL STARTUP FOLDER (5).

Accessing Menus

You can access menu commands with the mouse or with the keyboard. The commands which have an ellipsis (…) will call another menu or a dialog box.

♦ To access menu commands with the mouse, click on the menu and then click on the command.

Find File vs. File Manager The advantage of using Find File over File Manager is that it can search through Excel Summary Information. It can also preview the documents. It works in a very logical way, but if you have any questions, open the Find File dialog box, then choose the Help button for step-by-step instructions.

The Title Shortcut Menu Depending on whether a window is maximized or reduced, and depending on whether it was reduced by the down arrow at the far right corner of the menu bar or by the Restore command on the control box at the top left corner of the screen, the Title bar will be either above or below the menu bar. (When it's below the menu bar, the title at the top of the screen will read Microsoft Excel.)

If the Title bar is above the menu bar, Ⓦ right+click Ⓜ Control+click on the background of the menu bar. If it is below, click on the title bar itself to bring up the Title shortcut menu.

♦ To access menu commands with the keyboard, Ⓦ press **Alt** Ⓜ press /, then press the underlined letter within the command you want.

Changing the Command Options on the File and Edit Menus

The menu commands are different, depending on whether you are in a worksheet, chart, or Visual Basic module.

To change the commands in the File and Edit menus when you are in worksheet mode:

1 Hold down the Shift key as you click on the File menu (**Alt/**, **F**). The Close command changes to Close All.

2 Hold down the Shift key as you click on the Edit menu (**Alt/**, **E**); the Copy and Paste commands change to Copy Picture and Paste Picture.

Windows and Panes

You can use multiple windows, panes, and zoom control to work to your advantage. Three of the Window menu commands, New Window, Arrange, and Zoom are also available on the Title shortcut menu.

Opening a New Window

If you would like to have two or more windows of the same workbook open, you can open another copy and move to different places in each window. As you work, your changes will affect all open copies.

To open another window (copy) of the same workbook:

1 Ⓦ Right-click or Ⓜ Control+click on the Title bar.

2 Choose New Window.

Switching Workbook Windows

To switch between workbook windows, click on the window you want if it is visible. Press Ctrl+Tab to switch to the next workbook window, or press Ctrl+Shift+Tab to switch to the previous workbook window. If there are only two workbooks open, you do not need to use the Shift key.

Freeze Panes

To keep the headings of the top row or the left column visible, you can freeze the panes.

1 Select the cell where you want the panes to freeze (see Figure 2.3).

2 Choose Window, Freeze Panes (**Alt/**, **W**, **F**), or press the Freeze Pane button ⊞.

The Freeze Pane button is in the Utility category of the Customize dialog box. For More about customizing toolbar buttons, see Chapter 5.

Split a Worksheet Window

Once you split a window, you can view and work in two areas simultaneously. Splitting a window works the same as when you freeze panes.

	A	B	C	D	E	F	G
				BEEPER.XLS			
1	Beeper's Airline 1Q Ticket Sales						
2							
3		Jan	Feb	Mar			
4	LAX	$7,530	$8,290	$9,315			
5	OAK	$2,893	$3,346	$3,454			
6	SFO	$5,460	$6,978	$7,272			
7							
8							

Active cell—panes freeze above and to the left

Figure 2.3 Frozen panes

The split will be above and to the left of the active cell. To split a window:

 Select the cell where you want the split.

Choose Window, Split (**Alt/**, **W**, **S**); or drag the Split bar to where you want it.

 ### Remove a Split

To remove the split, you can choose the same command you used to make the split (**Alt/**, **W**, **S**), drag the Split bar back its original position, or double-click on the Split bar.

Too Many Splits

 Depending on where you have your tab split box and where you place a vertical split, you may not be able to see your sheet tabs at all. This does not happen when you freeze the panes.

Magnifying the View

You can enlarge the view of your screen and the toolbar buttons with the Full Screen command, the Zoom command, and the Toolbar dialog box. You can also zoom out to see the layout of your screen, rather than read the detail. For slick tricks using these features, see Chapter 6, "Views, Outlining, and Printing."

 ### Closing the Active Window

If there is only one window of the workbook open, when you close that window, the workbook will close. Otherwise, any other copies of the workbook will remain open.

♦ Ⓦ Double-click Ⓜ click the window control box, or

♦ Press Ctrl+F4.

Exiting

If you click on the Excel control box, you can select Close or you can double-click on it to end your session. There are two other ways to end your session:

♦ On the Main menu, Ⓦ File, Exit (**Alt/, F, X**) Ⓜ File, Quit (**Alt/, F, Q**), or

♦ Press **Alt/+F4**.

Printing

When you want to print, you have numerous options, some of which are new in Excel 5.0. For slick tricks above and beyond these basic instructions, see Chapter 6, "Views, Outlining, and Printing."

To preview before you print: Choose File, Print Preview (**Alt/, F, V**); or press the Print Preview button ⬚.

To print without previewing:

❶ Ⓦ Right-click Ⓜ Control+click on the Menu bar or a workbook Title bar.

❷ Choose Print to bring up the Print dialog box.

To bypass the Print dialog box, click on the Print button ⬚ on the Standard toolbar. This will print one copy of the open document, bypassing the Print dialog box.

Print Preview with the Print Button

If you hold down the Shift key when you press the Print button, it converts to the Print Preview button. The same is true with the Print Preview button: Pressing the Shift key causes it to behave like the Print button. Therefore, if you prefer, you can remove one of the Print buttons, thus making more room on the Standard toolbar. For more about this and other ways to customize toolbars, see Chapter 5, "Toolbars and Workspace Options."

Saving Your Work

Saving Files

This feature has not changed. The easiest way to save a workbook is to click on the Save button ▣. If your workbook has not been saved, the Save As dialog box will appear. If it has been saved and you want to save it in a different name, a different directory, or in a different format, choose File, Save As (**Alt/**, **F**, **A**).

Protect a Workbook

You can protect a workbook, a worksheet, or particular cells. You can do this by preventing the entire workbook from being opened without a password, or by hiding selected sheets or formulas by locking cells, or initiating read-only status. You can also cause Excel to recommend, but not require, that users open a workbook as read-only. This creates a built-in warning that requires users to consider carefully before making changes.

To prevent a workbook from being opened:

1 Press F12, and choose Options.

2 Type in your password in the Protection Password check box, and choose OK.

3 Type the password a second time in the next dialog box, and choose OK.

4 Choose OK in the Save As dialog box.

5 Don't forget your password.

To prevent a workbook from being saved, follow the same instructions as above, but in step 2, type your password in the Write Reservation Password box. Note that passwords are case-sensitive. They can be up to 15 characters long and contain any combination of letters, numbers, and symbols.

To remove passwords:

1 Press F12, and choose Options.

2 Paint the asterisks that represent the password, and press Delete; then choose OK.

To recommend that users read-only:

1 Press F12, choose Options.

2 Turn on the Read-Only recommended check box and choose OK.

3 Choose OK in the Save As dialog box.

Protect Part of a Workbook

You can protect the structure or windows in a workbook. The structure affects the sheets. When they are protected, they cannot be deleted, re-named, or hidden, and you cannot add another sheet.

When you protect the Windows, they cannot be resized, rearranged, or closed. When you protect windows in Windows, the maximize and minimize icons, the Control-menu box, and the window-sizing borders are hidden. In the Macintosh, protected workbook windows do not display the close box or the zoom box, and the size box is disabled.

When a password dialog box says a password is optional, it means that you can protect the selected features without adding one. This allows you and others to unprotect them without a password.

To protect workbook structure or windows:

1 Choose Tools, Protection (**Alt/, T, P, W**), and Workbook.

2 Type in a password if you want one.

3 Turn on the Structure and/or Windows check boxes, and choose OK.

Protecting a Worksheet

1 Choose Tools, Protection (**Alt/, T, P, P**), then Worksheet.

2 Type in a password if you want one.

3 Turn on the Contents, Object, and/or Scenarios check boxes, and choose OK.

Protecting Individual Cells

You may want to protect part of a worksheet rather than the whole thing. For instance, you may have created a form. You can lock the labels and format the entry cells to remain unlocked. There are two steps to locking a portion of a worksheet:

1 Set the cell range that you want to remain unlocked (using the next set of instructions).

2 Protect the worksheet (using the steps in the previous trick).

You can use the lock button or the menu commands to lock and unlock cells. The lock button toggles the lock status on and off.

To use the lock button:

1 W Right-click M Control+click on a toolbar, and choose Customize, then Utility.

2 Drag the Lock button 🔒 to a toolbar and choose Close.

To set a cell range to remain unlocked:

1 Select the range you want to unlock (it can be nonadjacent).

2 Click on the Lock button, or press Ctrl+1 or W right-click M Control+click the selection and choose Format Cells.

3 Select the Protection tab.

4 Turn off the Locked check box and choose OK.

Move among Unlocked Cells

Once a portion of a worksheet has been locked, you that can move among the unlocked cells using the Tab key. To move in the reverse direction, press Shift+Tab.

Hiding Formulas

You can hide the formula of a cell or cell range so that when a cell with hidden formulas is selected, the formula won't show in the Formula bar.

1 Select the range (it can be nonadjacent).

2 Press Ctrl+1 or W right-click M Control+click the selection and choose Format Cells.

3 Select the Protection tab.

④ Turn on the Hidden check box and choose OK.

⑤ Protect the worksheet using Tools, Protection (**Alt/**, **T**, **P**, **P**).

Saving the Workspace

You can save a list of all open files, including the glossary files that you opened in a session, by saving the workspace. Excel proposes the name Ⓦ RESUME.XLW. Ⓜ RESUME. You might prefer to name it Ⓦ FRI-DAY.XLW or Ⓜ B4 VACATION, or some other meaningful title. Choose File, Save Workspace (**Alt/**, **F**, **W**).

When you open a saved workspace, everything will be arranged as you left it.

Prompt for Summary Information

Each time you save a workbook for the first time, you are prompted to add Summary Information. This may be very helpful if you are sharing your files on a network. If you are working alone, however, and have already had a hard enough time trying to think of a filename, and you don't want to have to answer a bunch of hard questions like what key words and comments you would ascribe to each memorable workbook, turn off the Prompt for Summary Info dialog box:

❶ Choose Tools, Options (**Alt/**, **T**, **O**), and activate the General tab.

❷ Turn off the Prompt for Summary Info check box, then choose OK.

Help Features

There are two new features in Windows (and one in the Macintosh) that are like having a friend looking over your shoulder, waiting to tutor you when you ask a question.

TipWizard

Each time you perform an action in the Macintosh or Windows, the TipWizard is analyzing and deciding if the task could have been done more simply. If it thinks so, the little light bulb will light up (turn yellow). The light bulb will turn off when you click the scroll arrows in the TipWizard box.

Reading the Tips

To read the TipWizard tips, click on the TipWizard button [image]. The Tip-Wizard box will appear above the Formula bar and stay there until you click the TipWizard button again, or hide it using the Toolbar menu. Regardless of whether you make the TipWizard box visible or not, tips will continue to be recorded while you are working.

To scroll through previously recorded tips:

1 Click the TipWizard button to make it visible.

2 Use the scroll arrows to view the tips.

The first tip will always be a "tip of the day," which is actually a tip of the session. When you leave a session and return on the same day, you get a new tip of the day.

To read more about the tip presently displayed, click on the TipWizard Help button [image].

Making a Suggested Tool Available Immediately

When an arrow appears at the end of the TipWizard box, look for a button image to the left of the TipWizard help button. If you want to move the suggested button to a toolbar immediately, without having to search for it on an existing toolbar or in the Customize dialog box:

1 Choose View, Toolbars (or use the Toolbars shortcut menu— see the next slick trick).

2 Drag the button image from the TipWizard to a toolbar, and close the Toolbar dialog box.

This can also be done with the Customize dialog box open.

Use the Toolbar Shortcut Menu

Excel considers the TipWizard box to be a toolbar, so if you would like to make a toolbar visible or you want to access the Toolbar or Customize commands, you can use the TipWizard box, as well as a toolbar to access the Toolbar shortcut menu:

1 [W] Right-click or [M] Control+click on the TipWizard box or on a toolbar (on an area not occupied by a button).

2 Select the toolbar want to make visible or select the Toolbar or Customize commands.

Just like any built-in or custom toolbars, the TipWizard box will be visible when you start a new session if it was visible when you ended the last. For more about toolbars and buttons, see Chapter 5, "Toolbars and Workspace Options."

TipWizard Can Slow You Down

 If you are an experienced user, TipWizard is like momentarily "Alt/-tabbing" over to an interactive game. It's fun, but it can slow you down.

ToolTips

In Windows, the second tutor "friend" ready to help you is ToolTips. It is a tiny bubble with information about button images, which appears when your mouse is positioned over toolbars.

Turn ToolTips On or Off

To turn ToolTips on or off:

1. Right-click on a toolbar and choose Toolbars.
3. Click the Show ToolTips check box and choose OK.

Reading Button Descriptions

To read a description of any button image, place the mouse cursor above a button image, and a small text box appears with a description.

A similar, but more complete description of the tiny bubble also appears in the status bar. If you turn ToolTips off, you turn off only the small text box, not the description in the status bar.

Helpful Help

Excel 5.0's Help system is very complete and, in most cases, easy to use.

To get Help on a specific command or toolbar:

1. Click on the Help button 📐, located on the Standard toolbar.
2. Click on a menu command or a toolbar button.

To go directly to the Help Search dialog box, double-click on the Help button.

Chapter 3

. . . .

Worksheet Editing

THIS CHAPTER CONTAINS SLICK TRICKS for selecting, entering, moving, copying, and deleting worksheet data. It covers AutoFill and contains instructions for the easiest ways to Go To, Find, or Find and Replace.

Slick Tricks for Selecting

. . . .

All the conventional ways to select are still in effect in version 5.0, but here are some slick tricks for selecting that may be new to you.

Use the Mouse to Select the Whole...

To select the whole:	Click on the:
Worksheet	Select All button at the intersection of row and column headings
Row	Row heading
Column	Column heading

Use the Keyboard to Select the Whole...

To select the whole or all:	Press:
Worksheet	Ctrl+Shift+Spacebar
Objects—if one object is selected	Ctrl+Shift+Spacebar
Row	Shift+Spacebar
Column	Ctrl+Spacebar

For tables containing all the keyboard shortcuts, see the appendix at the end of the book.

Shift+Click to Select

The easiest way to select a large area on a worksheet is to click on one corner of the selection, then Shift+click on the other.

Select Nonadjacent Cells or Ranges

Hold down Ⓦ Ctrl Ⓜ Command and select each cell or range by clicking or dragging.

Use Go To

There is a great 5.0 slick trick for Go To, but it did not replace the former Excel Go To feature; it only enhanced it. You can use the name area to the left of the Formula bar or press F5.

To Go To, type the name or cell reference you want to go to into the name area to the left of the Formula bar, then press Enter. Or you can display a list of all the names in the workbook, then Go To one of them:

1 Click on the drop-down arrow next to the name area on the Formula bar.

2 Select the name you want from the list.

Don't Double-Click

When you use the Go To drop-down list to select a name, click only once.

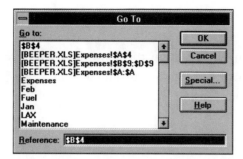

Figure 3.1 Go To dialog box

To bring up the Go To dialog box shown in Figure 3.1, press F5. The dialog box displays the last four active cell locations and all names in the workbook. There is also a new button which calls the Go To Special dialog box, shown in Figure 3.2, which further enhances the Go To capabilities. In former versions, you could accomplish most of these tasks with the Formula Select Special command. For a complete description of each Go To Special check box, click on the Help button.

After you have selected one of these special sets with Go To Special, you can move within the selection by pressing Tab or Shift+Tab. If the selection is nonadjacent, use Ⓦ Ctrl+F6 and Ctrl+Shift+F6 or Ⓜ Command+Tab or Command+Shift+Tab.

Use Find to Go To

One way to get somewhere quickly on a worksheet or within a workbook is to use Find, which is now located on the Edit menu. It works in a very logical way, but for step-by-step instructions press the Help button in the Find dialog box.

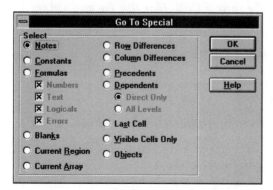

Figure 3.2 The Go To Special dialog box

There are two slick ways to bring up the Find dialog box; press Ctrl+F or press Shift+F5.

The Find What box within the Find dialog box remembers the last thing typed into it during the current session, regardless of whether it was typed in from Find or Replace.

Entering and Deleting Data

The Active Cell and the New Enter Key Action

The active cell is the cell that responds to the keyboard when you start typing. If it has any contents, the contents will display in the Formula bar. It is also highlighted (selected), but often a whole range has been highlighted. Only one cell within the range can be the active cell.

When you press Enter, the cell below the active cell becomes the new active cell. To complete an action and stay in the same cell, you need to click the check mark ▨ on the Formula bar or you can change the action of the Enter key in the Options dialog box.

Changing the Enter Key Action

If you do not like the way the Enter key moves down to the next cell in Excel 5.0, and you want it to stay in the same cell as it did in former versions:

① Choose Tools, Options (**Alt/**, **T**, **O**) and select the Edit tab.

② Turn off the Move Selection after Enter check box, then choose OK.

Type Directly into a Cell, Not the Formula Bar

In Excel 5.0, you can type either directly into the active cell or at the Formula bar.

♦ To enter data into the active cell, click on the cell and start typing.

♦ To edit a cell, double-click on the cell or select the cell, press F2, then place the cursor where you want it, using the mouse or the Home or arrow keys.

♦ To type in the Formula bar, select a cell and click in the Formula Bar.

When you are editing a formula, you will see the formula in the Formula bar and the results in the cell (unless you press W Ctrl+ ' M Command+ ').

Enter Data into a Range

If you select a range before entering data, the data will progressively fill the selection as you type. This is true even if the range is nonadjacent.

1 Select the range.

2 Type an entry and press Enter.

3 Keep typing and pressing Enter.

When the last entry of a column is filled, the selection will jump to the top of the next column without your help. Instead of pressing Enter, you can press Tab, Shift+Enter, or Shift+Tab to move in directions other than down one cell. If you try to use the arrow keys or the mouse, however, you will deselect the range.

When you select a nonadjacent range and start typing, your first entry may not start at what you consider the start of your range, unless you select in a particular order. For instance, in Figure 3.3, to have your first entry start in the cell that contains the first entry, you need to select Block 2 first, then hold down the Ctrl key and select Block 1 from the top. You can circumvent this inconvenience if you:

1 Select all of the nonadjacent ranges in any order you wish.

2 Ctrl+click the cell where you want the first entry.

3 After you type the first entry, press Enter twice.

4 Continue typing and pressing Enter as in the instructions above.

first entry		fifth	
second		sixth	
third		seventh	
fourth		eighth	

Block 1   Block 2

Figure 3.3 A nonadjacent range filled by continuous typing

Fill a Block of Cells with the Same Entry

To fill to the right:

1 Select the cell which contains the entry.

2 Paint as far right as you want it to fill.

3 Press Ctrl+R.

To fill down:

1 Select the cell which contains the entry.

2 Paint as far down as you want it to fill.

3 Press Ctrl+D.

To fill a selection, including a nonadjacent range:

1 Select the block(s) you want to fill.

2 Type your entry.

3 Press Ctrl+Enter.

Fill Up and Fill Left Have Changed

If you are used to former versions of Excel, don't look for Ctrl+H or Ctrl+W to fill up or fill left anymore.

Entering Data with the Fill Handle

You can fill a range by clicking on a cell or a selection, then dragging the fill handle.

If a cell/selection contains:	Excel will *usually* fill with:
A single entry (not in a list)	The entry
A list that Excel recognizes	The list
A range with a set pattern	The continuation of the pattern
A date	Incremental dates
An ordinal, such as 1st	Incremental ordinals

Excel will also increment two of these at the same time, such as 1st Quarter 94.

Sometimes it's hard to out-guess how Excel will recognize your initial entry, but if the range does not fill the way you want it to, you can press the Ctrl key to reverse the increment/nonincrement action.

For instance, if you type in a zip code such as **94526** and you drag the fill handle, it will increment to 94526, 94527, 94528, etc. If you hold down the Ctrl key as you drag, it will fill each cell of the selection with 94526.

Or, if you type **Jan** and drag the fill handle it will fill with Feb, Mar, Apr, etc. If you hold down the Ctrl key while you drag, it will fill each cell of the selection with Jan.

Or, if you type **1** and drag the fill handle, it will fill the each cell of selection with 1. If you hold down the Ctrl key and drag, it will increment with 1, 2, 3, etc.

Beware of Deleting with the Fill Handle

When you drag to fill, you can go in any direction from your initial entries. If you drag a selection from the fill handle to the upper left corner of the selection and let go, you will delete the selection. It's a convenient way to delete, but it's a lousy surprise if you are trying to automatically fill. Remember, you can Undo if you get an unpleasant surprise (see "Undo and Repeat" later in this chapter).

Double-Click to Fill a Column

If a column is set up to the left of a blank column, you can place an entry in the top row, select it, and then double-click the fill handle to fill down as far as the adjacent column to the left. You can also hold down the Ctrl key to reverse the increment/nonincrement action (the same as when you drag the fill handle). For instance, to fill the last three columns in Figure 3.4:

1 Select the two cells that contain Danville and CA.

2 Double-click on the fill handle.

120 Garden Creek Place	Danville	CA	94526
1070 Sunshine Circle			
543 Dimaggio Way			
51 South Gate Road			
8756 Linda Lane			
98 Homestead Ave			

120 Garden Creek Place	Danville	CA	94526
1070 Sunshine Circle	Danville	CA	
543 Dimaggio Way	Danville	CA	
51 South Gate Road	Danville	CA	
8756 Linda Lane	Danville	CA	
98 Homestead Ave	Danville	CA	

120 Garden Creek Place	Danville	CA	94526
1070 Sunshine Circle	Danville	CA	94526
543 Dimaggio Way	Danville	CA	94526
51 South Gate Road	Danville	CA	94526
8756 Linda Lane	Danville	CA	94526
98 Homestead Ave	Danville	CA	94526

Figure 3.4 **Double-clicking the fill handle**

3 Select the cell that contains 94526.

4 Hold down the Ctrl key and double-click on the fill handle.

Autofill Shortcut Menu

W Drag with the right mouse button M hold down Control as you drag to bring up a shortcut menu that gives you choices when you fill (Figure 3.5).

Create a Custom List to Use with AutoFill

You can now create your own custom list to use with AutoFill. In version 4.0 you could continue a series, such as Jan, Feb, Mar, or 1, 5, 10. In version 5.0 you can also create your own list to fill automatically, such as a list of product or department names.

To create a custom list from an existing list on your worksheet:

1 Select the list.

2 Choose Tools, Options (**Alt, T, O**).

3 Choose the Custom Lists Tab; NEW LIST will be proposed. (See Figure 3.6.)

4 Choose Import.

120 Garden Creek Place	Danville	CA	94526
1070 Sunshine Circle	Danville	CA	
543 Dimaggio Way	Danville	CA	
51 South Gate Road	Danville	CA	
8756 Linda Lane	Danville	CA	
98 Homestead Ave	Danville	CA	

Copy Cells
Fill Series
Fill Formats
Fill Values

Fill Days
Fill Weekdays
Fill Months
Fill Years

Linear Trend
Growth Trend
Series...

Figure 3.5 The AutoFill shortcut menu

5 Choose OK (you need to use the mouse or the Tab key to initialize OK to respond to Enter).

To create a custom list directly into the Options, Custom Lists dialog box:

1 Choose Tools, Options (**Alt, T, O**).

2 Choose the Custom Lists tab.

3 Type the list into the List Entries box, separating each item by pressing Enter.

4 Choose OK.

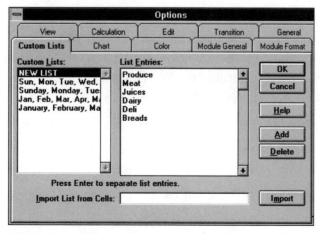

Figure 3.6 The Custom Lists dialog box

Enter Numbers As Text

There are times when you want to enter numbers as text, such as a list of phone numbers or postal codes. You can precede the entry with an apostrophe, or:

1 W Right-click M Control+click the range, column, or row you want to format.

2 Choose Format Cells.

3 Choose the Number tab.

4 Select the Text category that has the @ format code.

If your entry has any characters that are not numerical, such as 208B, it will be recognized as text.

Not all alphanumeric combinations will be read as text. If your entry has a 0 or a number to the right of an E–, E+, e–, or e+, Excel recognizes it as a number and will enter it in scientific format.

Recording a Macro to Enter Numbers As Text

If you need to enter numbers as text frequently, record a macro to expedite the process. See Chapter 14, "Macros and Programming," where entering numbers as text is used as an example for recording a macro.

Entering Dates and Times

Let Excel Finish Entering Dates and Times for You

Excel recognizes dates and times when you enter them. If you type in enough of the date or time for Excel to recognize it, it will complete your entry according to the first date or time format it comes to on the Format, Cells, (Ctrl+1) Number tab. For instance:

If you type:	Excel will place in the cell:
4/5 (or 4–5)	4/5/94 (or whatever year it is when you are typing)
3:4	3:04
3:4 p	3:04 PM
4/5 3:4	4/5/94 3:04

When you change a number format, if you get ####, make the cell larger by double-clicking on the Column heading.

Add a New Date or Time Formatting Code

If the date or time does not print into the cell the way you want it to, you can change it. For instance, if you type **4/5 3:4 p**, Excel will place 4/5/94 15:04 in the cell.

If you want the output to be 4/5/94 3:04 PM, you must create a custom format to be m/d/yy h:mm AM/PM.

To create a custom format:

1 W Right-click M Control+click on a cell.

2 Choose Format Cells (or press Ctrl+1).

3 Choose the Number tab.

4 Type a new format into the code box (see Figure 3.7).

5 Choose OK.

Date and Time Shortcuts

You can use the following shortcut keys to enter the present date and time from your computer clock into a cell. You can also use them consecutively in the same cell to enter the date, then the time.

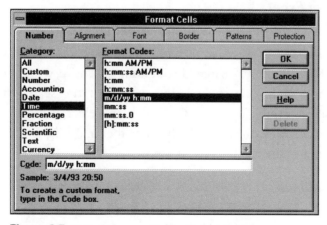

Figure 3.7 The Format Cells dialog box

To Enter:	Press:
Date	W Ctrl+;
	M Command+Hyphen
Time	W Ctrl+Shift+:
	M Command+;

The format will default to the first format in the Format Cells dialog box.

Correct Your Computer's Date and Time

If your clock doesn't know it's daylight savings time, or you didn't change the date on leap year, you may need to correct it using the Windows Control Panel or Macintosh Apple Menu Alarm Clock.

Use Double Quotation Marks

When you enter the date in a formula, you need to enclose it in double quotation marks. Excel will convert it to a corresponding number when it calculates. For instance, ="11/19/94"-"8/18/94" will calculate to 93.

Editing

Find and Replace within a Workbook

Find and Replace can be used on all sheets except Visual Basic modules. If you want to search throughout an entire workbook, you can select more than one sheet before you start the search. Use Shift+click to select contiguous, or Ctrl+click to select noncontiguous sheets. To Select All from the Tab shortcut menu, W right-click M Control+click on any sheet tab.

Replace

One of the greatest timesavers is the Replace command. With it, you can change the contents of a series of complex formulas, such as a name contained within them, by simply pressing Ctrl+H to call the Replace dialog box. Within the Replace dialog box, you can decide to replace all occurrences of particular data by selecting Replace All, or you can choose to go to each occurrence by selecting Replace. You can also call the Replace dialog box by choosing Replace in the Find dialog box.

Use Wildcard Characters in Find and Replace

When you are doing a search, you can use a question mark (?) or an asterisk (*) in the Find What box to simplify your input. A question mark takes the place of one character; an asterisk takes the place of several. If you want to actually search for a question mark or an asterisk, precede them with a tilde (~).

Undo and Repeat

Most edits can be undone by choosing Edit, Undo (**Alt/**, **E**, **U**); or repeated by choosing Edit, Repeat (**Alt/**, **E**, **R**); but there are shortcuts for both:

Function	Keyboard	Mouse Click
Undo	Ctrl+Z or Alt+Backspace	↰
Repeat	F4	↱

Undo and Repeat Last Edit Only

If you have done a series of edits, the Undo and Repeat buttons undo or repeat only the last edit. For instance, if you have formatted text with the Bold button and then with the Italic button, it will undo or repeat only the italic action. If, however, you have formatted text with the Format Cells dialog box, it will undo or repeat all changes you initiated in the dialog box before you chose OK.

Edit Tab Options

Before you look at the following slick tricks, you should be aware of the options available on the Edit tab, particularly the "Drag-and-Drop" and Alert Before Overwriting Cells check boxes. You can move and copy by dragging and dropping, but if it is awkward for you, you may want to disable this feature. Also, if you like to drag-and-drop and you are confident about your placement when you "drop," you may want to disable the alert box that warns you that you are about to drop on top of cells containing data. Remember, you can always Undo.

To make changes in the Edit tab:

1 Choose Tools, Options.

2 Select the Edit tab (see Figure 3.8).

3 Make your selections.

4 Choose OK.

Editing within Cells

If you select a cell and start typing, the contents of the cell will be replaced. You need to activate the cell in order to edit within it.

To activate a cell:

1 Select the cell.

2 Double-click on it or press F2.

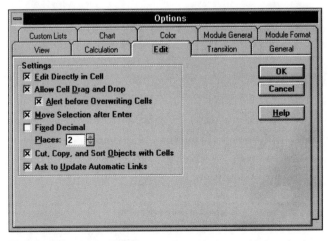

Figure 3.8 The Edit tab in the Options dialog box

Working in an Active Cell

Once a cell is activated, you can select individual characters within the cell and edit and format individual characters as if you are word processing. If, however, you press Enter or type more than 255 characters, Excel will remind you that you are not writing a book. The following three tricks can be used when a cell has been activated:

♦ To select a word within a cell, double-click on the word to select it.

♦ To place a carriage return within a cell, press Alt+Enter. This starts a new line within a cell. (You may prefer to wrap text within the cell; if so, see "Wrapping and Justifying Text within a Cell" in Chapter 4, "Worksheet Formatting.")

♦ To place a tab within a cell, press Ⓦ Ctrl+Alt+Tab Ⓜ Command+Option+Tab.

Adding More than 255 Characters of Text

If you need to add more than 255 characters of text, you can create a text box or embed a Word 6.0 document. For those slick tricks, see Chapter 13.

Cut, Copy, and Paste Inside or Outside a Cell

Remember, if you want to cut or copy actual characters from one cell to another using the clipboard, Excel needs to know whether you want to be within a cell or if you want to replace the contents. For instance, if you don't want to retype the word *Antidisestablishmentarianism* (which used to be the longest word in the dictionary—I'm probably dating myself), you can double-click on it to select it then copy it, but then comes the tricky part. If you want the word to replace the contents of another cell entirely, no problem: Just select the cell and paste away. If, however, you want the word to be inserted into a sentence, you will need to double-click on the cell (or select and press F2), then position the insertion point with the mouse or Home or arrow keys before you paste.

Moving and Copying

When you move and copy, you are essentially cutting or copying to the clipboard and then pasting (except when you drag-and-drop). Moving and copying can be done using the Edit menu, but there are four shortcuts:

+ The Edit/Format shortcut menu
+ Drag-and-drop
+ Click on toolbar buttons
+ Keyboard shortcut keys

The Edit/Format Shortcut Menu

If you normally select with the mouse, then this slick menu is the fastest way to do almost all the actions listed on it.

+ ⓦ Right-click ⓜ Control+click on a selection to bring up the menu shown in Figure 3.9a.
+ ⓦ Right-click ⓜ Control click on a row or column heading to bring up the variation of it, shown in Figure 3.9b.

But if you can master it, drag-and-drop is probably even faster for moving and copying.

Drag-and-Drop

If you drag-and-drop a selection, you move it (as shown in Figure 3.10); if you hold down the ⓦ Ctrl key ⓜ Option key as you drag, you copy it. When you drop it, it replaces the selection it lands on top of,

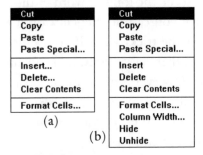

Figure 3.9 The Edit/Format shortcut menus

120 Garden Creek Place	Danville	94526	CA
1070 Sunshine Circle	Danville	94526	CA
543 Dimaggio Way	Danville	94526	CA
51 South Gate Road	Danville	94526	CA
8756 Linda Lane	Danville	94526	CA
98 Homestead Ave	Danville	94526	CA

120 Garden Creek Place	Danville	94526	CA
1070 Sunshine Circle	Danville	94526	CA
543 Dimaggio Way	Danville	94526	CA
51 South Gate Road	Danville	94526	CA
8756 Linda Lane	Danville	94526	CA
98 Homestead Ave	Danville	94526	CA

120 Garden Creek Place	Danville	CA	94526
1070 Sunshine Circle	Danville	CA	94526
543 Dimaggio Way	Danville	CA	94526
51 South Gate Road	Danville	CA	94526
8756 Linda Lane	Danville	CA	94526
98 Homestead Ave	Danville	CA	94526

Figure 3.10 **Dragging and dropping**

but you can use the Shift key to make it "drop in" politely. When the Shift key is held down, the selection in the new location is moved over to the right, or down, rather than replaced.

To move or copy:

1 Make a selection.

2 Place the mouse pointer over one of the lines in the border of the selection until it changes from a cross to an arrow. If you are copying, you will also see a tiny plus sign next to the arrow.

3 Hold down the mouse button and drag the selection to a new location. If you hold down the Shift key, the outline will become a ghost I-beam (instead of a box) which can be placed between two columns or rows.

4 When the ghost outline is where you want it, let go of the mouse.

To copy instead of move, hold down the Ⓦ Ctrl key Ⓜ Option key.

Move and Copy Shortcuts

There are three quick ways to move and copy, besides drag-and-drop. The first is part of what I consider a four-part set. If you hold the little finger of your left hand on top of the Ⓦ Ctrl key Ⓜ Command key, you can undo, cut, copy, and paste with the bottom four keys: Z, X, C, and V. All of these are familiar methods to users of Word for Windows and the Mac. The second is consistent with the methods used by Word 6.0 for DOS, so if you are used to using these keys, you may prefer to use them in Excel 5.0.

Cut	**Copy**	**Paste**
Ctrl+X	Ctrl+C	Ctrl+V
Shift+Delete	Ctrl+Insert	W Shift+Insert M Enter
✂	📋	📋

You could think of the X as a tiny pair of scissors.

Using Paste Special

Paste Special allows you to copy a selection, then give Excel specific directions to paste an attribute of the selection or specify how you would like the data pasted. For instance, you may be writing a macro that needs to use the value of the result of a formula in a function, such as the ROUND function. Paste Special also makes it possible to perform a mathematical operation as you paste, such as add the copied data to the pasted area. The Paste Link button causes the new area to update when the copied area is changed. Do all of this and more with the Paste Special dialog box shown in Figure 3.11. For more about Paste Special, see the next two slick tricks or choose the Help button in the Paste Special dialog box.

To use Paste Special:

1 Copy a selection to the clipboard (it doesn't work when you cut).

2 W Right-click M Control+click the top left cell where you want to paste.

3 Choose Paste Special from the shortcut menu.

Paste Special Shortcut Buttons

You can use the Paste Values and Paste Formats buttons as shortcuts for paste special. To use them, copy them to a toolbar from the Edit category

Figure 3.11 The Paste Special
dialog box

in the Customize dialog box. (For more about customizing toolbars,
see Chapter 5.)

To paste values:

1 Copy the cells you want to "paste special."

2 Select the area where you want to paste.

3 click on the Paste Values button ▦ to paste values.

To paste formats:

1 Copy the cells you want to "paste special."

2 Select the area where you want to paste.

3 Click on the paste formats button ▦ to paste formats only.

The Format Painter button is probably faster, but the Paste Formats
button is a shortcut in its own right and it is a "great reverso" of the
Paste Values button. This means that you can press the Shift key when
you click on one of them, and cause the action of the other.

Transpose

One of the check boxes in the Paste Special dialog box is Transpose.
This is a great option if you have several sources sending you information in worksheets, but the authors have arranged the information in
rows, and you need it lined up in columns, or visa versa. Figure 3.12
shows how the selection in A3 through D9 would paste into A12
through G15 with the Transpose check box turned on. It's nearly perfect. For other possibilities of transposing worksheet data, see Chapter
10, "Pivot Tables."

	A	B	C	D	E	F	G
1	Beeper's Airline 1Q Expenses						
2							
3		Jan	Feb	Mar			
4	Salary	$3,800	$4,200	$4,200			
5	Maintenance	$980	$1,340	$1,120			
6	Overhead	$1,000	$1,000	$1,000			
7	Fuel	$1,800	$2,500	$3,100			
8							
9	Expenses	$7,580	$9,040	$9,420			
10							
11							
12		Salary	Maintenance	Overhead	Fuel		Expenses
13	Jan	$3,800	$980	$1,000	$1,800		#REF!
14	Feb	$4,200	$1,340	$1,000	$2,500		#REF!
15	Mar	$4,200	$1,120	$1,000	$3,100		#REF!

Figure 3.12 Tranposing columns and rows

Formulas Don't Transpose

Notice in Figure 3.12 that relative formulas do not transpose. You need to rewrite relative formulas or turn on the values check box in Paste Special to paste them as values when you transpose. For slick ways to transpose sections of a worksheet and keep formulas intact, see Chapter 10, "Pivot Tables."

Deleting

You can delete the contents of cells or you can delete cells completely. Either way, you will affect formulas which refer to those cells.

Clearing Contents

There are several quick ways to clear the contents of a cell. Select the cells you want to clear, then:

Action	Result
Ⓦ Press Delete Ⓜ Del	Clears contents.
Click on 🖌	Clears contents.
Drag the fill handle to the upper left corner of the selection	Clears contents.
Ⓦ Press Backspace Ⓜ Delete (use to clear one cell only)	Clears contents and leaves the insertion point ready to type in the cell. It's like pressing Delete and then pressing F2 all in one stroke.

You can also use any of the Cut shortcut methods, which clear the contents of a cell and place them in the clipboard. You don't have to reuse the clipboard contents just because it's there.

The Difference between Clearing and Deleting

When you clear a cell, you empty its contents—you don't actually delete the cell. When you delete the cell itself, remaining cells shift to accommodate. You can also delete a cell by deleting the entire row or column which contains it. Be sure you are aware of the effect the deletion will have on existing formulas and the layout of your worksheet.

For instance, in Figure 3.13, if you clear the contents of cell B5, it will affect the formula in cell B9. If you delete cell B5, you will need to shift the cells up or left, which would mess up the logic of the worksheet. It would be better to delete cells A5 through D5 or the whole row.

Insert and Delete Cell Shortcuts

There are five quick methods for deleting and inserting cells.

To insert or delete using the Edit shortcut menu shown in Figure 3.9:

1 Ⓦ Right-click Ⓜ Control+click on the cell or range you want to delete or insert, and choose Insert or Delete.

2 Choose how you want to shift cells from the dialog box, then choose OK.

B9		=SUM(B4:B8)	
A	**B**	**C**	**D**
1	Beeper's Airline 1Q Expenses		
2			
3	Jan	Feb	Mar
4 Salary	$3,800	$4,200	$4,200
5 Maintenance	$980	$1,340	$1,120
6 Overhead	$1,000	$1,000	$1,000
7 Fuel	$1,800	$2,500	$3,100
8			
9 Expenses	$7,580	$9,040	$9,420

Figure 3.13 Deleting

To use the Delete Cells and Insert Cells buttons, copy them to a toolbar from the Edit category in the Customize dialog box. (For more about customizing toolbars, see Chapter 5.)

To insert or delete using a keyboard shortcut or the insert or delete cells button:

1 Select a range the size you want to delete or insert, in the location where you want to insert or delete.

2 Press Ctrl+minus sign (–) to delete, or click on the Delete Cells button 圕. To insert, either press Ctrl+plus sign (+) or click on the Insert Cells button 圕. (Use the numeric keypad.)

To insert, dragging with the mouse:

1 Select a range of cells as wide as those you want to insert, in the location where you want to insert them.

2 Hold down the Shift key as you drag the fill handle down as far as you want to insert them.

To delete by dragging with the mouse: Hold down the Shift key as you drag the fill handle to the upper left corner of the selection, then let go.

Insert and Delete Entire Rows and Columns

To insert or delete a row or column using the shortcut menu:

1 Select the number of row or column headings you want to insert, in the location where you want them inserted.

2 Ⓦ Right-click Ⓜ Control+click on the selection and choose insert or delete.

To use the Delete Rows, Delete Columns, Insert Rows, and Insert Columns buttons (shown below), copy them to a toolbar from the Edit category in the Customize dialog box. (For more about customizing toolbars, see Chapter 5.)

Delete Rows	🔳
Insert Rows	🔳
Delete Columns	🔳
Insert Columns	🔳

To insert or delete a row or column using the Insert or Delete Rows or Columns buttons:

1 Select the number of rows or columns you want to insert anywhere in the row or column (you do not have to select the heading).

2 Click on the appropriate button to delete or insert rows or columns.

You Can Lose Everything when You Delete a Row or Column

🚫 When you delete rows or columns you will not get an alert box. The rows or columns and everything contained within them will be deleted. Remember, you can always undo immediately.

Edit Multiple Sheets Simultaneously

Very often a cloned worksheet is used for each division, each quarter, or whatever. One of the greatest new conveniences in Excel 5.0 workbooks is the ability to edit more than one worksheet at the same time.

To select all tabs:

1 Ⓦ Right-click Ⓜ Control+click one of the sheet tabs.

2 Choose Select All Sheets.

To select contiguous sheets, Shift+click on the first tab and the last tab in the selection.

To select noncontiguous tabs, Ⓦ Ctrl+click Ⓜ Command+click on each tab you want to select.

Once the worksheets have been grouped, you can add column or row headings, move, copy, delete, format or name nonadjacent ranges, or spell-check all selected sheets simultaneously.

Spelling

You can check the spelling of more than one sheet, including chart sheets, by selecting all the sheets you want included in the spelling check; then press F7 or click on 📖.

Chapter 4

· · · · · · · · · · · · · · · · · · · ·

Worksheet Formatting

EASE OF FORMATTING IS ONE OF THE reasons Excel is becoming the spreadsheet industry standard. You can create beautiful presentations with a few slick tricks.

Excel 5.0 has six tabs in the Format Cells dialog box, which contain most of the formatting commands you will need. If you are looking for Excel 4.0 formatting commands, you will find them on one of the tabs in the Format Cells dialog box.

Bringing Up the New Format Dialog Box

You can bring up the new Format dialog box in one of four ways:

- ◆ Press Ctrl+1.
- ◆ W Right-click M Control+click a cell or row or column header, then choose Format Cells.
- ◆ Choose Format, Cells (**Alt, O, E**) from the main menu.
- ◆ Press Ctrl+F to open it with the Font tab activated (see Figure 4.1). If the Formatting toolbar is visible, you will need to press it twice—the first time activates the Font Name box on the Formatting toolbar.

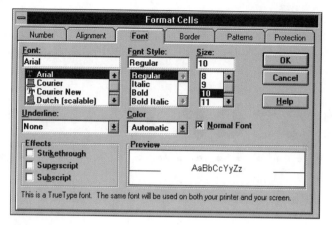

Figure 4.1 The Format Cells dialog box with the Font tab active

The six tabs in the Format Cells dialog box contain many of the formats with which you may be familiar:

Number	Border
Alignment	Patterns
Font	Protection

Most of the formatting that can be done in the formatting dialog box can also be done by clicking on buttons on the toolbars. Many of these tool buttons are on the built-in Formatting toolbar (see Figure 4.2).

The Formatting Toolbar

When Excel opens initially, the Formatting Toolbar is already visible. If not, choose View, Toolbars from the main menu, then choose Formatting. You can also use the Toolbar Shortcut menu to make the Formatting Toolbar visible: Ⓦ Right-click Ⓜ Control+click on a toolbar or the TipWizard box and choose Formatting.

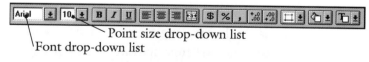
Point size drop-down list
Font drop-down list

Figure 4.2 The Formatting Toolbar

Jump to the Formatting Toolbar

Sometimes it's easier to keep your hands on the keyboard, rather than to reach for the mouse. When the Formatting toolbar is visible, you can jump to the Font list and Font Point size drop-down lists with the keyboard. If the Formatting toolbar is not visible, the following two instructions will open the Format Cells dialog box at the Font tab.

To change the font with the keyboard and the Font drop-down list:

1 Select the cell or range you want to change, and press Ctrl+Shift+F.

2 Press the Down arrow key to display the list.

3 Press the arrow keys to choose the font you want, then press Enter.

To change the point size with the keyboard and the Point drop-down list:

1 Select the cell or range you want to change, and press Ctrl+Shift+P.

2 Press the Down arrow key to display the list.

3 Press the arrow keys to choose the point size you want, then press Enter.

Using ToolTips or Balloon Help

Until you are familiar with all of the tool buttons, you can use ToolTips in Windows and Balloon Help in Macintosh to read a description of button images. To see a description of any button image, place the mouse cursor above it. The desciption will also appear in the status bar.

Formatting with a Toolbar Button

To format with most of the toolbar buttons:

1 Select the range, cell, or text you want to format.

2 Click on a toolbar button.

The Format Painter Button

The Format Painter button works a little differently than the rest of the toolbar buttons.

To copy the format of a cell (or object) to other cells (or objects):

1 Click on the cell that has the format you want to copy.

2 Click on the Format Painter button ⬛. (If you change your mind, click on the button again or press Esc.)

3 Click on the cell, or paint the cells, where you want the format copied to.

To copy the format to more than one place:

1 Click on the cell that has the format you want to copy, and double-click on the Format Painter button.

2 Click and drag wherever you want the format copied to.

3 Continue to paint (it's sort of like the Midas touch, only different).

4 Click on the Format Painter button or press Esc to turn it off.

A Format Painter Limitation

If you want to copy the format of a cell that contains more than one text format, only the formatting of the first character will be pasted into the cells you paint. For instance, if a cell contains the following:

| **Activity** |
| Testing |

and you copy and paste it with Format Painter, all of the text will be copied in bold print.

More Formatting Tools

There are several formatting buttons available, such as the Double Underline ⬛ and Strikethrough ⬛ buttons, which are not located on built-in toolbars. These can be placed on a toolbar by themselves or placed on an existing toolbar.

To access additional formatting buttons:

1 Ⓦ Right-click Ⓜ Control+click on a toolbar and choose Customize, then choose Formatting or Text Formatting.

2 Click on each button to see a description of it at the bottom left corner of the dialog box.

3 Drag the buttons you want to use to an existing toolbar, or to the workspace to create a new toolbar.

For more customizing toolbar slick tricks, see Chapter 5, "Toolbars and Workspace Options."

Rows and Columns

Row Height and Column Width

When you place the mouse pointer on top of a row or column heading boundary, it changes from a fat, white cross to a slim, black cross with two arrows (see Figure 4.3). The arrows point horizontally when on a column and vertically when on a row. Once it is centered on one of these boundaries, you can change the size of a row or column using the eyeball approach rather than by precise measurements.

♦ To change the height of a row, drag the bottom boundary of the row heading to the desired height.

♦ To change the width of a column, drag the right boundary of the column heading to the desired width.

♦ You can also select several rows or columns and then drag the boundary of one to change them all.

	A	B	C	D
1	Beeper's Airline 1Q Expenses			
2				
3		Jan	Feb	Mar
4	Salary	$3,800	$4,200	$4,200
5	Maintenance	$980	$1,340	$1,120
6	Overhead	$1,000	$1,000	$1,000
7	Fuel	$1,800	$2,500	$3,100
8				
9	Expenses	$7,580	$9,040	$9,420

Figure 4.3 The mouse pointer changes into a slim, black cross.

Format Best Fit Rows and Columns

1 Select a row or column, or several rows or columns.

2 Place the mouse pointer at the top of one of the header boundaries until it changes into the slim, black cross shown in Figure 4.3, and double-click.

Precise Measurements for Row Height and Column Width

If you would like to determine the height or width of a row or column with precise measurements, you can bypass the main menu by choosing Format Row (**Alt/, O, R**); or Format, Column (**Alt/, O, C**).

To use the shortcut menu:

1 W Right-click or M Control+click on a row or column header.

2 Choose Column Width or Row Height, and type in your measurement.

The Effect of Clicking on Hidden Rows and Columns

If you have hidden rows and columns, you may accidentally unhide them if you try to change the size of rows and columns with the mouse. Make sure the cross looks like the one shown in Figure 4.3 before dragging. If it appears to have a double line, as shown in Figure 4.4, instead of a single line, it is about to unhide rows or columns. For more about hiding and unhiding, see Chapter 6.

Text

· ·

Change the Default Font Format

1 Choose Tools, Options (**Alt/, T, O**); then choose the General tab.

2 Select the font you want in the Standard Font box and choose OK.

Figure 4.4 The mouse pointer ready to unhide rows or columns

Format Text before, after, or during Typing

You can apply format to text as you are typing or after you type it. Select the range, format it, then enter the data. Or enter the data, then format the range.

You can also format individual characters within a cell before or after you type them. For example: To apply the bold format to part of the text in a cell such as:

Percentage: **15% allowed**

1 Type **Percentage:**.

2 Press Ctrl+B and type **15%**.

3 Press Ctrl+B again, and type **allowed**.

Alternatively, you can type the text, select the portion you want to format, and then apply the format. In the example above, you would:

1 Type **Percentage: 15% allowed**.

2 Select **15%**, and press Ctrl+B.

You can also click on the Bold button **B** to apply bold.

Alignment

There are three obvious formatting options on the Formatting toolbar to align data in cells:

Left	
Right	
Center	

Three less obvious options are also available: Text Wrap, Justified Wrapped Text, and Text Centered Across Columns.

Wrapping and Justifying Text within a Cell

After you have wrapped or justified text, you may need to double-click on the row heading, using Best Fit to bring all text into view.

To wrap text automatically within cells:

1 Adjust the column to the width you want.

2 Select the cells containing the text you want to wrap and Ⓦ right-click Ⓜ Control+click on the selection to bring up the shortcut menu.

3 Choose Format Cells and turn on the Wrap Text check box, then choose OK.

To justify text:

1 Adjust the column to the width you want.

2 Select the cells containing the text you want to justify and Ⓦ right-click Ⓜ Control+click the selection to bring up the shortcut menu.

3 Choose Format Cells, and turn on the Horizontal Justify radio button, then choose OK.

It's not necessary to turn on the Wrap Text check box when you justify text, because the text wraps automatically.

Centering across Columns

To center text across a selection:

1 Place the text in the left cell of the selection.

2 Select across to the right edge of the selection.

3 Click on the Center Across Columns button ▦.

Borders

· ·

Applying borders, patterns, and shading can add professionalism and pizzazz to your spreadsheets. Even if you don't have a color printer, using color can still add color to your screen and shading to your printouts.

Adding Borders and Patterns

To use the shortcut menu:

1 W Right-click M Control+click on the selection you want to format, and choose Format Cells.

2 Activate the Border or Patterns tab.

3 Choose the border or pattern you want, and choose OK.

To use a button on the built-in toolbars:

1 Select the range you want to format.

2 Click on one of the following buttons:

Border		on the Formatting toolbar
Color		on the Formatting toolbar
Pattern		on the Drawing toolbar

Each of these have tear-off palettes, which you can drag to your workspace after clicking on the drop-down arrow. Once you tear off a palette, you can use it like a visible toolbar. For more on how to use toolbars and palettes, see Chapter 5.

Tear-Off Palettes

You can now place a palette of the borders, colors, patterns, and font colors that you will be using frequently right at your mousetips:

1 Click on any of the tools that have drop-down arrows.

2 Drag the palette off the button image onto your workspace.

3 When you are through with the palette, click (once) on the close box in the top left corner.

Once you place a palette on your worksheet, you can format a range or cell by clicking on the palette.

Apply a Border

To apply a default outline border:

1 Select a cell or range.

2 Press W Ctrl+Shift+& (ampersand). (M Look for a comparable shortcut key. Excel 5.0 for the Macintosh was not available at the time of this printing.)

Remove All Borders

To remove all borders, make your selection and press Ⓦ Ctrl+Shift+_ (underscore). (Ⓜ Look for a comparable shortcut key. Excel 5.0 for the Macintosh was not available at the time of this printing.)

Make Borders and Patterns Stand Out

You can remove gridlines to make borders and patterns more vivid.

❶ Choose Tools, Options (**Alt/, T, O**); then activate the View Tab.

❷ Turn off the Gridlines check box and choose OK.

If you turn off the gridlines from the Options dialog box, they will not be visible on your screen, nor will they print. If you turn them off in the File, Page Setup (**Alt/, F, U**) dialog box, you can prevent them from printing but still keep them visible on your screen.

Borders Are Shared

The appearance of borders on your worksheet may be misleading: Adjoining cells share lines. This can cause frustration when you print or copy the format. A cell that seems to have a line on one side may only be sitting next to the cell that actually contains the border. You can use Print Preview to save trees; then make changes, if necessary, before you actually print.

Numbers

You can format a row or column before or after you enter numbers. For instance, if you want a column to display numbers in the currency format, you can select the column and click on the currency button, regardless of whether or not you have entered the data. Table 4.1 demonstrates the formatting of numbers.

Table 4.1 Applying Number Formats

Format	Shortcut Key	Toolbar Button	Example
Currency	Ctrl+Shift+$		456 becomes $4.56
Percent	Ctrl+Shift+%	%	.56 becomes 56%
Comma	Ctrl+Shift+!	,	4567 becomes 4,567.00

Enter Decimal Points without Typing Them

1 Choose Tools, Options; then select the Edit tab.

2 Turn on the Fixed Decimal check box.

3 Type in the number of decimal places you want, then choose OK.

If you format decimal places from the Edit tab, it affects the operation of your session, not the format of a range of cells. If you turn off the Fixed Decimal check box, the data you have previously entered will not be reformatted.

Accounting Number Formats

Excel has four built-in Accounting number formats that keep the dollar sign to the left of a cell, show negative values in parentheses, and show zero values as hyphens. They are shown in Figure 4.5.

To select an Accounting format:

1 Select the range then Ⓦ right-click Ⓜ Control+click on it. Choose Format, Cells. Or, press Ctrl+1.

2 Activate the Number tab and choose Accounting.

3 Click on the format you want.

4 Leave the dialog box open if you want to add underlines to currency entries.

To add single or double underlines to currency entries:

1 Select the Font tab.

2 Choose Single Accounting or Double Accounting from the Underline drop-down box.

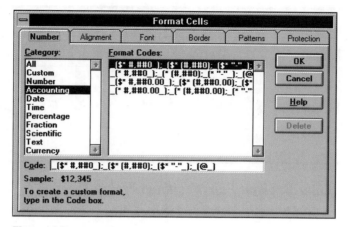

Figure 4.5 The Accounting number formats

Creating Custom Number Formats

The easiest way to create a custom format is to select a built-in format that is close to what you want and then edit it.

When you create a custom number format, it is available throughout the workbook in which it was created, but will not be in other workbooks that you open. It will be located in the appropriate category, as well as in the Custom category. For instance, if you create a currency format, it will be available in the Currency and in the Custom categories. The format can contain up to three number sections and a text section, separated by semicolons. Formats must be in the following syntax:

positive number format;negative number format;zero format;"text format"@

Commas are used as delimiters to separate arguments. If only the first argument is used, the rest of the commas may be left off. For instance, if you create the following formats:

Example format 1: $#,##0.00;[Red]($#,##0.00);0;"Total for "@

If you type:	The data in the cell will read:
45678	$45,678.00
-45678	($45,678.00) *in red*
0	0
January	Total for January

Example format 2: 000-000-000

If you type:	**The data in the cell will read:**
8005551212	800-555-1212

Example format 3: ;;;"Reading for the day: "

If you type:	**The data in the cell will read:**
Psalm 100	Reading for the day: Psalm 100

Increase or Decrease Decimal Places

Two buttons on the Formatting toolbar make it easy to change the decimal places of a selection:

To increase

To decrease

Format vs. Stored Value

The number you see in a cell may be different than the one Excel is storing, due to the format. You can see the difference if you look at the cell and the number in the Formula bar. For instance, 12,346 in the cell may be 12,345.97 formatted without decimal places. If you want Excel to calculate on the displayed values, you can permanently change the constant values (they *cannot* be changed back) to their displayed values:

1 Choose Tools, Options (**Alt/, T, O**).

2 Activate the Calculation tab.

3 Turn on the Precision as Displayed check box, then choose OK.

Enter Fractions As Mixed

If you enter a fraction as mixed, you avoid having Excel read it as a date format; for instance, enter ¼ as **0 1/4**.

Remove All Formats

To use the Clear Format button, copy it to a toolbar from the Edit category in the Customize dialog box. For more about customizing toobars, see Chapter 5.

To remove all formats:

1 Select the cell or range from which you want to clear formats.

2 Click on the Clear Formats button 📝.

AutoFormats

• •

AutoFill Formats

If you drag the fill handle with the Ⓦ right mouse button Ⓜ Control key held down, when you let go, a shortcut menu will appear. You can then choose Fill Formats.

AutoFormats

It's easy to apply combinations of formats to a selected range. The AutoFormat dialog box lets you preview each one before making a decision. If you click on the Options button you can turn off some of the check boxes and keep the formats you have already applied to your selection (see Figure 4.6).

To Apply an AutoFormat:

1 Select a cell in your range. (If Excel can't figure out the whole range, it will prompt you to select it.)

2 Choose Format, AutoFormat (**Alt/, O, A**).

3 Click through the choices until you find the one you want.

To remove an AutoFormat, you can Undo immediately; or select the range later and choose None from the AutoFormat dialog box.

Repeating AutoFormats

There is a button in the Formatting category of the customize dialog box which causes Excel to AutoFormat with the default choices, or repeat the last table format you selected in your session. If you are going to use AutoFormat a lot, it would be worth adding this button to a toolbar 🔲. For more about customizing toobars, see Chapter 5.

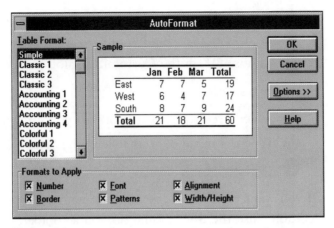

Figure 4.6 The AutoFormat dialog box after
clicking on Options

Styles

You can define several formats for a cell and then name the formats with
a style. In a new workbook, only the built-in styles will be available, but
once you have created a style, you can copy it between workbooks. A
key element assisting you with styles is the Style Name box. It displays
the name of the current style and allows you to change it by selecting
from the drop-down list.

The great advantage of using a style is that even if it is a simple one—
readily available from the Formatting toolbar—you can redefine the
style to automatically change all the cells to which that style has been
applied. For instance, you could apply a currency style, which includes
decimal places, to several ranges in a workbook. If you decide later that
you would like to remove the decimal places from those ranges, you
need only to redefine the style.

There are two ways to bring up the Style Name box: Choose Format,
Style (**Alt/, O, S**); or press Alt+ ′ (apostrophe).

You can also add the Style Name box to a toolbar:

1 Ⓦ Right-click Ⓜ Control+click on a toolbar.

2 Choose Customize, then Formatting.

③ Drag the Style Name box to a toolbar, or to the workspace to make it a toolbar by itself.

④ Choose OK in the Customize dialog box.

To create a style:

① Select a cell that has the formats you want to use.

② Type the name of your style in the Style Name box.

③ Press Enter.

If you want to turn off the effect of your style on some of the formats, don't use the Style Name box on a toolbar; use the one in the Style dialog box Ⓦ (Alt+ ') and turn off appropriate check boxes before you press Enter. (Ⓜ Look for a comparable shortcut key. Excel 5.0 was not available at the time of this printing.)

Select Multiple Formats before Creating a Style

You can create a new style from cells that are not exactly the same but have some formats in common. Select several cells (instead of one) before creating your style. The new style will reflect the formats in common and ignore those that are not.

To apply a style to another selection:

① Select the cells to which you want to apply the style.

② Select the style from the Style Name box.

To copy a style to another workbook:

① Open both workbooks and activate the one without the style.

② Press Alt+ ' , click on the Merge button.

③ Ⓦ Select the workbook that has the styles you want.
(Ⓜ Look for a comparable shortcut key. Excel 5.0 was not available at the time of this printing.)

④ Choose OK to copy them into the new workbook.

Duplicate Style Names

  If the active workbook contains styles that have the same names as those being copied, you will be asked if you want to replace them. If you say yes, it will overwrite all conflicting style names without prompting you for each one.

To redefine a style:

① Select a cell that has the formats you want and press Ⓦ Alt+'. (Ⓜ Look for a comparable shortcut key. Excel 5.0 was not available at the time of this printing.)

② Type the name of the style you want to redefine in the Style Name box.

Alternatively:

① Select a cell that has the formats you want and press Ⓦ Alt+'. (Ⓜ Look for a comparable shortcut key. Excel 5.0 was not available at the time of this printing.)

② Select the style you want to redefine from the Style Name box and click on the Modify button.

③ Make the changes you want in any of the tabs in the Format, Cells dialog box.

④ When you press OK, you can still make more changes by turning off check boxes in the Style dialog box.

To delete a style:

① Press Ⓦ Alt+'. (Ⓜ Look for a comparable shortcut key. Excel 5.0 was not available at the time of this printing.)

② Select the style you want to delete from the Style Name box.

③ Click on Delete.

When you delete a style, all cells formatted with that style revert to Normal.

Chapter 5

Toolbars and Workspace Options

Some of the slickest tricks can be orchestrated from toolbars. This chapter gives tips on how to optimize the toolbar buttons to best suit your needs. You will also find tips on how to set the defaults in your workspace to make it the most convenient launching pad for your personal taste, whether you're a rocket scientist or any sort of creative genius.

The Workspace

Most of the workspace attributes and defaults can be changed in the Options dialog box (**Alt**, **T**, **O**). The trick is in trying to remember which tab contains which feature.

 ### A Quick Reference to Tools, Options

This section will orient you to the eight tabs in the Options dialog box. Its purpose is to apprise you of workspace option possibilities and minimize the number of times you need to search through the Options tabs. I have divided these tabs into three groups:

Five of the tabs have obvious purposes:

Tab:	Used to:
Chart	Set chart options
Color	Set color options
Calculation	Set calculation options
Custom Lists	View existing lists and create new lists
Transition	Assist in Lotus 1-2-3 and other spreadsheet transitions

Two Visual Basic Application (VBA) options used for programming:

Tab:	Used for:
Module General	VBA procedures and display
Module Format	VBA font format and color of code

If the old adage about the word value of pictures is true, the first three figures in this chapter (Figures 5.1, 5.2, and 5.3) are worth three thousand words. Three worksheet tabs used to adjust workbook and worksheet options:

Tab:	Used to:
General	Set workbook and worksheet options
View	Change display
Edit	Change how editing takes place

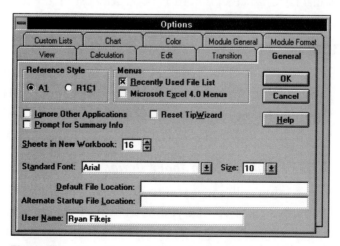

Figure 5.1 The **General** tab

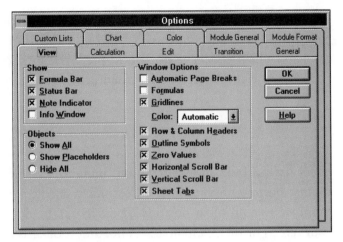

Figure 5.2 The View tab

Tab Reminders

Remember that you can switch between tabs with the keyboard as well as with the mouse by pressing Ctrl+Tab.

Remember also that a detailed description of each tab feature is at your mousetips: Click on the Help button within the dialog box.

When you make changes to your workspace, Excel saves them for you at the end of the session and brings them back in the next. For instance, if you have deactivated the Prompt for Summary Info check box on the General tab, you will not be prompted with that dialog box each time

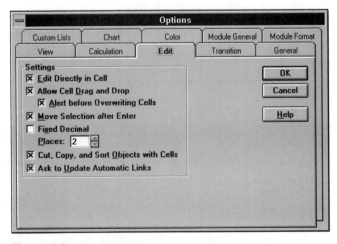

Figure 5.3 The Edit tab

you save a new workbook in future sessions. This includes toolbars; any custom toolbars you create will still be in the Toolbar menu. Visible toolbars, which you have docked in preferred locations, will be visible and docked right where you left them when you start the next session.

Toolbars

Excel has 13 built-in toolbars (and numerous additional ready-to-use toolbar buttons) hiding in the Customize dialog box. You can also assign macros to toolbar buttons. Toolbars can be docked at the edge of your screen or they can "float." A floating toolbar is not as independent as it may sound; it only moves when you move it. The word "floating" merely indicates that it is not docked and that it contains a title bar with a close box. A toolbar will change from horizontal to vertical when you drag it to one side. Figure 5.4 shows several different types of toolbars in various positions.

Make Toolbars Visible

The easiest way to make a toolbar visible is to use the Toolbar shortcut menu. But if no other toolbars are visible, use the main menu.

To make a toolbar visible with the shortcut menu:

1 W Right-click M Control+click on an existing toolbar or check the TipWizard box.

2 Select a toolbar, or select Toolbars from the Toolbar dialog box, if the toolbar you want is not on the shortcut menu.

To make a toolbar visible using the main menu:

1 Choose View, Toolbars (**Alt/, V, T**).

2 Choose the toolbar you want and choose OK.

There are more toolbars listed in the Toolbar dialog box than on the shortcut menu.

Standard Toolbar

To show or hide the Standard toolbar, press Ctrl+7.

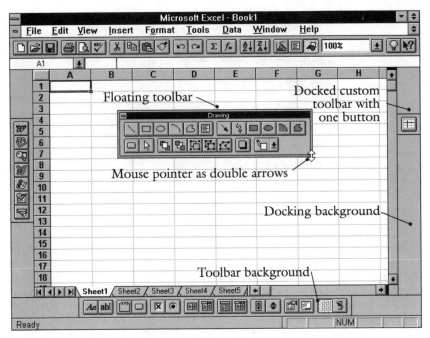

Figure 5.4 Various toolbar positions and attributes

Moving Toolbars—Docking or Floating

You can drag a toolbar around by its background, or title bar if it has one. When you you drag the toolbar near the edge of the screen and let go, the toolbar usually docks. However, if it is a toolbar with a drop-down list box or a palette, such as the zoom box on the Standard toolbar, it will only float or dock horizontally. A floating toolbar has a title bar and a close box. You can double-click on the close box to hide it.

When the mouse pointer changes to a double-arrow on a floating toolbar, you can drag the side to change the toolbar's shape.

Double-Click to Float or Dock

Double-click on the background of a toolbar to toggle between a floating or docked toolbar. It will return to its last floating or docked position.

Double-Click to Bring Up the Toolbar Dialog Box

If a portion of a toolbar docking background is visible, double-click on it to bring up the Toolbar dialog box (Figure 5.5).

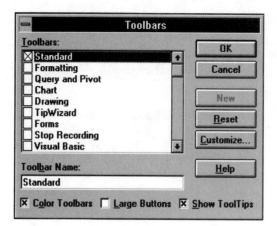

Figure 5.5   The Toolbar dialog box

Controlling Toolbar Attributes

At the bottom of the Toolbar dialog box, three self-explanatory check boxes give you control over the appearance of the toolbar buttons. All three—Color Toolbars, Large Buttons, and Show Tooltips (in Windows)—are extras that use up power. If you turn them off, your system will run faster.

Ⓦ Remember that if you turn off ToolTips, you will still be able to read descriptions of the toolbar buttons in the status bar.

Customizing Toolbars

You can customize existing toolbars or you can create new ones. All of these fun things can be done when the Customize dialog box is open. It can be opened in three ways:

♦ Ⓦ Right-click Ⓜ Control+click on a toolbar and choose Customize.

♦ Press the Customize button in the Toolbar dialog box.

♦ Type a name for a new toolbar in the Toolbar Name box in the Toolbar dialog box. Click on New.

A new floating toolbar, with the title you gave it, will appear on your screen and the Customize dialog box will open.

Find Hidden Treasures in the Customize Dialog Box

There are quite a few button images in the Customize dialog box, which are not located on any built-in toolbar. Most of them have commands attached to them. For instance, the handy button ⊞ that freezes and unfreezes panes is located in the Utility category, but you will not find it on any built-in toolbar. The last category, appropriately named Custom, has several unattached buttons.

To browse through the Customize buttons on-line:

1 Ⓦ Right-click Ⓜ Control+click on a toolbar and choose Customize.

2 Click on each button in each category to see a description of it in the lower left corner of the dialog box.

3 Choose Close when you are through browsing

If you would prefer to read a list describing the buttons:

1 Double-click on the Help button 🔳 and type in **button**.

2 Click on Show Topics and choose Button Category Summary.

The Great Button Reverso

As you browse through the buttons in the Custom dialog box or in Help, you will notice that quite a few buttons do reverse actions. For instance, there are Ascending and Descending Sort buttons 🔳🔳. If you hold down the Shift key while you press the Ascending Sort key, it will sort with a descending sort, and vice versa. The same is true for the Repeat and Undo buttons 🔳🔳, Print and Print Preview buttons 🔳🔳, the filled and not-filled shape buttons—such as the Rectangle 🔳🔳 and Ellipse 🔳🔳 buttons—as well as many other logical reverses. As you re-arrange buttons and customize toolbars, this information can be very helpful. You can eliminate a lot of buttons from toolbars and use their "partners" in reverse.

Rearranging Toolbar Buttons

While the Customize dialog box is open, you can drag buttons from any of the categories within the Customize dialog box, or from any visible toolbar. If you drag a button from an existing toolbar, it removes the button from that toolbar. If you drag a button from the Customize categories, one copy of the button remains in the dialog box and an-other copy is placed where you dragged it to. There are two places to which you can drag a button image:

♦ If you drag to an existing toolbar, the button becomes a new button on that toolbar. If you were dragging from an existing toolbar, it moves it from one to the other. If you hold down the Ctrl key as you drag, it copies the button.

♦ If you drag to the workspace, the button becomes a toolbar with one tool on it. (Do this only from the Customize dialog box—not from an existing toolbar.)

Making Toolbars Visible When the Customize Dialog Box Is Open

When most dialog boxes are open, normal Excel operations, such as menus, commands, drag-and-drop, etc., are suspended. When the Customize dialog box is open, however, you can still use the Toolbar shortcut menu. This is very handy if you would like to customize a toolbar that is not visible.

1 Ⓦ Right-click Ⓜ Control+click on a visible toolbar.

2 Select the toolbar you want to make visible from the list.

Create a New Toolbar

The pieces of this puzzle are scattered above, so you may be way ahead of me; but so you will have a one-stop place, here's the slickest way to create a brand-new toolbar:

1 Open the Toolbar dialog box and type a name into the Toolbar Name box.

2 Click on New, which opens the Customize dialog box.

3 Drag any buttons you want to appear on it from the Customize categories, the TipWizard, or any existing toolbar.

4 Close the Customize dialog box.

Remember that a button from an existing toolbar will move from its original present location unless you hold down the Ctrl key as you drag.

You can also create a new toolbar without giving the toolbar a name. Open the Customize dialog box from the shortcut menu and drag buttons to the workspace. Excel will name the new toolbars Toolbar1, Toolbar2, etc.

Resetting Built-In Toolbars or Deleting Custom Toolbars

One of the buttons in the Toolbar dialog box is a chameleon: When you have a built-in toolbar selected, the Reset button returns the built-in toolbar to its original state (as it was when Excel was shipped). If you have custom toolbar selected, the Reset button becomes a Delete button. Need I say more?

Restore Toolbars or Save a Toolbar Configuration

Perhaps you have customized your toolbars, and one day you decide to change them again—but then you decide you want them back to the way they were when you started your session. To restore toolbar settings from the beginning of a session, all you need to do is open the toolbar file:

- ◆ W Open the file EXCEL5.XLB. It is located in the EXCEL5\EXCELCBT subdirectory.

- ◆ M System 7—Open the file EXCEL TOOLBARS(5) in the PREFERENCES folder in the SYSTEM folder.

- ◆ M System 6—Open the file EXCEL TOOLBARS(5) in the SYSTEM folder.

If you have created a particular configuration of toolbars that you don't want to use at every session but would like to use again, you can save it under a different name. To create an alternate toolbar file:

1 Customize and arrange toolbars and buttons as you want them.

2 Exit from Excel.

3 Make a copy of the file with a different name (W use .XLB), storing it in the proper directory or folder listed above.

4 Open the file from the File menu whenever you want to use the custom configuration

Copy a Button Image

You may want to copy a button image so that you can attach a macro to it, or use it as a graphic for some other reason. You may want to edit it first (see the next trick). You can also paste the face of one button image on top of another, and the button will still respond the way it did with its old image. For instance, if you copy the image from the Print button to the Print Preview button, it will look like Print button, but respond like the Print Preview button.

Copying and Pasting Buttons

When the Customize dialog box is open and a button is selected, the Edit menu changes the Copy and Paste commands to Copy Button Image and Paste Button Image. It also activates a Button Image shortcut menu (see Figure 5.6).

To bring up the Button Image shortcut menu:

1 Open the Customize dialog box.

2 W Right-click M Control+click on any button image on a visible toolbar.

To copy a button image to the clipboard:

1 Follow the two steps above to bring up the shortcut menu.

2 Choose Copy Button Image.

After you close the Customize dialog box, you can paste the image back onto your spreadsheet. It will be merely a graphic object, and not a button (unless you attach a macro to it). You can also paste the image into other programs by using the clipboard or by dragging.

To copy one button image to another:

1 Follow the steps above to copy a button image.

2 W Right-click M Control+click on a button on a visible toolbar and choose Paste Button Image.

If you have copied the image of one button to another, you can select it with a W right-click M Control+click and then use the shortcut menu to reset it back to its original image using the Reset Button Image command.

Copy Button Image
Paste Button Image
Reset Button Image
Edit Button Image...
Assign Macro...

Figure 5.6 The Button Image shortcut menu

Edit a Button Image

If you select Edit Button Image from the shortcut menu, you bring up the Button Editor (Figure 5.7). This slick editor is logical and easy to use, but if you have any questions concerning its operation, click on the Help button. You can edit buttons from built-in toolbars, or from the Customize dialog box after copying them to a toolbar.

Attaching a Macro to a Toolbar Button

The last category in the Customize dialog box is Custom. It contains several button images which are not assigned to macro commands. If you drag one of these to a toolbar, the Assign Macro dialog box will open. If you do this, you can skip the first three steps in the following example and the first two steps in the next one.

To assign a macro to a button image located on a toolbar:

1 Write or record a macro.

2 Open the Customize dialog box and Ⓦ right-click Ⓜ Control+click on the button you want to assign the macro to.

3 Choose Assign Macro.

4 Type in the name of the macro or select it from the list, then choose OK.

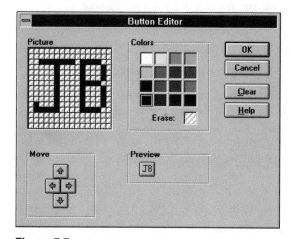

Figure 5.7 The Button Editor

Alternatively:

1 Open the Customize dialog box and W right-click
Ⓜ Control+click on the button you want to assign a
macro to.

2 Choose Assign Macro.

3 Choose Record, then type a name for your macro in the
Record New Macro dialog box and choose OK.

4 Record your macro and click on the Stop Recording button
when you are through.

For more information about recording and editing macros, see Chapter 14, "Macros and Programming."

Placing a Button Image without Attaching a Macro

You may prefer to design your toolbars before attaching macros. You can do this and still use the unassigned button images in the Customize dialog box.

1 Open the Customize dialog box and choose Custom.

2 Drag the button you want to a toolbar.

3 Choose Close in the Assign Macro dialog box.

4 Choose Close in the Customize dialog box.

Attach Custom Toolbars to a Workbook

You can arrange for custom toolbars to appear each time you open a workbook—just as the Chart floating toolbar appears each time you press F11 to create a new chart sheet.

1 Insert a module sheet or open an existing module. The commands on the Tools menu change when a module is active.

2 Choose Tools, Attach Toolbars (**Alt/, T, T**).

3 Copy any of your custom toolbars into the current workbook, using the Attach Toolbars dialog box.

When you open that workbook again, the custom toolbars you copied will be available.

Chapter 6

. . . .

Views, Outlining, and Printing

WORKSHEETS AND EXCEL MACRO SHEETS can be gigantic, but using these tricks with Excel Views and Outlines can help you manage monster workbooks. This chapter also contains more advanced printing slick tricks.

Views

. . . .

You can create a view of your workbook, which includes the active cell, the print area, hidden rows, and window attributes. For instance, you might have one view for each division in your organization. If you select the view of one of the divisions from View Manager, Excel will switch to the worksheet which contains that division, place the active cell where you want to start, zoom the window to the level of magnification at which you saved it, split panes where you need them, and have the print area defined to print only the portion you need for a report. Whew.

This first slick trick teaches you how to create a view. The rest of this chapter contains slick tricks for using screen or printing attributes that you may like to include in a saved view, such as a zoomed view, hidden rows or columns, an outline view, or printing attributes.

Create a View

1 Set up the view the way you want it, including the way you would like it to print.

2 Choose View, View Manager (**Alt/**, **V**); and choose Add.

3 Type a unique name into the Add View dialog box, then choose OK.

If you don't define a print area in a view, it will print the whole worksheet.

Switch to a View

1 Choose View, View Manager (**Alt/**, **V**, **V**).

2 Select the view you want from the View Manager dialog box, and choose Show.

When You Cannot Show Views

You cannot show views when a workbook is protected or when an object or chart is selected.

Delete a View

1 Choose View, View Manager (**Alt/**, **V**, **V**); and select the view you want from the View Manager dialog box.

2 Choose Delete, then Close.

Magnify the View

You can enlarge the view of your screen and the toolbar buttons with the Full Screen command, the Zoom command, and the Toolbar dialog box. You can also zoom out to see the layout of your screen, rather than small detail.

Switch to Full Screen

Excel 5.0 makes it easy to switch to a full screen view. In so doing, you hide everything on the screen except the worksheet area and menus. It's just as easy to switch back, placing all the convenient toolbars, the title bar, and the status bar back into view.

♦ To switch to Full Screen using the Main menu, choose View, Full Screen (**Alt/**, **V**, **U**). Your screen will switch to full and the Full toolbar will become visible. All you have to do to switch back is click on:

♦ To switch to Full Screen using the toolbar button, 🖩 right-click or 🍎 Control+click a toolbar, choose Toolbars; then turn on the Full Screen check box.

The Full toolbar will stay on your screen in both modes, so you can click on it to switch back and forth.

Zoom a Worksheet

You can control the magnification level of a selection within workbooks with the Zoom command on the Workbook Shortcut menu, the Zoom Control box on the Standard toolbar, or one of the magnification buttons. You can zoom a selection within a worksheet, or zoom several sheets simultaneously to help you navigate, overview worksheet contents, or see the detail in an enlarged section.

When you zoom in or out on a worksheet, it does not affect the way the worksheet prints—it will print at 100%.

You can also bring up the Zoom dialog box from the main menu (see Figure 6.1). Choose View, Zoom (**Alt/**, **V**, **Z**).

To Zoom from the Workbook Shortcut menu:

1 Select the sheet or sheets that you want to zoom.

2 🖩 Right-click 🍎 Control+click the menu bar or the title bar of a workbook.

3 Choose Zoom to bring up the Zoom dialog box.

4 Select a magnification level or Fit Selection from the dialog box and choose OK.

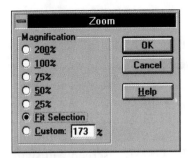

Figure 6.1 The Zoom
dialog box

To Zoom with the Control box:

1 Select the sheet or sheets that you want to zoom.

2 Type or select a size in the Zoom Control box ⌜Zoom⌐ on the Standard toolbar.

To zoom with the magnifying buttons:

1 Ⓦ Right-click Ⓜ Control+click on a toolbar.

2 Choose Customize, then Utility.

3 Drag the magnifying glass buttons 🔍🔍 one at a time to a toolbar.

4 Close the Customize dialog box.

5 Select the sheet or sheets that you want to zoom.

6 Click on the magnifying glass buttons to increase or decrease the magnification level.

When you use the magnifying glass buttons, they zoom to the next increment in the Zoom dialog box.

The Great Reverso Reminder

You can hold down the Shift key on either of the magnification buttons to zoom in the opposite direction.

Zoom a Selection

Sometimes you would like as much of a selection as possible on your screen at one time. Rather than adjust the magnification level using the trial-and-error method, you can tell Excel that you want to see the selection fit within the window.

1 Select the area you want to fit in the window.

2 Choose Selection from the Zoom Control box; or choose View, Zoom (**Alt/, V, Z**).

3 Select the Fit Selection button and choose OK.

Panoramic Views

If you have a selection that will be a large, panoramic view and the detail will be difficult to see, switch to Full view or hide some of the toolbars before you choose Fit Selection. This will give you a greater magnification level.

Make Toolbar Buttons Larger

1 Ⓦ Right-click Ⓜ Control+click on a toolbar and choose Toolbars.

2 Turn on the Large Buttons check box and choose OK.

Focusing the View

There is often a great advantage to focusing the view to a portion of the worksheet data. For instance, you may want to view only titles, subtotals, and totals. This can be done very simply by hiding rows or columns that contain detailed information. The hiding and unhiding process can be used for selected rows or columns, or the entire sheet can be outlined to expand or collapse to various levels of detail.

When you hide or unhide rows and columns, it changes the way the worksheet prints. It is therefore an excellent way to create reports that focus on the "bottom line."

Hiding/Unhiding Rows and Columns

You can tell a row or column is hidden, because the row or column headings are also hidden. For instance, if you have hidden column E, you will see D, then F.

There are three shortcut methods for hiding and unhiding: You can use the mouse, the shortcut menu, or the keyboard.

♦ To hide rows/columns with the mouse, point to a row or column heading border and drag to the edge of the row above or the column to the left.

- To unhide rows/columns with the mouse, point to the border above or to the left where the row or column is hiding. When the pointer turns into a thin, black cross with a space between the direction arrows 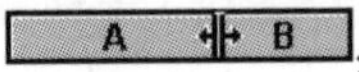

, drag backwards and let go.
- To hide or unhide rows and columns with the shortcut menu, Ⓦ right-click Ⓜ Control-click on a row or column heading or a range of headings, then choose Hide or Unhide.

The hide and unhide commands can also be accessed by choosing Format Row or Column to call their submenus (**Alt/**, **R** or **Alt/**, **C**).

Hide/Unhide Keyboard Shortcuts

Select the rows or columns you want to hide or unhide, or the area where they are hidden, then:

To Hide:	Press:	To Unhide, Press:
Rows	Ctrl+9	Ctrl+Shift+((left parenthesis)
Columns	Ctrl+0 (zero)	Ctrl+Shift+) (right parenthesis)

Group Rows or Columns before You Hide Them

You can expedite the hide/unhide process by grouping rows and columns. This is especially helpful if you are using the mouse shortcut.

To group rows or columns, press Alt+Shift+Right arrow or Ⓦ right-click Ⓜ Control+click on the selection, and choose Group.

To ungroup:

1. Select the rows or columns.
2. Press Alt+Shift+Left arrow.

Or,

1. Select the area where the rows or columns are hidden.
2. Ⓦ Right-click Ⓜ Control+click on the selection and choose Ungroup.

If you are getting ready to create a chart, you can hide everything you don't need, such as unnecessary detail or blank rows or columns used to break totals from the body of data.

Outlines

Outlining a worksheet defines up to eight levels of vertical or horizontal groups. It gives you the ability to focus on summary information and then look at detail with a click of the mouse.

You can save summary information as one view and various levels of detail information as other views. You can then switch between them or print them differently. It is particularly helpful to outline large Excel 4.0 macro sheets on which the code is divided into categories.

You Can Have Only One Outline per Worksheet

If you would like to have separate outline levels for sections of your worksheet, you can copy the sections you want outlined differently to other sheets in the workbook, but you cannot have more than one outline per worksheet. Sorry.

Outline Automatically

If your worksheet has logical formulas and direction of reference, Excel can outline for you. It's worth a try, because you can always Undo or remove the outline if your logic differs from that which Excel considers easy to read.

1. Select the data you want to outline.
2. Choose Data, Group, and Outline (**Alt/, D, G, A**).
3. Choose Auto Outline.

Automatic Styles for an Outline

Excel applies styles to an outline automatically, which makes it easy for you to change the format of the level or heading which Excel applies the style to. For instance, if you decide that you want all of your RowLevel_1 cells to have a pattern in them, you can define the format of RowLevel_1 with a pattern, which then fills all RowLevel_1 cells in your workbook with a pattern.

You need to set Automatic styles *before* you automatically outline. To set automatic styles:

1 Choose Data, Group And Outline (**Alt/**, **D**, **G**, **E**).

2 Choose Settings to display the Outline dialog box.

3 Turn on the Automatic Styles check box and choose OK.

For more about the Outline dialog box options, click on the Help button within it.

For more about adding, redefining, or deleting styles, see Chapter 4, "Worksheet Formatting."

Create an Outline Manually

If the automatic outline doesn't work the way you expected it to, you can remove it, then select individual rows or columns and apply outlining to them. Sometimes an automatic outline is nearly perfect; for instance, Excel may not recognize the first few rows correctly, but everything else may be fine. If that happens, rather than removing the entire automatic outline, remove only a portion of it, then outline that portion manually.

To manually outline:

1 Select the rows or columns.

2 Choose Data, Group And Outline (**Alt/**, **D**, **G**, **G**).

3 Choose Group.

Remove or Hide Outlining

You can remove all outlining or only a portion of it. Anything that is selected before you choose Clear Outline will be affected. You can also keep the outline structure but hide the outlining symbols.

To remove outlining:

1 Select the rows, columns, or range you want to remove the outline from.

2 Choose Data, Group And Outline (**Alt/**, **D**, **G**, **C**).

3 Choose Clear.

Using the Outline Structure

Excel's outlining is very logical. To expand individual outlined areas, click on the plus button. To collapse, click on the minus button. To expand or collapse the entire worksheet to the level you want, click on the number button of the level you want displayed. For instance, if you want to see only the highest level of detail, click on the outline button that has a 1 on it. Figures 6.2, 6.3, and 6.4 show outlines at varying levels.

Select by Using the Outline Plus and Minus Buttons

You can select the entire section represented by the plus or minus sign by holding down the Shift key before you click on it.

Printing

Printing in Excel 5.0 is greatly simplified. It is more logical and user-friendly than ever before. The choices for printing are no longer scattered over the main menu. They are now all located on the File menu

	A	B	C	D	E	F	G	H	I
1		Installer		Jan	Feb	Mar	Apr	May	YTD TOTAL
2	1	I. BOOGIE							
3			Installations	127	111	134	121	143	636
4			Repairs	3	13	7	2	17	42
5			Total	130	124	141	123	160	678
6	2	B. COOL							
7			Installations	105	98	110	101	114	528
8			Repairs	22	15	30	19	26	112
9			Total	127	113	140	120	140	640
10	3	M. BEEPER							
11			Installations	91	100	97	94	89	471
12			Repairs	0	0	11	0	0	11
13			Total	91	100	108	94	89	482
14	4	S. ALADDIN							
15			Installations	100	92	89	90	92	463
16			Repairs	7	6	5	4	17	39
17			Total	107	98	94	94	109	502
18	5	M. MOUSE							
19			Installations	86	85	80	89	86	426
20			Repairs	5	3	0	8	6	22
21			Total	91	88	80	97	92	448
22	6	D. DUCK							
23			Installations	83	85	98	76	76	418
24			Repairs	7	9	5	6	3	30
25			Total	90	94	103	82	79	448
26	8	H. CLINTON							
27			Installations	62	63	66	54	61	306
28			Repairs	64	66	71	81	42	324
29			Total	126	129	137	135	103	630
30	9	M. JACKSON							
31			Installations	69	60	43	59	72	303
32			Repairs	0	0	23	3	0	26
33			Total	69	60	66	62	72	329

YTD SUMMARY \ INSTALLER PERFORMANCE

Figure 6.2 Outline with two levels, both expanded

		A	B	C	D	E	F	G	H	I
			Installer		Jan	Feb	Mar	Apr	May	YTD TOTAL
	1	1	I. BOOGIE							
	2			Total	130	124	141	123	160	678
	5	2	B. COOL							
	6			Total	127	113	140	120	140	640
	9	3	M. BEEPER							
	10			Total	91	100	108	94	89	482
	13	4	S. ALADDIN							
	14			Total	107	98	94	94	109	502
	17	5	M. MOUSE							
	18			Total	91	88	80	97	92	448
	21	6	D. DUCK							
	22			Total	90	94	103	82	79	448
	25	8	H. CLINTON							
	26			Total	126	129	137	135	103	630
	29	9	M. JACKSON							
	30			Total	69	60	66	62	72	329
	33	10	B. DONE							
	34			Total	148	152	147	138	164	749

Figure 6.3 Outline with rows collapsed to level 1

in the Page Setup, Print, or Print Report commands. Each of these will bring up a dialog box. Each dialog box has a Help button, where you can find step-by-step instructions for each option. To get you started with these options, here are a few printing slick tricks.

Set a Print Area

If you do not set a print area, Excel will print the entire active worksheet. You may want to set one print area in one view and a different print area in another view.

To set a print area:

1 Select the area you want to print.

2 Choose File, Page Setup (**Alt/**, **F**, **U**).

		A	B	C	I
			Installer		YTD TOTAL
	1	1	I. BOOGIE		
	2			Total	678
	5	2	B. COOL		
	6			Total	640
	9	3	M. BEEPER		
	10			Total	482
	13	4	S. ALADDIN		
	14			Total	502
	17	5	M. MOUSE		
	18			Total	448
	21	6	D. DUCK		
	22			Total	448
	25	8	H. CLINTON		
	26			Total	630
	29	9	M. JACKSON		
	30			Total	329
	33	10	B. DONE		
	34			Total	749

Figure 6.4 Outline with rows and columns collapsed to level 1

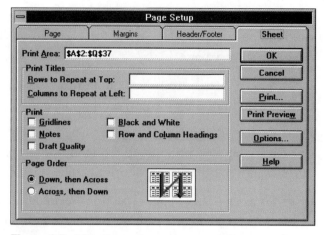

Figure 6.5 The Page Setup Sheet tab

❸ Choose the Sheet tab (Figure 6.5). The Print Area box will contain the area you selected. Choose OK.

There are other ways to get to Page Setup dialog besides (**Alt/**, **F**, **U**): You can press the Page Setup button in the Print dialog box or the Setup button in the Print Preview dialog box.

Print the Whole Worksheet after Setting a Print Area

If you have set a print area but want to change it back to include the whole worksheet, you do not have to paint the entire range of the worksheet that contains data.

You can select a whole worksheet by pressing Ctrl+A or clicking on the Select All button. The Select All button is the blank button to the left of the column headings and above the row headings.

❶ Click on the Select All button or press Ctrl+A.

❷ Choose File, Page Setup (**Alt/**, **F**, **U**).

❸ Select the Sheet tab. The Print Area box will contain the coordinates of the area of your worksheet that contains data.

❹ Choose OK.

Other Sheet Tab Choices

In Figure 6.5, notice that you can also:

Add Titles—You can type in the row or column headings that contain headings for your data in the Print Titles box. This causes them to print on every page.

Print Screen Attributes—You can print gridlines, row and column headings, and notes by turning on the appropriate check boxes.

Print Faster—Choose draft quality, which will not only print with less density on your printer—it also won't print the graphics. You can also choose other levels of print quality on the Page tab.

Print Sharper—If the pages you print seem a little fuzzy, it could be that your screen colors are not sending the right messages to your printer. To clear things up, tell Excel to convert the colors to black-and-white before sending output to the printer.

Add Headers and Footers

Use the Headers/Footers tab to view the default headers and footers that Excel places on your Worksheets, or to create custom headers and footers.

1 Choose File, Page Setup (**Alt/**, **F**, **U**).
2 Select the Headers/Footers tab, and make your changes.
3 Choose OK.

Print Best Fit

When a worksheet is almost the size of one page but it spills over only slightly, instead of spending your time rearranging the margins, use the best fit option:

1 Choose File, Page Setup (**Alt/**, **F**, **U**); and choose the Page tab (Figure 6.6).
2 Choose Fit to 1 by 1, and choose OK.

The Page Setup Page tab is also where you determine other page layout choices or start page numbers at a number other than 1.

Print As Wide As You Want

You can also proportionately best-fit several pages in the Page Setup Page tab. For instance, if you have a worksheet that print previews at 10

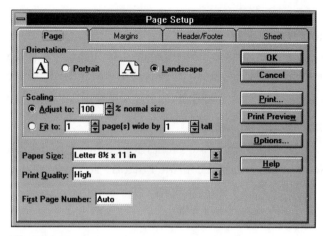

Figure 6.6 The Page Setup Page tab

pages long and one half of those pages are one column wide, you can set the Fit To option to five pages long by 1 page wide to proportionately scrunch your document. You can also leave one of the Fit To check boxes blank to cause your worksheet to print one page wide for as many pages as necessary.

Designate Page Breaks

You can override Excel's choice of where to break pages when your worksheet is printed.

If the entire worksheet is selected or the active cell is directly below or to the left of a page break, the Insert, Page Break command changes to Remove Page Break. Choosing it will remove all page breaks or the one to which the active cell is pointing.

1 Select the cell that you want to be the first row or first column of your new page.

2 Choose Insert, Page Break (**Alt/, I, B**).

Print Multiple Copies or Selected Pages

To control the number of copies of a worksheet to be printed, or to designate selected pages, use the Print dialog box.

1 Press Ctrl+P.

2 Make your selections, and choose OK.

There are several ways to bring up the Print dialog box besides choosing File, Print (**Alt/**, **F**, **P**). You can press Ctrl+P, or click on the Print button in the Print Preview or Page Setup dialog boxes. If you click on the Print button 🖨 on the Standard toolbar, you bypass the Print dialog box, using all of the currently selected print choices.

Print Multiple Sheets

To print more than one sheet, hold down Ctrl or Shift as you select the sheets, then press the print button. You can also turn on the Entire Workbook check box in the Print dialog box (Ctrl+P).

Worksheet Overload Alert

If there is ever a time that your system or Excel will overload, it will be when you are printing—especially if you are trying to print several sheets or a whole workbook. Before you try it, save your workbook and any other significant files open in other applications—just in case.

Avoid Margin Overlap

Margins are set within the Margin tab or in Print Preview (see the following trick). You can also make an adjustment that prevents the footer from overlapping worksheet data:

1 Choose File, Page Setup (**Alt/**, **F**, **U**); and select the Margins tab.

2 Type a number in the Footer box that is smaller than the number in the Bottom box and choose OK.

The Header is already set up this way, but if you have made margin adjustments that overlap the header, type a smaller number in the Header box than in the Top box.

The Eyeball Approach to Margins

When a worksheet almost fits a page in width or length and you want to keep the output of your printer at 100%, instead of going to Page Setup and using the trial-and-error method to reset the margins, you can rearrange them in Print Preview.

1 Click on the Print Preview button 🔍.

2 Click on the Margins button if the margins are not designated with lines and handles, as shown in Figure 6.7.

3 Place the mouse pointer on top of one of the margin handles. It will turn into a thin, black cross.

4 Drag the margins to the size you want them.

It takes patience on your part to wait until Excel readjusts the graphics on the screen, but when you see that the screen contains all the rows or columns you want, press the Print button to print or return to the worksheet by pressing Close.

Adjust Column Width in Print Preview

You can now change the width of columns in Print Preview, rather than returning to the worksheet in the main screen. Just drag the columns where you want them, using the handles shown in Figure 6.7.

Other Print Options

If you can't find the print options you are looking for on any of the four Page Setup tabs or in the Print dialog box, click on the Options button in any of the Page Setup tabs.

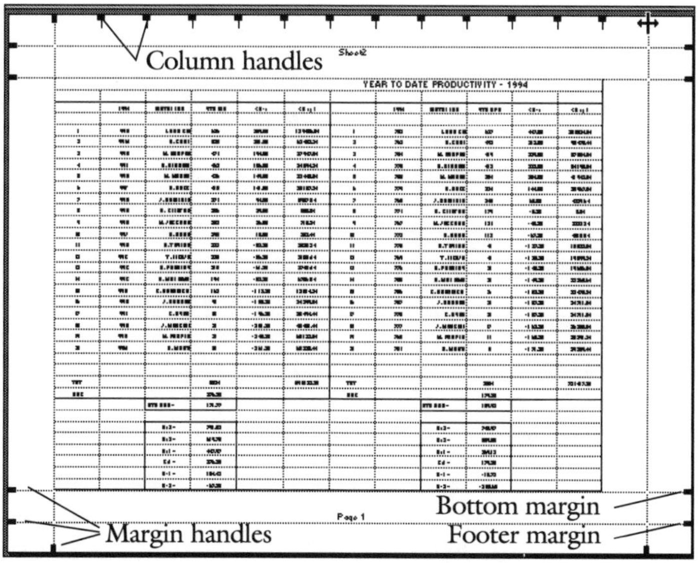

Figure 6.7 **Adjustments that can be made in Print Preview**

Print a View or Scenario

You can print a view or scenario, using the Print Report command. First, you need to create a report that contains the view you want:

1 Choose File, Print Report (**Alt/**, **F**, **E**).

2 Choose Add—the Add Report dialog box will appear.

3 Type a name for your report.

4 Select a sheet, the View and/or Scenario; choose Add.

5 When you have added all the pages you want to print in your report, choose OK.

For more step-by-step instructions on using the Add Report dialog box, click on the Help button. For more about scenarios, see Chapter 9, "Analyzing Data."

To print a report:

1 Choose File, Print Report (**Alt/**, **F**, **E**).

2 Select the report you want to print and choose Print.

Chapter 7

· ·

Slick Tricks for Formulas

FORMULAS ARE THE BACKBONE OF SPREADSHEETS. They are the multi-faceted calculators you put into place to produce information automatically to help you measure or attain success. This chapter contains slick tricks for Excel 5.0 that will take the fear out of writing formulas.

A formula uses mathematical operators to define a relationship between numbers. Excel knows you are about to enter a formula when you type an equal sign (=). The numbers within formulas are often represented by references to cells.

A formula is an equation with one side located in the Formula bar and the other located in the active cell.

Operators perform mathematical operations that combine the values of numbers to produce numeric results—most of the time. Sometimes they produce errors rather than numeric results. Excel's Help has a complete list of the error codes that Excel generates and a description of what each of them means.

References

References identify a location in workbook and they tell Excel where to find the numbers to be used in a formula. They can refer to a cell, a cell range, or a name that represents a cell or cell range. There are three kinds of references: relative, absolute, and mixed. References save you time because formulas are automatically updated when the value in a reference changes.

Relative References

Relative references refer to a cell location that is relative to another. For instance, in Figure 7.1, the cell reference in B4 refers to the cell range consisting of the two cells above it (B2 through B3). If this formula is copied to C2, as in Figure 7.1, it still refers to the two cells above it.

Absolute and Mixed References

Absolute references refer to a particular location, regardless of where the formula is placed. You designate absolute cell references by placing a dollar sign in front of the column and row letter. If you refer to a sheet name as part of a reference, it is always absolute and does not require a dollar sign. Figure 7.2 shows a formula that contains a relative reference subtracting an absolute reference. It is not a mixed reference—it's a "mixed" formula. A mixed reference is one that is half relative and half absolute. It has the dollar sign in front of the column or row letter, but not in front of both.

Point to Cells, Rather than Type In Their References

Once you type an equal sign in a cell or Formula bar, you can use your mouse to point to the cell references you want entered into your formula, type another operator point, and keep adding operators and cell references. When you are through, press Enter or click on the check mark on the Formula bar ☑.

B4	↨	=SUM(B2:B3)		
	A	**B**	**C**	**D**	**E**
1		Jan	Feb	Mar	Apr
2	REG HRS	5427.75	5324.5	6154	6039.5
3	OT HRS	563	1069.75	888.25	830.5
4	TOT HRS	5990.75	6394.25	7042.25	6870
5					
6	% OT	10.37%	20.09%	14.43%	13.75%

Refers to the two cells above

Figure 7.1 **A relative reference**

| G4 | ↓ | =SUM(F4-$F$27) |

	A	B	C	D	E	F	G	H
1				Provisioning Productivity - Year to Date				
2		1994	INSTALLER	INSTALATIONS	DISCONNECTS	TOTAL	TOTAL-AVE	TOTAL-AVE SQ
4	1	9YU	I.BOOGIE	530	106	636	360.40	129888.16
5	2	9YW	B.COOL	459	69	528	252.40	63705.76
6	3	9YR	M.BEEPER	128	347	475	199.40	39760.36
7	4	9YF	S.ALADDIN	399	64	463	187.40	35118.76
8	5	9YE	M.MOUSE	351	75	426	150.40	22620.16
9	6	9YT	D.DUCK	370	48	418	142.40	20277.76
10	7	9YH	J.SEINFELD	326	45	371	95.40	9101.16
11	8	9YS	H.CLINTON	291	15	306	30.40	924.16
12	9	9YH	M.JACKSON	264	39	303	27.40	750.76
13	10	9YJ	B.DONE	291	4	295	19.40	376.36
14	11	9YA	E.TAYLOR	216	7	223	-52.60	2766.76
15	12	9YG	T.FIKEJS	206	14	220	-55.60	3091.36
16	13	9YK	E.PRESLEY	170	45	215	-60.60	3672.36
17	14	9YC	R.WILLIAMS	185	9	194	-81.60	6650.56
18	15	9YQ	C.SANDIEGO	138	25	163	-112.60	12670.76
19	16	9YL	J.BANNAN	65	15	80	-195.60	38259.36
26	TOTAL			4550	962	5512		597072.80
27	AVG			227.50	48.10	275.60		

Figure 7.2 A relative and absolute reference

Don't Use Dollar Signs in Formulas to Indicate Currency

If the numbers within a formula represent money, use currency number formatting to format the result in the cell. Save the dollar sign for the higher cause of absolutes. For more about formatting numbers, see Chapter 4, "Formatting Worksheets."

The Copy and Cut Commands Control Adjustments in Relative References

When you copy and paste a relative reference, the reference is adjusted. When you cut and paste a relative reference, the reference is not adjusted. For instance, in Figure 7.3, if you cut and paste the formula in cell D10 to cell C10, it will paste as the same formula, =SUM (D1:D9). If you copy and paste it, it will paste as =SUM(C2:C9).

Copy a Formula or Paste a Value from the Cell Above

There are two slick shortcuts, one for copying a formula and the other for copying the value of the formula. The first copies the formula from the cell above into the active cell without adjusting the reference. The second copies the value of the cell above it into the active cell.

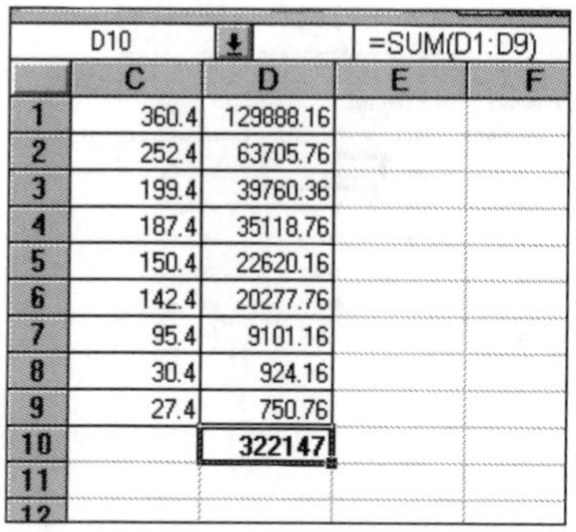

D10	↓		=SUM(D1:D9)	
	C	**D**	**E**	**F**
1	360.4	129888.16		
2	252.4	63705.76		
3	199.4	39760.36		
4	187.4	35118.76		
5	150.4	22620.16		
6	142.4	20277.76		
7	95.4	9101.16		
8	30.4	924.16		
9	27.4	750.76		
10		322147		
11				
12				

Figure 7.3 Cut and paste or copy and paste

To copy a formula exactly from the cell above to the active cell, select the cell beneath the cell which contains the formula you want to duplicate, and press Ctrl+' (apostrophe). For instance, in Figure 7.4, after cell D11 was selected, I pressed Ctrl+'. The formula =SUM(D1:D9) was copied into D11.

To paste the value of the cell above it into the active cell, select the cell beneath the cell that contains the formula value you want to duplicate, and press Ctrl+Shift+" (quotation marks). For instance, in Figure 7.5, after cell D11 was selected, I pressed Ctrl+Shift+". This is a shortcut for using copy, selecting the target cell, then using paste special with the value option selected.

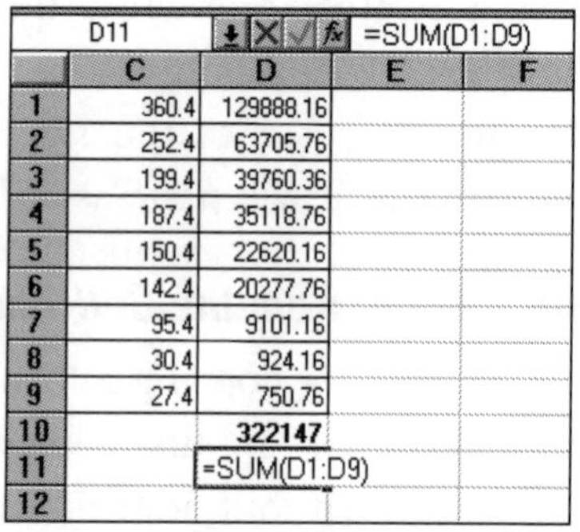

D11	↓ X ✓ ƒ		=SUM(D1:D9)	
	C	**D**	**E**	**F**
1	360.4	129888.16		
2	252.4	63705.76		
3	199.4	39760.36		
4	187.4	35118.76		
5	150.4	22620.16		
6	142.4	20277.76		
7	95.4	9101.16		
8	30.4	924.16		
9	27.4	750.76		
10		322147		
11		=SUM(D1:D9)		
12				

Figure 7.4 The results of pressing Ctrl+'

	C	D	E
1	360.4	129888.16	
2	252.4	63705.76	
3	199.4	39760.36	
4	187.4	35118.76	
5	150.4	22620.16	
6	142.4	20277.76	
7	95.4	9101.16	
8	30.4	924.16	
9	27.4	750.76	
10		322147	
11		322147	
12			

(D11 — 322147)

Figure 7.5 The Results of Pressing Ctrl+Shift+"

"Copy" a Reference

You can combine two of the slick tricks above to "copy" a formula to a location other than the one directly beneath it, without adjusting a relative reference.

All of these copy and paste slick tricks are especially helpful when the formulas that you are working with are very complex.

1 Select the cell beneath the cell that contains the formula you want to duplicate.

2 Press Ctrl+' (apostrophe).

3 Cut and paste the contents of the active cell to the new location.

Make Room for These Copy and Paste Tricks

If the formula you want to copy does not have a blank cell beneath it, you can insert a row and then delete it after you have pasted your copy.

Enter a Reference to an Entire Row or Column

To enter a reference to an entire row or column, type the row or column number twice, separated by a colon. For instance, type B:B or 2:2.

Use Named References

Names can simplify your life immensely. Think how much easier it would be to remember why a reference was used in a formula if it was named total, average, or tax_rate, rather than B2:H2. Also, when you insert columns within rows (or rows within columns) within a named range, the range automatically includes the additions. For instance, in Figure 7.6, B3 through B6 was named Feb before a row was inserted. If a formula elsewhere in the workbook referred to B3:B6, it would need to be updated. If it referred to Feb, no changes would need to be made.

You can name a cell or cell range in two ways:

♦ Select the range you want to name, then type the name into the name box to the left of the Formula bar.

♦ Select the range you want to name, and press Ctrl+F3 to bring up the Define Name dialog box. Type the name and choose OK.

Chapter 9 has other examples of how names can simplify formulas.

The Name box and the Go To box are one and the same. Once a name is defined on a worksheet, it stays unique. If you type it into the box or select it from the drop-down list, you Go To the named range. You can still press F5 to call the Go To *dialog* box, though.

Feb	↓		4200	
	A	**B**	**C**	**D**
1	Month	Jan	Feb	Mar
2	Revenues	2,543.00	4,200.00	3,245.00
3	Expenses	2,123.00	2,206.00	2,215.00
4	Materials	1,023.00	1,106.00	1,115.00
5	Rent	1,100.00	1,100.00	1,100.00
6	Total Income	420.00	2,309.90	2,313.65

	A	**B**	**C**	**D**
1	Month	Jan	Feb	Mar
2	Revenues	2,543.00	4,200.00	3,245.00
3	Expenses	2,123.00	2,206.00	2,215.00
4	Materials	1,023.00	1,106.00	1,115.00
5				
6	Rent	1,100.00	1,100.00	1,100.00
7	Total Income	420.00	2,309.90	2,313.65

Feb	↓		4200	
	A	**B**	**C**	**D**
1	Month	Jan	Feb	Mar
2	Revenues	2,543.00	4,200.00	3,245.00
3	Expenses	2,224.45	2,309.90	2,313.65
4	Materials	1,023.00	1,106.00	1,115.00
5	Utilities	101.45	103.90	98.65
6	Rent	1,100.00	1,100.00	1,100.00
7	Total Income	318.55	2,309.90	2,313.65

Figure 7.6 A row inserted into a range named February is automatically included in that range.

Use Intersected Named References As a Formula

If you have both a column range and a row range named, you can refer to the cell at the intersection of those ranges by typing both names separated by a space. For instance, in Figure 7.7, the rows are named Expenses, Revenues, Materials, etc.; and the columns are named Jan, Feb, Mar, etc. The formulas in cells B10 through B13 are the intersection of the named references for each quarter. Cell B10 contains the formula, =Jan Revenues+Feb Revenues+Mar Revenues.

Apply Names

In Figure 7.7, the formulas could have been created by clicking on the cells to insert the references, and then using the Apply Names command to change the references into names. For instance, the following method could have been used to create the formula in cell B10:

1 Select cell B10 and press =.

2 Click on cell B2 and press +.

3 Click on cell C2 and press +.

4 Click on cell D2 and press Enter.

5 Choose Insert, Names (**Alt/, I, N, A**); choose Apply from the submenu.

6 Select the names Revenues, Jan, Feb, and Mar; choose OK.

B10	↓		=Jan Revenues+Feb Revenues+Mar Revenues			
	A	B	C	D	E	F
1	Month	Jan	Feb	Mar	Apr	May
2	Revenues	2,543.00	4,200.00	3,245.00	3,561.00	3,456.00	4,5
3	Expenses	2,224.45	2,309.90	2,313.65	2,417.35	2,430.33	2,4
4	Materials	1,023.00	1,106.00	1,115.00	1,228.00	1,245.00	1,3
5	Utilities	101.45	103.90	98.65	89.35	85.33	
6	Rent	1,100.00	1,100.00	1,100.00	1,100.00	1,100.00	1,1
7	Total Income	318.55	2,309.90	2,313.65	2,417.35	2,430.33	2,4
8						
9						
10	1 Q Revenues	$ 9,988.00				
11	2 Q Revenues	$11,540.00				
12	3 Q Revenues	$12,657.00				
13	4 Q Revenues	$13,732.00				

Figure 7.7 A formula using the intersection of named ranges

Name References Using the Titles on Your Worksheet

If the logical name for a cell or names for a range are already on your worksheet, you can create the names all at the same time, as shown in Figure 7.8. The Create Names dialog box will propose the most logical location to find the names. Isn't Excel smart?

To create names from existing titles:

1 Select the range, including the row or column titles.

2 Press Ctrl+Shift+F3.

3 If Excel proposes correctly, choose OK. Otherwise, change the check box before choosing OK.

A Name without a Home

You can establish a name without having it refer to a particular cell. For instance, you may want to establish a rate of $10 per hour to be used in calculating payroll throughout your workbook, as shown in Figure 7.9. When the hourly rate changes, you can change the amount **rate** refers to and leave your formulas and workbook intact.

To create a name that doesn't refer to a range:

1 Press Ctrl+F3 to call the Define Name dialog box.

2 Type the name in the Name box.

3 Type an equal sign (=), then the value you want the name to be equal to in the Refers To box.

4 Choose Add, then choose OK.

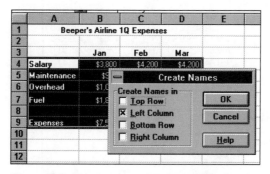

Figure 7.8 Names created (almost) automatically

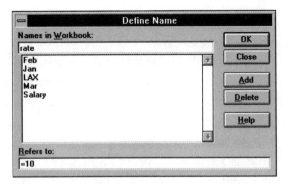

Figure 7.9 **A name without a home to Go To**

Sometimes a Name Won't Appear

A name you defined without a worksheet range reference will not appear in the drop-down list of the name box to the left of the Formula bar because you cannot Go To it.

Formula Toolbar Buttons

There are several toolbar buttons in the Formula category which you may find useful if you prefer to click rather than type. The only one I find useful is the Paste Name button ; but if you are using a pen, you may appreciate the last button in the selection, which constrains pen recognition to digits and punctuation ⟐.

To view or copy the Formula toolbar buttons:

1 Ⓦ Right-click Ⓜ Control+click on a toolbar, and choose Customize.

2 Choose the Formula category.

3 Click on each of the buttons to read their functions in the bottom of the Customize box.

4 Drag the ones you want to use to a toolbar, and choose Close.

Paste a Name

When you are going to use one of the names you have created in a formula, you can avoid misspelling it if you paste it. This is particularly helpful if you have a large workbook with an intricate naming convention. It also confirms that you have actually gotten around to naming the reference as you intended.

Start typing your formula. When you get to the place where you want to use a name as a reference, press F3 or click on the Paste Name button . Then double-click on the name.

Select from the Name Box

You can paste a name into a formula in process from the name box to the left of the Formula bar, rather than bringing up the Paste Name box. The only problem is that some names may not be listed in the name box if they are names without a home, such as the one in Figure 7.9.

Type the First Letter of a Name to Jump through the List

If the list of names in your Create Names dialog box is lengthy, you can jump through it alphabetically.

1 Select any name in the list box (unless one is already selected).

2 Type the first letter of the name you want.

Paste the List of Names

If you would like a list of all the names in your workbook and their references, you can use the Paste List button in the Paste Name dialog box.

1 Select a cell where you want the names to be listed.

2 Press F3 and choose Paste List.

Double Names

Sometimes a cell is named with more than one name. For instance, you may have a cell being referred to by a formula that calls it division_tot, and another formula that calls it jan_tot. It may also be part of two intersecting named ranges; one named January and the other named Totals, which would give it two *more* names that wouldn't show up in the name box unless the entire range was selected. Excel records and remembers all the names of a cell, and uses them appropriately when the cell is referred to in formulas or when the Go To range is used. But only the first name (alphabetically) will show up in the name box when the cell is selected. If you are confused by a different name than you expected showing up in the name box, there's a way to find out all of the names attributed to a cell.

1 Select the cell.

2 W Right-click M Control+click on a toolbar and choose Toolbars.

3 Turn on the Auditing check box.

4 Click on the Info window button.

5 Click on the Names command to display all of the names of the cell.

For more about the Info window and the Auditing toolbar, see the section, "Locating Problems in Formulas," later in this chapter.

Paste the Value of Formulas

1 Copy a selection to the clipboard (it doesn't when you cut).

2 W Right-click M Control+click the top left cell where you want to paste.

3 Choose Paste Special from the shortcut menu.

4 Turn on the Values check box and choose OK.

5 Press Esc to turn off the marquee around the copied area.

Paste Values Shortcut and Its Great Reverso, Paste Formats

You can use the paste values and paste formats buttons as shortcuts for paste special.

To use the paste special buttons, copy them to a toolbar from the Edit category in the Customize dialog box.

To paste values:

1 Copy the cells you want to "paste special."

2 Select the area where you want to paste.

3 Click on the Paste Values button to paste values 🔲.

To paste formats:

1 Copy the cells you want to "paste special."

2 Select the area where you want to paste.

3 Click on the Paste Formats button 🔲 to Paste Formats only.

Refer to Other Workbooks or Other Sheets in a Workbook

You can tell Excel to find a cell reference on another worksheet within your workbook or on another workbook entirely.

Type the name of the workbook (enclosed in brackets), followed by the name of the worksheet, an exclamation point, and a reference.

For example:

Ⓦ [CABLE_CO.XLS]PRODUCTIVITY YTD!$F$27

Ⓜ [CABLE_CO]PRODUCTIVITY YTD!$F$27

Let Excel Place the Exclamation Point

This trick is really the same trick as pointing to references, but it's really slick when you point to another workbook or worksheet. Excel places the worksheet name and the reference into the formula for you.

1 Start your formula with an equal sign.

2 Click on the tab of the worksheet you want (change workbooks if necessary).

3 Paint the range of the reference.

4 Press Enter; or keep adding to your formula until you are done, and press Enter.

3-D References   A 3-D reference spans two or more sheets in a workbook. For instance, you can have a column that contains actual expenses for several regions on several worksheets, and refer to all of them in your formula.

For example:

=SUM(North:South!$F$2:$F$23)

This reference adds the values in column F, from row 2 to row 23, on the sheets named North and South and on all the sheets in between them in the workbook.

To create a 3-D reference:

1 Start typing your formula in a cell.

2 Press the Shift key and click on the first worksheet you want included in the 3-D range (it can be the one you are in or another).

3 Click on the last worksheet you want contained in the range.

4 Paint the range you want and press Enter.

3-D Names

You can name a 3-D range. For instance, as in the example above, North:South!$F$2:$F$23 could be named Actuals.

To create a 3-D name:

1 Go To the first sheet where you want the range to start (it doesn't matter which cell is active).

2 Press Ctrl+F3 to call the Define Name dialog box, and type a name in the name box.

3 Place the mouse pointer in front of the exclamation point in the Refers To box.

4 Paint everything to the right of where you placed the insertion point so it will be deleted when you click again.

5 Click on the Sheet tab of the last sheet you want in the 3-D range, and paint the range you want.

6 Choose Add, then OK.

Functions

· ·

A function is a formula built into Excel that can be used in place of a formula you would write yourself. For instance, instead of typing =+C2+C3+C4+C5+C6, you can type =SUM(C2:C6). The cell range in this example, C2:C6 (contained in parentheses), is the *argument* of the SUM function. Functions always require at least one argument placed in parentheses after the function. Sometimes more arguments are required, and often a function can take optional arguments as well. All this arguing may sound negative, but it's worth it.

The function uses arguments to perform its action. Arguments are separated by commas that designate which argument to use for each calculation. When you leave off arguments at the end, you no longer need the commas to mark their place. If you leave out arguments before the end, you need to mark their place so that the function will know to skip an argument and look for one that accommodates the next calculation. Are you still with me? The following example will help.

The PV function is used to calculate the present value of a loan. The acceptable arguments for PV are (***rate,nper,pmt,fv,type***). The first three arguments are required for the calculation; the last two arguments are not required.

Argument	Requires
rate	A number to calculate the rate.
nper	A number to designate the total number of payment periods.
pmt	A number to designate the amount of each payment.
fv	Zero or a number to determine the future value. If this argument is omitted, it's assumed to be zero. Zero would be the most likely future value of a loan at the end of its life. A number value would be most likely in the case of an annuity—hopefully.
type	Can be zero or one. If this argument is omitted, Excel assumes the type to be zero. Zero means the payment is due at the end of each period. One means it's due at the beginning.

Whew. All of this explanation is to show you how to separate arguments with commas, remember? You could use the PV formula to calculate the content of cells on your worksheet in the following way:

The syntax again: **PV(*rate,nper,pmt,fv,type*)**

PV(B12,B13,B14,,1)	The payment of a loan that will have a future value of 0 is due at the beginning of each period.
PV(B12,B13,B14)	The payment of a loan that will have a future value of 0 is due at the end of each period.
PV(B12,B13,B14,20000)	The payment of an annuity that will be worth $20,000 is due at the end of each period.

Name Remainder

You could name the cells containing the loan data, in the example above, as *rate*, *pay_per*, *payment*, etc. Your formula would make more sense, and you could easily use Go To to find each one.

Type Formulas and Functions in Lowercase

Type function names in lowercase letters. If you have typed them correctly, they will convert to uppercase when you press Enter. If anything stays lowercase, you will know immediately that there is an error.

Use the Function Wizard f_x

This latest, greatest wizard (Figure 7.10) helps you step through the process of writing formulas in a worksheet, just as the Chart Wizard helps you step through the process of creating a chart.

These are some of the Features of the Function Wizard dialog box shown in Figure 7.10:

- If you select a category from the Function Category box, the Function Name box displays a list of names in that category.
- Choosing the next button inserts the list of arguments for a selected function into the Formula bar.

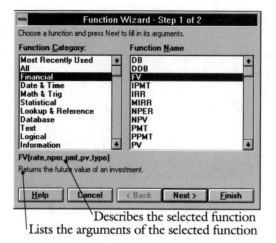

Describes the selected function
Lists the arguments of the selected function

Figure 7.10   The Function Wizard dialog box

Bringing Up the Function Wizard

The following methods can be used to bring up the Function Wizard:

+ Press Shift+F3, then click on the Function Wizard button f_x on the Standard toolbar.

+ Press F2 to activate the Formula bar, then click on the Function Wizard button on the Formula bar.

Turn the Function Wizard into a Formula Edit Wizard

If you have a long formula with several embedded functions, you will appreciate the way the Function Wizard displays the references for each function. To use the Function Wizard as an Editing Function wizard, you can bring it up using Shift+F3 or one of the Function Wizard buttons. If you press F2 first, the Edit Function dialog box (Figure 7.11) will not be brought up when you click on the Function Wizard button.

Select the cell that contains the function or functions you want to examine or debug. Press Shift+F3 or click on the Function Wizard button.

Fill In the Arguments

If you want to see the arguments for a function without using the Function Wizard:

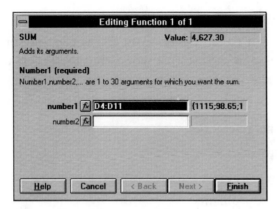

Figure 7.11 The Editing Function dialog box

1 Type an equal sign (=) and a valid function.

2 Press Ctrl+Shift+A.

AutoSum

AutoSum is definitely the favorite tool of avid worksheet builders.

To bring up AutoSum, click on the AutoSum button ⎣Σ⎦ or press Alt+=.

If you select a row or column before you call AutoSum, Excel automatically totals the selection in a the cell or cells to the right of a row or at the bottom of a column.

If you do not make a selection first, Excel will propose a formula from the location of the active cell, which you can accept or change. For instance, it will look to the left in a row, up in a column, and then look for a blank cell to end its proposal. If you don't agree with the proposal, you can drag the range you want to be summed, then press Enter. If you have subtotals in the range, Excel will read them and assume that you want to total the subtotals, and it will ignore the other values.

Entering Array Formulas

To enter a formula that will pick up an array, type the formula, and press Ⓦ Ctrl+Shift+Enter Ⓜ Command+Return.

Linking Formulas and Workbooks

When you fill in a formula by selecting a cell in another worksheet, the reference links. When you update the original reference, the new reference will reflect the change. This is also true if the reference is in a workbook other than the one you are writing the formula in. You can link by typing in the external syntax, but the easiest way is to open the other workbook, then select the reference. For more about linking, Double-click on the Help button ▇ and browse the following topics:

- ♦ External references
- ♦ Links, workbook
- ♦ Saving workbooks (topic—saving unnamed linked workbooks)
- ♦ Source documents
- ♦ Source workbooks
- ♦ Auditing

Auditing

Watch the Formula Bar

The Formula bar gives you clues about your formula input. For instance, when you enter a simple formula containing a left parenthesis, Excel inserts the right parenthesis automatically when you press Enter.

When you type in a right parenthesis, the matching left parenthesis is temporalily emphasized in bold. If you would like to see each set of parentheses matched with bold, use the arrow keys to move the insertion point through the formula. Each time a matching parenthesis is passed by the insertion point, the pair appears bold temporarily. This is particularly helpful when you are nesting references and functions, which require several sets of parentheses.

If you get an alert box telling you something is wrong with the formula you are trying to enter, and you press OK to return to the formula, Excel will select the area that caused the alert if possible. For instance, if you have typed too many parentheses and then press Enter, you will get an Error in Formula alert. When you choose OK, Excel will return you to the formula, and the insertion point will be placed where you should have stopped, as in the following example:

```
=sqrt(h26/(A23))))
```

Switch to Formulas instead of Values

If you would like to see the formulas and functions on your worksheet instead of the values, you can toggle between the two modes (see Figure 7.12).

♦ Ⓦ Press Ctrl+ʹ (the accent with the tilde above it, to the left of 1 on the main keyboard).

♦ Ⓜ Press Command+ʹ (the accent).

Display the Calculation Button

The next few slick tricks can be enhanced by using the Calculation button.

1 Ⓦ Right-click Ⓜ Control+click on a toolbar, and choose Customize, then Utility.

2 Drag the Calculation button 🖩 to a toolbar and choose Close.

Calculate a Formula or Part of a Formula

If a formula is returning an error, you can check the nested portions of it.

1 Select the reference or formula within the formula.

2 Press F9 or click on the Calculate button 🖩.

After you have reviewed the result, be sure to press Esc.

	A	B	C	D	E	F	G	H
1								
2		1994	INSTALLER	INSTALATIONS	DISCONNECTS	TOTAL	TOTAL-AVE	TOTAL-AVE SQ
4	1	9YU	I.BOOGIE 530	106		=SUM(D4:E4)	=SUM(F4-$F$27)	=SUM(G4*G4)
5	2	9YW	B.COOL 459	69		=SUM(D5:E5)	=SUM(F5-$F$27)	=SUM(G5*G5)
6	3	9YR	M.BEEPER 128	347		=SUM(D6:E6)	=SUM(F6-$F$27)	=SUM(G6*G6)
7	4	9YF	S.ALADDIN 399	64		=SUM(D7:E7)	=SUM(F7-$F$27)	=SUM(G7*G7)
8	5	9YE	M.MOUSE 351	75		=SUM(D8:E8)	=SUM(F8-$F$27)	=SUM(G8*G8)
9	6	9YT	D.DUCK 370	48		=SUM(D9:E9)	=SUM(F9-$F$27)	=SUM(G9*G9)
10	7	9YN	J.SEINFELD 326	45		=SUM(D10:E10)	=SUM(F10-$F$27)	=SUM(G10*G10)
11	8	9YS	H.CLINTON 291	15		=SUM(D11:E11)	=SUM(F11-$F$27)	=SUM(G11*G11)
12	9	9YH	M.JACKSON 264	39		=SUM(D12:E12)	=SUM(F12-$F$27)	=SUM(G12*G12)
13	10	9YJ	B.DONE 291	4		=SUM(D13:E13)	=SUM(F13-$F$27)	=SUM(G13*G13)
14	11	9YA	E.TAYLOR 216	7		=SUM(D14:E14)	=SUM(F14-$F$27)	=SUM(G14*G14)
15	12	9YG	T.FIKEJS 206	14		=SUM(D15:E15)	=SUM(F15-$F$27)	=SUM(G15*G15)
16	13	9YK	E.PRESLEY 170	45		=SUM(D16:E16)	=SUM(F16-$F$27)	=SUM(G16*G16)
17	14	9YC	R.WILLIAMS 185	9		=SUM(D17:E17)	=SUM(F17-$F$27)	=SUM(G17*G17)
18	15	9YQ	C.SANDIEGO 138	25		=SUM(D18:E18)	=SUM(F18-$F$27)	=SUM(G18*G18)
19	16	9YL	J.BANNAH 65	15		=SUM(D19:E19)	=SUM(F19-$F$27)	=SUM(G19*G19)
26	TOTAL		=SUM(D4:D23)	=SUM(E4:E23)	=SUM(F4:F23)			=SUM(H4:H23)
27	AVG		=SUM(D26/20)	=SUM(E26/20)	=SUM(F26/20)			

Figure 7.12 The worksheet shown in Figure 7.2, displaying formulas instead of values

Turn Off Automatic Calculation to Speed Things Up

If you have a large worksheet, every time you make a change that requires calculation, you have to wait. If you would prefer to wait only
when you choose to, you can turn on Manual Calculation.

To turn on manual calculation:

1 Choose Tools, Options (**Alt/**, **T**, **O**); and select the
Calculation tab.

2 Turn on the Manual Calculation check box and choose OK.

Notice the cool check box beneath Manual, which automatically calculates before you save. Never turn it off. While you are working with
manual calculation in effect, if the workbook needs calculation, the
status bar displays the word Calculate.

♦ To calculate the workbook manually, press F9 or click on the Calculation button ▦.

♦ To calculate the active worksheet manually, press Shift+F9.

Large Hidden Ranges

When you have linked formulas that are referring to large ranges, your
worksheet may run very slowly. Here is another way to speed things up:

1 Choose Tools, Options (**Alt/**, **T**, **O**); and select the
Calculation tab.

2 Turn off the Update Remote References check box and choose
OK.

Making Notes on Your Worksheet

One way to make sense of a complex formula (three months after you
struggled to figure out how to enter it) is to make a note in the cell. If
you have recording hardware and sound driver software installed, you
can even have the note play back an audible message or sing a little song
about your memorable formula.

To attach a note to a worksheet:

1 Click on the Attach Note button 📇 located on the auditing
toolbar, or press Shift+F2.

2 Type the note into the Cell Note dialog box, and choose Add, then OK.

You can also bring up the Cell Note dialog box by choosing Insert, Note (**Alt, I, N**).

To select the next cell with a cell note, press Ctrl+Shift+? (question mark).

Other Notes on the Worksheet

You can also draw a text box on your worksheet and write a note in it. These boxes can be hidden or left visible, and printed or not. For more about text boxes, see Chapter 12, "Graphics."

Locating Problems in Formulas

It's now possible to display precedent, dependent, and error tracers directly on the worksheet. The new Auditing toolbar (Figure 7.13) makes it easy to place tracer arrows which indicate the direction of data flow on your worksheets. You can also use the Tools, Auditing submenu (**Alt/, T, A**) to perform some of the auditing actions.

Precedents and Dependents
Precedents are cells that are referred to by a formula. A direct precedent is referred to by the formula in the active cell. An indirect precedent is a cell referred to by a formula in any cell other than the active cell.

Dependents are cells containing formulas with references to other cells. A direct dependent contains a formula that refers to the active cell. An indirect dependent contains a formula that refers to any dependent cell other than the active cell.

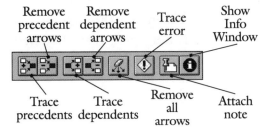

Figure 7.13 The Auditing toolbar

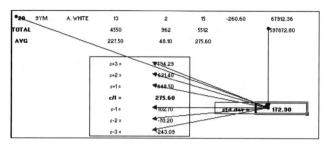

Figure 7.14 Tracer arrows pointing to precedents
and dependents

Display Worksheet Precedents and Dependents

1 Select the cell which contains the formula you want to trace.

2 Click on the Trace Precedents or Trace Dependents button to display those which are direct.

3 Click again to display those which are indirect (see Figure 7.14). You may continue repeating this step until you get an obnoxious beep telling you there are no more.

Display External Precedents and Dependents

You can use the same method as above to find external precedents and dependents, but the only information you will receive is that the precedents or dependents are external. The arrow leads to an external reference icon, shown in Figure 7.15. When you see this external reference icon and you need more information, you can click on the Info window button **ⓘ**.

Double-Click on the Arrow

Double-click on a trace arrow to go to the cell the arrow is pointing to. This works even if the cell is an external reference—but the file needs to be open, and you will then pass through the auspices of the Go To dialog box. If the file is not open, read the reference in the Go To

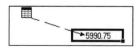

Figure 7.15 An external
reference trace arrow

dialog box to know which file to open and which cell to Go To after opening it.

List Precedents and Dependents in the Info Window

To get information about a cell:

1 Select the cell.

2 Click on the Info button .

When this window opens, you can display the level of information you need by clicking on each command on the Info menu. These commands are: Cell, Formula, Value, Format, Protect, Names, Precedents, Dependents, and Note. All nine of these commands have been checked to display information about the cell in Figure 7.16.

Once you open the Info window, it stays open during your session. You can select any cell and switch to it by clicking the Info button or by using the Window menu.

Switching between Your Worksheet and the Info Window

It's easy to switch to the Info window (click on the Info button), but it's not quite as easy to switch back. If you will be using the Info window a great deal, shrink the Info window so that you can see the main worksheet behind it. Then all you have to do is click on your main worksheet window when you want to return to it.

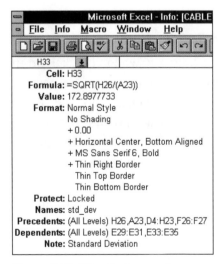

Figure 7.16 The Info window

The Restore and Maximize Buttons The Restore and Maximize buttons will affect the Info window and the main worksheet window simultaneously. That means if you click on the Restore and Maximize buttons in one, it affects the other in the same way. This simultaneous action affects only the worksheet that was active when you initially opened Info.

To shrink the Info window:

1 Click on the Restore arrow at the top left corner of the Info window screen.

2 Size the main worksheet window by dragging the lower right corner.

Tracer Arrows Do Not Appear if Objects Are Hidden

If you have hidden objects, you will need to unhide them if you want to use tracer arrows.

1 Choose Tools, Options (**Alt/**, **T**, **O**); and select the View tab.

2 Select Show All or Show Placeholders, and choose OK.

The Great Reverso Resides Here

If you hold down the Shift key when you click on the Trace Precedents or Dependents buttons, it removes the respective trace arrows. The reverse is also true; Shift-clicking on the Remove Precedents or Dependents arrows creates trace arrows. Actually, with the Remove All Arrows button available, the other two Remove Arrow buttons are almost superfluous. These dual roles are mentioned to inspire you to economize on your workspace, as well as to clear some confusion from this toolbar. For more about customizing toolbars and the workspace, see Chapter 5.

Select Precedents and Dependents with Go To Special

1 Select the cell and press F5.

2 Click on the Special button.

3 Select Precedents or Dependents.

4 Select Direct or All Levels, and choose OK.

Very often, selecting with the Go To Special in this manner will select a whole range that may be nonadjacent.

Select All Precedents and Dependents

♦ To select all direct precedents, press Ctrl+[.

♦ To select all precedents, press Ctrl+Shift+{.

♦ To select all direct dependents, press Ctrl+].

♦ To select all dependents, press Ctrl+Shift+}.

Finding Row and Column Differences

Excel makes it easy for you to find the cells in a column or row, which do not fit the pattern of the rest.

To find row differences:

1 Select the range that you want to compare. It will compare to the active cell.

2 Press Ctrl+\ to find row differences.

To find column differences:

1 Select the range that you want to compare. It will compare to the active cell.

2 Press Ctrl+Shift+| to find column differences.

To find row or column differences using Go To Special:

1 Select the range that you want to compare. It will compare to the active cell.

2 Press F5 and choose Special.

3 Select Row Differences or Column Differences, and choose OK.

Help

Step-by-step information on this subject is located under Tracer in the Help menu, and also under Arrows, Tracer. Double-click on the Help button to go directly to the Search dialog box.

Chapter 8

Lists, Tables, and Databases

THIS CHAPTER AND THE NEXT are for those of you who need to work with lists, tables, and databases. The new filtering and sorting features will simplify your tasks. The data form provides a simple way to view or change records in a list or database.

Important Terminology Change

Look for the word *list*. Excel 5.0 uses this word in dialog boxes and in Help. In Excel, a list is a labeled series of worksheet rows that contain similar sets of data. Excel can recognize a list as a database, and with the help of Text Wizard, as a table. It reads rows as records and columns as fields. Lists can be sorted, filtered, analyzed, and automatically subtotaled and totaled.

Set Up a List

Excel can help you manage and analyze data in a list. Setting up a list with certain specifications helps you take advantage of powerful features. The following is a list of guidelines for setting up a list.

List Setup Guideline:	Reason:
Use one list per worksheet.	Some of Excel's list management features are restricted to one list per worksheet.
Leave blank rows above and below a list, but not within it.	If you have other data on a worksheet, separate it with blank rows, but use borders to separate the data within the list so that Excel will recognize the list data.
Keep the areas to the left and right of the list clear.	If you are going to filter the list, Excel uses these areas.
Create column labels in the first row and format them differently than the data. Use the same format for all cells in a column.	Excel recognizes column labels as field names. The format confirms Excel's recognition.
Name the list.	You don't have to, but it will make it a lot easier for you each time Excel requests a reference to the list.
Don't insert extra spaces at the beginning of a cell.	Extra spaces affect sorting and searching.

Name Your List Database

If you name your list Database, Excel will always recognize the first row as field names.

Use a Dataform

· ·

You can add, find, edit, or delete records, using Excel's built-in dataform (see Figure 8.1). The dataform is a customized dialog box, which Excel creates for you after it reads the field names in your list.

Excel 5.0 doesn't require you to set the database as you did in Excel 4.0.

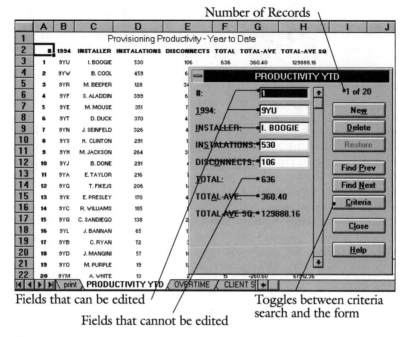

Figure 8.1 A dataform

In Excel, a field is a cell that contains part of a record. For instance, a field might contain a person's age, and might be grouped with other fields containing more embarrassing information about the same person, such as his or her weight. The age and weight fields would be located in the same row of the list. The row would therefore contain a record.

To open a dataform:

1 Select any cell or range on your worksheet (Excel will find the list).

2 Choose Data, Form (**Alt/, D, O**).

To move through records in the dataform, choose the Find Prev or Find Next buttons, or scroll with the scroll bar and arrows.

To add new records using the dataform:

1 Open a dataform and choose the New button.

2 Fill in the field.

③ Use the Tab key (or the mouse) to move between fields.

④ When you are through entering a record, W press Enter M press Return.

⑤ You may then add another new record or choose another button.

Since Enter is used within the dialog box to move to the next record, in order to access Close, you need to use the mouse, press Alt/+L, or tab to Close and then press Enter.

To edit records with the dataform:

① Open a dataform.

② Find the record you want to edit and make your changes.

③ When you are through editing a record, W press Enter M press Return.

To find particular records with the criteria button:

① Open a dataform.

② Choose the Criteria button and type in the criteria you want met.

③ Choose Find Prev or Find Next to find the previous or next record that meets your criteria.

To delete a record:

① Open a dataform and select the record you want to delete.

② Choose Delete to permanently remove the row containing the record, and shift all the rows below it up one position.

A Dataform Is Not Mutually Exclusive

 Just because the dataform is available, you don't have to use it. You can edit your list directly in Excel, as any worksheet.

Sorting

It is often necessary to get information in a list organized before you can work with it or report it. This can be done with the Sort command on the Data menu. Sorting arranges rows according to the contents of the column you select and according to the sort order you request. The sort order can be ascending or descending, chronologically, or according to a custom list that you create. For instance, besides being able to sort in alphabetic or numeric order, you could sort according to a list of the divisions in your company.

When sorting in ascending order:

♦ Numbers sorts from the smallest number to the largest; dates and times from earliest to latest.

♦ Text values sorts numbers entered as text first, then regular text.

♦ Logical values sorts FALSE, then TRUE.

♦ Error values, such as #VALUE OR #N/A, are listed in the order in which they are found.

♦ Blanks.

Sorting in descending order sorts in the opposite of ascending order except blanks, which will always be sorted to the end.

Before You Sort

Sorting can be confusing. Before you sort, there are a few safeguards you can put in place:

1 **Save your workbook**. Sorting can tax the memory in your computer. Press Shift+F12 or click on the Save button ▣.

2 **Make a copy of your worksheet**. Hold down the Ⓦ Ctrl Ⓜ Command key, and drag the worksheet tab to another place in the workbook. Perform the sort on one of the copies; the other will remain intact.

3 **Enter a "return to original" numbered column**. If you would like to sort several times and return to the original list, or you would like to have a record of the order in which you added records, you can add a column to your list numbered 1 to whatever. Insert a column, then place a 1 in the first row and a 2 in the second; select them, then drag the autofill handle to the end of the column. Then each time you want to add a record, add the next sequential number to that column.

4 **Be sure to calculate before you sort**. If you are sorting by a column that contains formulas and you have manual calculation in effect, don't forget to press F9.

A Simple Sort

If you are sure that Excel will select your list correctly, and you do not need to add any secondary Then By sort columns, you can use the Sort buttons on the Standard toolbar.

When you select a cell in a list and choose Sort, Excel selects the entire list for you. It identifies up to two column labels as the field names, using formatting as its clue. If it doesn't recognize labels, it will propose your list without them. It will also propose the column where your active cell was as the Sort By column. If it does not select the data you want to sort, select the data manually and choose the Sort command again, or turn on or off one of the My List Has check boxes in the Sort dialog box.

To Sort Using the Sort Buttons :

1 Select a cell in the column in which you want to Sort By.

2 Click on either the Ascending or Descending Sort button.

To sort using the Sort command:

1 Select a cell in your list.

2 Choose Data, Sort (**Alt/, D, S**) to bring up the Sort dialog box (Figure 8.2).

3 Select the column you want to Sort By from the drop-down list, and select Ascending or Descending.

4 Select Then By columns if you wish, and choose OK.

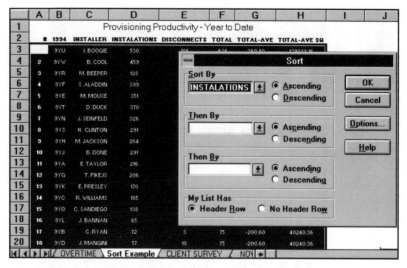

Figure 8.2 The Sort dialog box

The Great Reverso Sorts

If you like to customize your Standard toolbar to include fewer buttons, this is one more place where you can economize space. If you hold down the Shift key when you press the Ascending Sort button, Excel will sort in descending order, and vice versa.

Sort by a Custom Sort Order

You can sort by any list on the Custom List tab in the Tools, Options dialog box. This includes the chronological lists provided by Excel and any custom lists you create yourself. Instructions for creating a custom list are in Chapter 3.

To sort by a list on the Custom Lists tab:

1 Select a cell in the column that contains your custom list fields.

2 Choose Data, Sort (**Alt/, D, S**).

3 Choose the Options button.

4 Select the custom list you want to sort by in the drop-down list.

5 Choose OK in the Options dialog box.

6 Make any other selections in the Sort dialog box and choose OK.

You can only sort by a custom list in the Sort By box, not in the Then By boxes. Sorry.

Notice in the Sort Options dialog box (see Figure 8.3) that you can cause the sort to be case-sensitive. You can also choose to sort columns instead of rows by choosing Left to Right instead of Top to Bottom.

Sort Graphics along with Data

Unless you tell Excel not to, all graphics will be sorted with associated rows.

To exclude graphics from the sort:

1 Double-click on the border of one of the graphics to open the Format Object dialog box.

2 Select the Properties tab.

3 Turn on the Don't Move Or Size With Cells option button and choose OK.

When you select a cell to sort in a pivot table, you will receive a special Sort dialog box. Pivot Tables and this dialog box are discussed in Chapter 10.

Sort by Four or More Columns

You can sort three columns at a time. If you want to sort by more, you will need to sort several times.

1 Sort by the three least important columns.

2 Choose the Sort command and continue to sort in order of importance.

Figure 8.3 The Sort Options dialog box

Don't Sort a Portion of Your List

When you are sorting, you need to select one cell or the entire selection you want to sort. If you have a range selected, Excel will assume that the sort should apply to that range only. Sorting selected data does not move data in adjacent columns or rows. Fortunately, Excel warns you with a dialog box, which offers you the choice of expanding your list or continuing to sort a portion.

Automatic Subtotals

You can now summarize data in Excel without adding formulas. Using the groups of data you choose, Excel automatically calculates subtotal and grand-total values, inserts and labels the total rows, and outlines the list for you. You can then create a report or a chart, using the outline to display the level you want to see.

Automatically Summarizing a List

Before you have Excel automatically summarize a list, you need to prepare it. It needs to be labeled and sorted so Excel can read the detail information (see Figure 8.4).

To prepare a list for Subtotals, sort the rows so that the items to subtotal are grouped together.

Labeled columns

Grouped data

	A	B	C	D	E	F	G	H	I
1	Installer	Inst/Rep	Jan	Feb	Mar	Apr	May	
2	I. BOOGIE	Installations	127	111	134	121	143	636
3	I. BOOGIE	Repairs	3	13	7	2	17	42
4	B. COOL	Installations	105	98	110	101	114	528
5	B. COOL	Repairs	22	15	30	19	26	112
6	M. BEEPER	Installations	91	100	97	94	89	471
7	M. BEEPER	Repairs	0	0	11	0	0	11
8	D. DUCK	Installations	83	85	98	76	76	418
9	D. DUCK	Repairs	7	9	5	6	3	30
10	H. CLINTON	Installations	62	63	66	54	61	306
11	H. CLINTON	Repairs	64	66	71	81	42	324
12	M. JACKSON	Installations	69	60	43	59	72	303
13	M. JACKSON	Repairs	0	0	23	3	0	26
14	B. DONE	Installations	59	54	75	40	67	295
15	B. DONE	Repairs	89	98	72	98	97	454
16								

Figure 8.4 A list prepared for automatic subtotals

To insert subtotals:

1 Select a single cell with your list and choose Data, Subtotals (**Alt/, D, B**).

2 Change the criteria in the Subtotals dialog box (see Figures 8.5 and 8.6) if Excel has not proposed what you want. (You can select more than one column in the Add Subtotals To box.)

3 Choose OK.

Insert Nested Subtotals

You can subtotal smaller groups within existing subtotal groups.

1 Select a cell in your previously subtotaled list.

2 Choose Data, Subtotal (**Alt/, D, B**).

3 Select another column in the At Each Change In box.

4 Turn off the Replace Current Subtotals check box and choose OK.

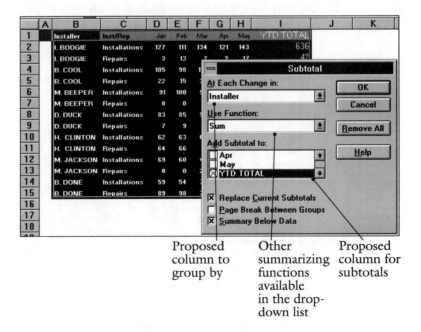

Proposed column to group by

Other summarizing functions available in the drop-down list

Proposed column for subtotals

Figure 8.5 The Subtotals dialog box

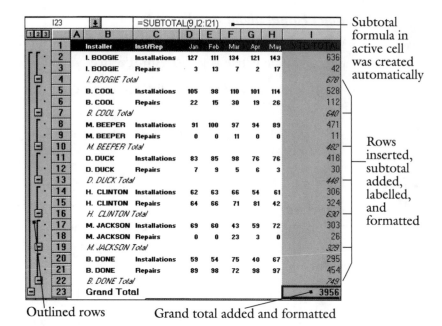

Figure 8.6 **A list subtotaled by Excel**

Choose More than One Summary Function

You can have Excel add another line to your outline with a another labeled summary. For instance, you may want subtotals and to add another line with an average or a count.

1 Select a cell in your previously subtotaled list.

2 Choose Data, Subtotal (**Alt/, D, B**).

3 Select another function in the Use Function box.

4 Turn off the Replace Current subtotals check box and choose OK.

Add Subtotals to a Filtered List

You can filter a list to create a subset before you insert subtotals. When you insert automatic subtotals in a filtered list, Excel summarizes only the visible data. For more about filtering, see the next section.

Don't Forget about AutoFormat

When you are adding subtotals, one way to make the worksheet easier to read immediately is to use AutoFormat.

1 Select a cell in your list and choose Format, AutoFormat (**Alt/, O, A**).

2 Select a format from the AutoFormat dialog box and choose OK.

Printing a Subtotaled List

A subtotaled list is a natural "bottom line" report. If you use AutoFormat as suggested in the slick trick above and then make a few adjustments using the following suggestions, you can have a beautiful report with a very small investment of your time.

To break pages at each group that was subtotaled:

1 Select a cell in your list and choose Data, Subtotal (**Alt/, D, B**).

2 Turn on the Page Break Between Groups check box and choose OK.

To use row or column headings as titles on each page:

1 Choose File, Page Setup (**Alt/, F, U**), and select the Sheet tab.

2 Type the range reference for column labels in the Rows to Repeat At Top box.

3 Type the range reference for row labels in the Columns To Repeat At Left box, then choose OK.

To hide unnecessary columns to simplify the report:

1 Ⓦ Right-click Ⓜ Control+click on the columns you want to hide.

2 Choose Hide from the shortcut menu.

Removing Subtotals

You can undo the last subtotal command, replace existing subtotals with new totals, or remove all subtotals.

To remove subtotals you have just inserted, press Ⓦ Alt+Backspace, Ctrl+Z; or click on the Undo button.

To replace existing subtotals with new totals:

1. Select a cell in your list and choose Data, Subtotal (**Alt/, D, B**).
2. Make your changes in the Subtotals dialog box.
3. Turn on the Replace Current Subtotals check box and choose OK.

To remove all subtotals and the outline:

1. Choose Data, Subtotal (**Alt/, D, B**).
2. Choose Remove All.

Filtering

If you want to work with a subset of the data in a list, you can filter it. A filtered list hides all rows that do not contain the criteria you specify. You can use AutoFilter for most filtering, but there is also an Advanced Filter command. These are both located on the Data, Filter submenu (**Alt/, D, F**).

When you set up a filtered list using AutoFilter, a drop-down arrow appears at the top of each column. When you click on one of the arrows, a drop-down list displays the unique values of the column and a menu selection for All and Custom. When you select one of the values, Excel automatically hides all rows that do not contain the selected value. Use All to unhide all rows. Custom is for filtering with custom criteria and is explained in the following trick. If there are blanks in the column, the drop-down list will also allow you to choose Blanks and NonBlanks.

Filter a List Using AutoFilter

When you filter a list with AutoFilter, you can select one cell in your list to filter the whole list. If you want a drop-down list on selected columns only, select the labels of those columns.

Blanks and NonBlanks   When you use AutoFilter to filter a list, the drop-down list at the top of a column will include Blanks and NonBlanks. This allows you to hide all rows that contain data or those that do not. The blanks may be insignificant or they could be very relevant. For instance, the column might contain the number of contacts with a client so far this year. Filtering the list to hide all but blank cells could bring to light those clients that have been ignored.

To apply AutoFiltering to a list:

1 Select a cell or selected column labels.

2 Choose Data, Filter (**Alt/, F, F**).

3 Choose AutoFilter from the submenu.

To hide all rows except for a selected value, select the value from the drop-down list.

To show all rows:

1 Select All from the top of the filtered column, or choose Data, Filter (**Alt/, D, F, S**).

2 Choose Show All from the submenu.

To remove AutoFilter:

1 Choose Data, Filter (**Alt/, F, F**).

2 Choose AutoFilter from the submenu to turn off the check mark.

Move Quickly through a Drop-Down List

If the contents of your column cause the drop-down list to be lengthy, you can move through it quickly by typing the first letter of the value you want.

Filter with Custom Criteria

The Custom option in the drop-down list allows you to filter the list with your own criteria. For instance, in Figure 8.7 you may want to hide all rows in column B except those which contain B. Cool *and* S. Aladdin. Or, you may want to filter a list to hide all except a value you give

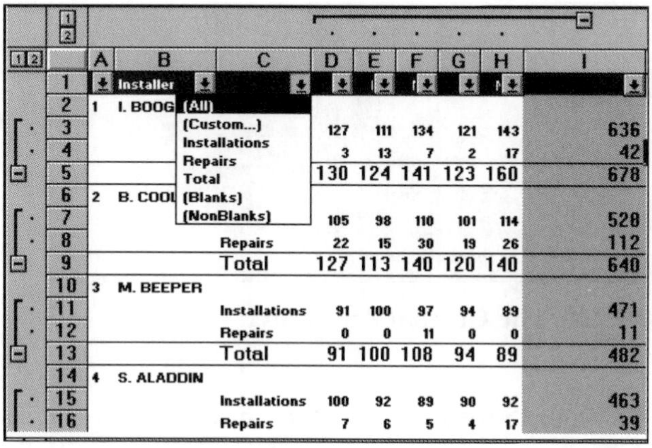

Figure 8.7 A filtered list displaying a drop-down list

it. For instance in Figure 8.8, after filtering column, you could filter the monthly installation columns to display only the installations that exceeded 100.

To filter with custom criteria:

1 Select Custom from the drop-down list at the top of a column.

2 Type the criteria, or select it from the drop-down list in the Custom AutoFilter dialog box (Figure 8.9).

3 Choose OK.

Custom AutoFiltering

If the AutoFilter dialog box does not meet your needs, you can use the Advanced filter command. This command filters your list in place as the AutoFilter command does, but it does not display a drop-down list on

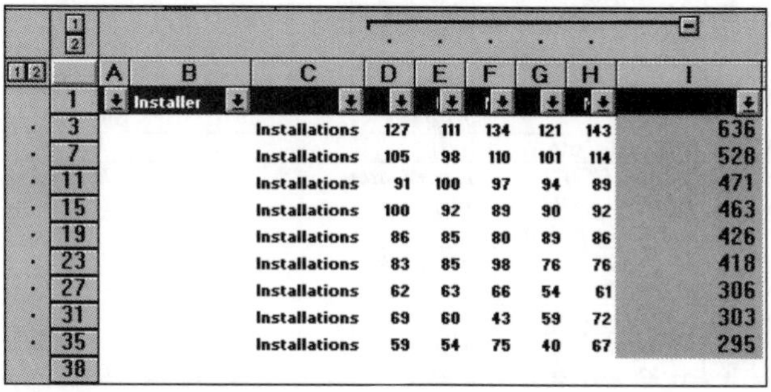

Figure 8.8 A filtered list with hidden rows

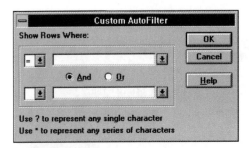

Figure 8.9 The Custom AutoFilter
dialog box

each column. Instead, you type criteria into a criteria range on your
worksheet (see Figure 8.10). In the criteria range, you can specify
exactly what you want. For instance, if you would like to display rows
containing more than two names, you cannot use AutoFilter and must
move into Advanced filtering.

Unlike AutoFiltering, you cannot filter again with Advanced Filter.
Each time you specify your custom criteria, it affects your entire list.

To filter with Advanced Filter:

1 Create a range where you are going to write your custom criteria.

2 Type your criteria into the range.

3 Select a cell in your list and choose Data, Filter (**Alt/, F, A**).

	A	B	C	D	E	F	G	H
1	Installer	ytd total	ytd total					
2	I. Boogie	>600	<700					
3	B. Cool							
4	H. Clinton							
5								
6								
8	*Installer*	*Inst/Rep*	*Jan*	*Feb*	*Mar*	*Apr*	*May*	*YTD TOTAL*
9	*I. BOOGIE*	*Installations*	127	111	134	121	143	636
10	*I. BOOGIE*	*Repairs*	3	13	7	2	17	42
11	I. BOOGIE Total							678
12	*B. COOL*	*Installations*	105	98	110	101	114	528
13	*B. COOL*	*Repairs*	22	15	30	19	26	112
14	B. COOL Total							640
15	*M. BEEPER*	*Installations*	91	100	97	94	89	471
16	*M. BEEPER*	*Repairs*	0	0	11	0	0	11
17	M. BEEPER Total							482
18	*D. DUCK*	*Installations*	83	85	98	76	76	418
19	*D. DUCK*	*Repairs*	7	9	5	6	3	30
20	D. DUCK Total							448
21	*H. CLINTON*	*Installations*	62	63	66	54	61	306
22	*H. CLINTON*	*Repairs*	54	66	71	81	42	324

Figure 8.10 Advanced Filter criteria range

4 Choose Advanced Filter from the submenu, and make any changes necessary in the Advanced Filter dialog box.

5 Choose OK.

Copy Filtered Data to Another Location

You can leave your original list as it is, and copy filtered data to another location.

1 Create a range where you are going to write your custom criteria.

2 Type your criteria into the range.

3 Select a cell in your list and choose Data, Filter (**Alt/, F, A**).

4 Choose Advanced Filter from the submenu and select the Copy To Another Location option button.

5 Type in the range where you want the filtered list and choose OK.

When you copy in Excel, you can select a cell and let Excel paste the entire range, or you can select the entire range before you paste. This is also true in the Advanced Filter dialog box (see Figure 8.11), except that you must type in the range rather than select it. If you enter a range that is smaller than what is needed or one that has data in it, you will get an alert box. If you enter a larger range or the top left cell, you will not get an error.

Copy Only to Columns You Specify As You Filter

You can specify a range that has column labels built in before you copy a filtered list. If you leave out some of the columns in the original list or rearrange them, Excel doesn't care. It will dutifully copy your filtered

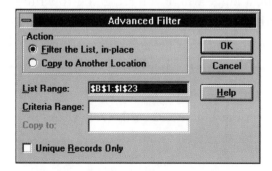

Figure 8.11 Advance Filter dialog box

list, matching column for column. It won't even alert you to tell you that things are not the same. Use the same steps as above, but specify the range that has your column labels set up the way you would like them copied.

Copy to Another Worksheet

The easiest way to copy a filtered list to another worksheet is to filter it on the original worksheet, then copy it using copy and paste. If, however, you would like to use the Advanced filter command, it's not that hard.

1. Switch to the worksheet where you want the filtered list copied.
2. Choose the Advanced Filter command.
3. Specify the list and criteria ranges including the sheet reference, with an exclamation point separating the sheet reference and the ranges.
4. Type the cell reference or range in the Copy to box and choose OK.

Whenever you refer to another sheet in a reference, you use an exclamation point to separate the sheet name and the reference. For instance, if you are on Sheet2 and you want to refer to a range on Sheet1 named TOTALS, you would type in **Sheet1!TOTALS**.

Filter All Duplicate Records

You can use the Advance Filter command to hide all duplicate rows in your list.

1. Create a range where you are going to write your custom criteria, and type your criteria into the range.
2. Select a cell in your list and choose Data, Filter (**Alt/, F, A**).
3. Choose Advanced Filter from the submenu.
4. Clear the data out of the Criteria Range box.
5. Turn on the Unique Records Only check box and choose OK.

Filtering a Subtotaled List

Excel does not recalculate automatic subtotals when you filter. Therefore, you need to sort and filter lists before you insert automatic subtotals.

Use AutoSum on a Filtered List

When you use AutoSum on a filtered list, it automatically adjusts to include correct totals as the list adjusts to include or exclude detail.

Printing a Filtered List

When you print a filtered list, only the displayed area prints. You can therefore use filtering to create different views. You can also save those views. For more about views and printing, see Chapter 6.

Removing an Advanced Filtered List

To remove an Advanced Filtered list that has been filtered in place:

1 Choose Data, Filter (**Alt/, D, S**).

2 Choose Show All.

Importing and Consolidating Data

There are times when you might have data in a text document, which would be much more useful to you if you imported it into Excel as a table. For instance, you may have received a note on electronic mail which lists anticipated income for a project, and you would like to use these figures in Excel. Figure 8.12 shows a worksheet where some data was copied from column B to column D, then parsed with the Text Wizard.

To parse is to distribute data from a single, delimited column into the correct number of columns of a table.

Converting Imported Text into a Table

To import the data:

1 Copy the data to the Clipboard (if possible).

	A	B	C	D	E
1					
2		January 225 * 20,4500		January 225 * 20	4500
3		Feb -May 203 * 15,3045		Feb -May 203 * 15	3045
4		Jan - May 5 * 600,3000		Jan - May 5 * 600	3000
5					
6		Anticipated June,3600		Anticipated June	3600
7		Anticipated July,600		Anticipated July	600
8		Anticpated August,7600		Anticpated August	7600
9		Anticipated September,4600		Anticipated September	4600
10		So far anticipated Oct -Dec,1800		So far anticipated Oct -Dec	1800
11					

Figure 8.12 **A single column converted into a table with the Text Wizard**

2 Switch to Excel.

3 Paste the data into Excel.

To parse the data from one column into a table:

1 Select the data.

2 Choose Data, Text to Columns (**Alt/, D, E**).

3 Go through the three steps of the Text Wizard to spread your data out into a table (see Figure 8.13).

Consolidating Data

One feature that can save you hours of time is the Consolidation command on the Data menu. With it, you can bring in data from past reports to create new ones. For instance, you can consolidate monthly

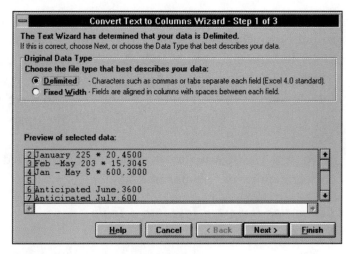

Figure 8.13 Step 1 of Text Wizard

reports into quarterly, then into annual reports. The source documents can be in the same workbook, in a different workbook, or saved in a different document in a different subdirectory. They can be saved in different applications or on the other Excel platform. If you can write a road map for Excel, Excel will consolidate the data for you.

There are two kinds of consolidation: position consolidation and category consolidation. Position consolidation brings data in from worksheets which have been created on templates or from each other. The data is located in exactly the same place on each. Category consolidation brings in data which has exactly the same labels on the source documents. When you consolidate by position you do not use labels. You will need to add them to your destination document.

To consolidate data:

1 Prepare your source documents with correct positioning or labels and make a note of the location of each document.

2 Prepare your destination area with enough space to hold the data and labels if possible.

3 Save all worksheets that are open (not necessary, but recommended).

4 Choose Data, Consolidation (**Alt/, D, N**). (See Figure 8.14.)

5 Select a function from the drop-down list or accept the proposed SUM function.

6 Type in or select the Reference box, then select the destination range.

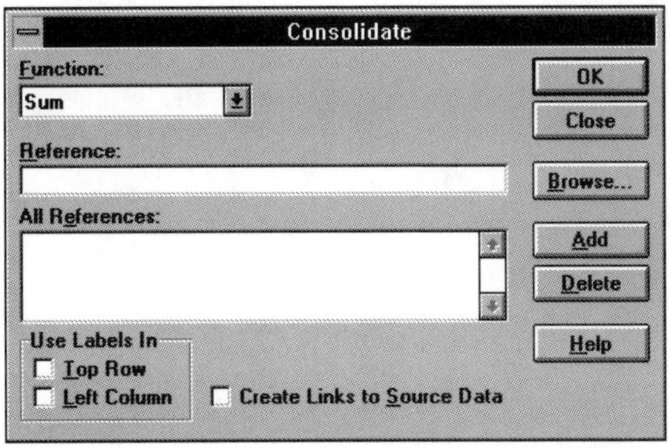

Figure 8.14 **The Consolidate dialog box**

7 Type in or select the All References box, then select within open workbooks or browse to select source documents.

8 Turn on the Use Labels check boxes if you are consolidating by category.

9 Turn on the Create Links to Source Data check box if you want the Links to continually update. Finally, choose OK.

If you do not turn on the Create Links to Source Data check box, Excel remembers where the source documents are and will update the destination document after you open it. Just choose Data, Consolidate (**Alt/, D, N**); then choose OK.

Remove Previous Links and Outlines before Consolidating

If your destination document has been previously outlined or linked, remove them before consolidating. You cannot Undo a consolidation in which you create links.

Add Identical Headers When Consolidating by Category

If you are preparing source documents for consolidation and you need to add identical headers on some of them, you can move them into a single workbook, then select them all before you add the headers. Use the W Ctrl M Command key or the Shift key to select more than one sheet.

Chapter 9

Analyzing Data

THIS CHAPTER, AND THE NEXT, contain slick tricks for the analyst. I didn't call you a nerd, but you know who you are. You like to forecast, to play with data to see possibilities, and you love Excel. For you, these slick tricks are fun. But keep reading; more fun is on the way. In Chapters 11 and 12, you will find tricks to chart the scenarios (real and imagined) that you will learn to create in this chapter. Then you will be able to razzle-dazzle others like you, who love to see what "the numbers" can do.

Getting Results

Goal Seek

When you know the result you want but you don't have all the input values to get there, you can use Goal Seek (Figure 9.1). Don't tell my eighth-grade algebra teacher, Mr. Zigler: It would break his heart. Excel makes it easy to find a specific value for a particular cell by adjusting the value of only one other cell. For more complicated calculations, you will need to use Solver.

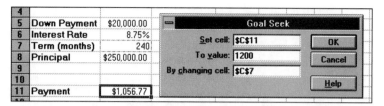

Figure 9.1   The Goal Seek dialog box

To use Goal Seek:

1 Choose Tools, Goal Seek (**Alt/, T, G**).

2 In the Set Cell box, enter the reference or select the cell containing the formula in which you want to place the goal.

3 Enter the goal value in the To Value box.

4 In the By Changing Cell box, enter or select the reference of the cell which you want Excel to change, and choose OK.

5 To Pause, choose Pause. After you pause, choose Step to step one goal at a time. To resume normal goal seeking, choose Continue.

6 To keep the solution on your worksheet, choose OK. To read the results of Goal Seek without changing your worksheet, choose Cancel.

If you change your mind, you can Undo by pressing Ctrl+Z or Alt+Backspace, or by clicking on the Undo button .

What if You Change One Input Cell?

You can create a data table which produces results dependent on what-if values you place in a list. The list of values replaces the value in an input cell. The formula picks up the variable values in the list, one at a time, to create a new table of values.

When you create a data table you use the Table command as a shortcut for calculating multiple variations in one operation. Your formulas can refer to existing worksheet rows or columns, and place the results next to the worksheet if there is room beneath the rows or to the right of the columns.

To fill in a one-variable input oriented table:

1 In a single column or row, list the variable values you want plugged into the initial formula instead of the value in the input cell.

2 Enter a formula that refers to the input cell:

♦ For a column—in the next column to the right, one row above your list of variable values (see Figure 9.2)

♦ For a row—in the row beneath your list of variable values, one column to the left (see Figure 9.3)

3 Select a range containing your list, the formula, and the blank cells that will make the selection a rectangle.

4 Choose Data, Table (**Alt/, D, T**).

5 Enter the cell reference of the input cell (you can type it in; or click in the box, then select the cell):

♦ For a column—in the Column Input Cell box

♦ For a row—in the Row Input Cell

6 Choose OK.

If the Table dialog box covers the input cell, you can use its title bar to drag it out of the way.

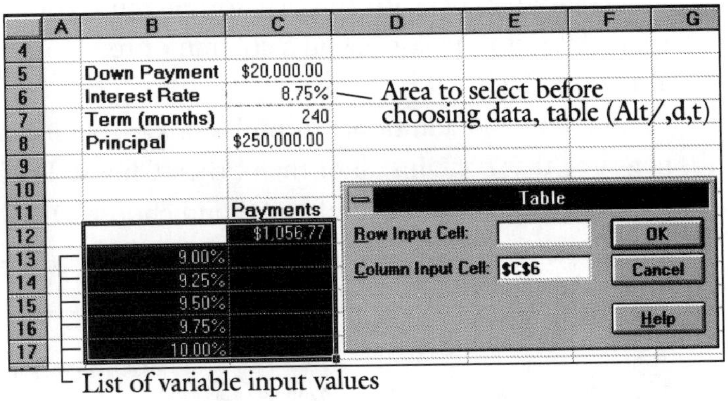

Figure 9.2 **One-Input Cell data table preparation when using columns**

Formula which computes with original value in input cell

E7		=((C8-C5)+((C8+C5)*C6))/C7							
	B	**C**	**D**	**E**	**F**	**G**	**H**	**I**	**J**
4									
5	Down Payment	$20,000.00							
6	Interest Rate	8.75%			9.00%	9.25%	9.50%	9.75%	10.00%
7	Term (months)	240	Payments	$1,056.77					
8	Principal	$250,000.00							

Placement of formula   List of variable input values

Figure 9.3 **The Placement of an initial Formula when using rows**

Use Names

In Figure 9.3, the following process was used to change the formula in cell E7 to read as it does in Figure 9.4. Isn't that easier to understand?

1 Select cells B5 through C8, painting from Down Payment to the amount of the principal.

2 Press Ctrl+Shift+F3, and choose OK.

3 Select Cell E7.

4 Choose Insert, Name (**Alt/, I, N, A**); and choose Apply from the submenu, then choose OK.

Add Additional Formulas

You can add as many formulas and variable input values as you need to a data table, but each formula must directly or indirectly refer to the same input cell. Add additional formulas to the right of the first formula in a column or beneath the first formula in a row. Add variable input values beneath the last one in a column or to the right of the last one in a row (see Figure 9.5).

After you add additional formulas or variable input values, select the new area that contains all of them, then Choose Data, Table (**Alt/, D, T**). Fill in the Input Cell reference and choose OK.

E7		=((Principal-Down_Payment)+((Principal+Down_Payment)*Interest_Rate))/							
	B	Term__months							
4									
5	Down Payment	$20,000.00							
6	Interest Rate	8.75%			9.00%	9.25%	9.50%	9.75%	10.00%
7	Term (months)	240	Payments	$1,056.77					
8	Principal	$250,000.00							

Figure 9.4 **What a difference a name makes!**

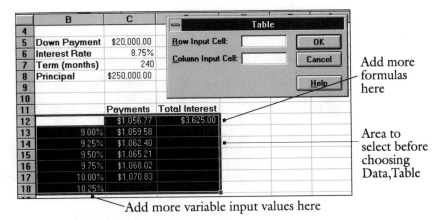

Add more formulas here

Area to select before choosing Data, Table

Add more variable input values here

Figure 9.5 Adding additional formulas to a data table

Two What-If Input Cells

You can use two variable input cells if they are laid out in rows and columns—as long as they are both variables in the same formula.

To fill in a two-variable input data table:

1 In a cell, enter the formula that will refer to both sets of variable input values.

2 In the column beneath the formula, enter the variable values for one of the column input cells.

3 In the row to the right of the formula, enter the variable values for the row input cells.

4 Paint the range to contain them all and choose Data, Table (**Alt/, D, T**).

5 Enter the column and row input cells referred to in the initial formula (see Figure 9.6), and choose OK.

Supply New Values

You can replace the variable values in data tables to recalculate the results.

Edit a Data Table

The results in a data table are entered in an array and therefore need to be edited accordingly. If you want to work with the table, you can copy the data using Paste Special to edit the values independently.

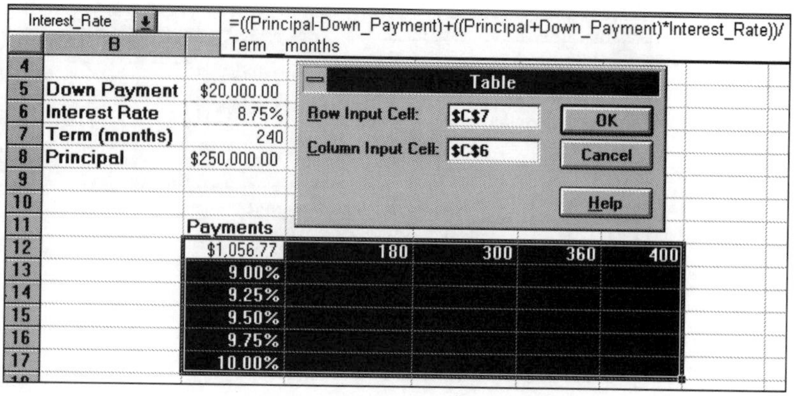

Figure 9.6 Two-Input cells data table preparation

To copy the range:

1 Select the range and copy it, using Ctrl+C or the shortcut menu.

2 Right-click ⌹ Control+click the upper left cell of the range where you want to paste, and choose Paste Special.

3 To paste the values and formats, choose OK.

4 To paste a linked formula, choose Paste Link.

Scenario Manager

With the new Excel 5.0 Scenario Manager, you can create, manage, protect, merge, and track changes in scenarios. A scenario is a group of up to 32 (named) input values called *changing cells.* Each set of changing cells represents a set of what-if assumptions that can be applied to a worksheet model.

When you are creating a scenario, you can start with existing values on your worksheet in the changing cells. Those cells will be overwritten when you run your scenarios. If you want to use the existing values again, give them the first of your scenario names. Then, to bring those original values back, run the scenario with that original name. For instance, if the contents of the changing cells were named Last Year, and you wanted to view last year's figures, you would choose the Last Year scenario in the Scenario box.

Creating a Scenario

To create a scenario:

1 Within a worksheet with dependent formulas, select the cells you would like to vary, up to 32 cells. The cells can be non-contiguous.

2 Choose Tools, Scenario (**Alt/ T, C**) to open the Scenario Manager dialog box.

3 Choose Add to open the Add Scenarios dialog box, shown in Figure 9.7.

4 Type in a name for your first scenario, then choose OK.

5 Type in the variable value for each changing cell in the Scenario Values dialog box, shown in Figure 9.8.

6 Choose Add to add another Scenario.

7 Choose OK to return to the Scenario Manager dialog box.

You can also create a scenario by changing the values in the changing cells, selecting them, then typing a name in the Scenario box of the Workgroup toolbar, shown in Figure 9.9.

To show a scenario:

1 Ⓦ Right-click Ⓜ Control+click on a toolbar.

2 Choose Workgroup (if the Workgroup toolbar is not a choice on the shortcut menu, choose Toolbars and turn on the Workgroup check box).

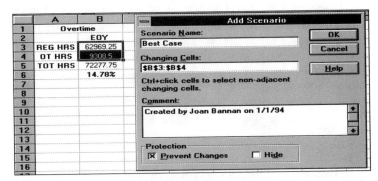

Figure 9.7 The Add Scenario dialog box

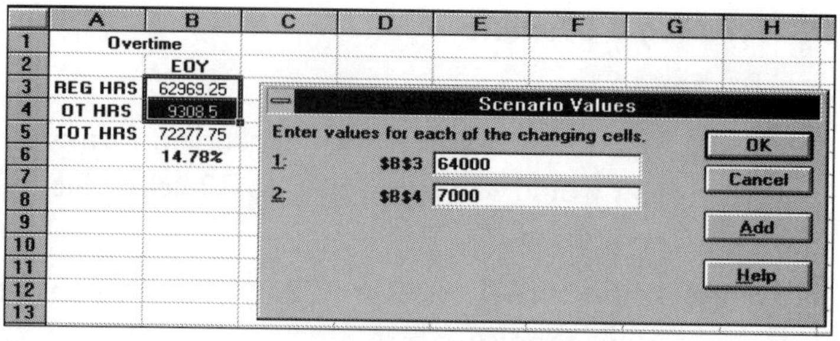

Figure 9.8 The Scenario Values dialog box

③ Click on the name of the scenario you want to show in the Scenario box.

You can also show a scenario by clicking the Show button in the Scenario dialog box on the Workgroup toolbar.

To delete a scenario:

① Choose Tools, Scenario (**Alt/, T, C**).

② Select the scenario you want to delete, and choose Delete.

To create a summary report:

① Choose Tools, Scenario (**Alt/, T, C**); and choose Summary.

② Enter the References or names for the result cells you would like in your report. If you have more than one reference, separate them with commas.

③ Choose OK.

When you tell Excel to create a Scenario Summary report, Excel opens a new sheet in the same workbook, outlines the worksheet, and uses an automatic format to format your report (see Figure 9.10).

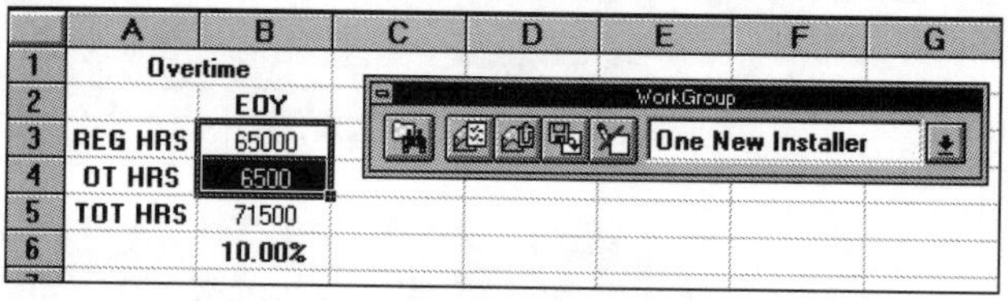

Figure 9.9 The Scenario Box on the Workgroup Toolbar

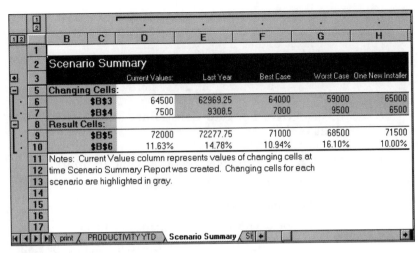

Figure 9.10 A Scenario Summary report

Solver

Solver is the most complex what-if analysis tool in Excel. With it, you can find the optimum value of a particular cell by adjusting the values of several cells. You can also apply specific limitations to one or more values involved in a calculation.

Before you put Solver to work, you need to identify the following cells on your worksheet that you want Solver to use:

♦ The target cell (objective) that you want to minimize, maximize, or set to a certain value.

♦ The changing cells (decision variables) that Solver will change to affect the value of the target cell.

♦ A constraint, which is a cell value that must fall within certain limits or satisfy target values for either the target cell or the changing cells.

Using Solver

Follow these instructions to use Solver:

1 Open the worksheet you want to use, and enter the reference or name of the target cell in the Set Target Cell box.

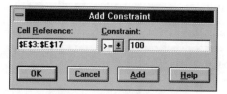

Figure 9.11 The Add Constraint dialog box

2 Enter the references or name of up to 200 cells you want changed in the By Changing Cells box.

3 Build a list of constraints in the Subject To The Constraints box with the Add, Change, and Delete buttons. The Add button opens the Add Constraint dialog box shown in Figure 9.11. The Change button opens an identical dialog box with the title, Change Constraint.

4 Choose the Solve button.

5 Wait—it may take a while for the problem to be solved. Don't panic if the hour glass hangs out for a while. When the Solver solution is complete, the Solver Results dialog box will appear (Figure 9.12). You can keep the solution, restore the original values, save the scenario, or generate one of three reports from this dialog box.

The target cell should contain a formula that depends on the changing cells. If the target cell does not contain a formula, it must also be a changing cell. If you don't specify a target cell, the solution will contain adjusted values for the changing cells which satisfy all of the constraints.

Changing cells can be restricted to integer values (use the "int" operator). When you are using the integer constraint, you can also use the

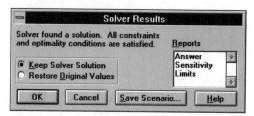

Figure 9.12 The Solver Results dialog box

Tolerance Setting in the Solver Options dialog box to adjust the allowable margin of error.

If you use the Guess button, you have to specify a target cell; but Solver will propose the changing cells for you based on the formula in the target cell.

For each problem, there can be two constraints: an upper and a lower bound for any cell, including the target cell and the changing cells. The cell referred to in the Cell Reference box usually contains a formula that depends on one or more of the changing cells.

The Effect of a Solver Solution on Formulas in Changing Cells

If you keep your Solver solution, and your changing cells contain formulas, the formulas will be replaced by constant values.

Chapter 10

· ·

Pivot Tables

T HIS CHAPTER IS AN OVERVIEW of how to create and customize pivot tables. Pivot tables are tables that you can change and rearrange by dragging field labels with the mouse. They are so slick that they deserve their own chapter. They are so tricky, they will probably be challenging to understand initially. The explanation is simple, but your input and Excel's pivot table capabilities make them very complex. The slickest trick I can offer you in this chapter is this suggestion: Open a worksheet that contains a fairly comprehensive list or table, use the slick tricks in this chapter to make the list into a pivot table, and "play" with it.

A pivot table is an interactive worksheet table that you use to summarize and analyze data from an existing list(s) or table(s). The source of the existing list(s) can be single or multiple worksheets or databases. They can be from within Excel or from external applications. With a pivot table, you can rearrange, organize, and analyze data by dragging and dropping fields.

Prepare Your Data for the PivotTable Wizard

Before you create a pivot table, there are a few things you can do to prepare.

♦ Remove any filters created, using the Filter command. The Pivot-Table Wizard ignores them anyway, but for your sanity and understanding—remove all filters.

♦ Remove any subtotals from your list. The PivotTable Wizard automatically includes subtotals and grand totals, unless you tell it not to in Step 4. If the data it is summarizing is numerical, it summarizes using the SUM function. If the data it is summarizing is text, it uses the COUNT function.

♦ Clarify in your mind what you would consider as a *field* or an *item*. The field is a category of data, such as the year or the month in the figures to follow. An item is a subcategory in a field, such as Expenses and Revenues. Figures 10.1 to 10.6 show how to create a pivot table step by step.

The PivotTable Wizard

The Pivot Table Wizard steps you through the creation of a pivot table.

1 Choose Data, PivotTable (**Alt/**, **D**, **P**).

2 In Step 1, shown in Figure 10.1, choose the source for your pivot table. A pivot table's source can be:

♦ An Excel worksheet range with labeled columns.

♦ A collection of worksheet ranges with labeled columns that contain data you want to consolidate.

♦ A database file or table from an external application.

♦ Data from an existing pivot table or Excel 4.0 Crosstab Table.

3 Choose Next.

4 In Step 2, enter the range of the data you want used from your source. (See Figure 10.2 and the next trick).

5 Choose Next.

6 In Step 3, drag the labels to the Page field, Column field, Row field or data field boxes, as shown in Figure 10.3. Or, to

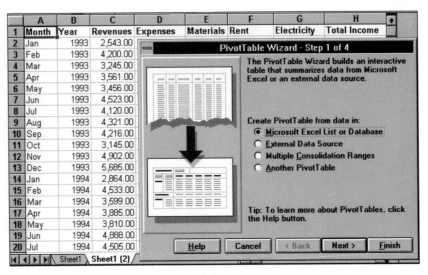

Figure 10.1 Step 1 of the PivotTable Wizard

customize or place the fields, double-click on the field buttons
to open the PivotTable Field dialog box shown in Figure 10.4.

7 Choose Next.

8 In Step 4, enter the upper left cell of the target range where
you want the pivot table to import (see Figure 10.5).

	A	B	C	D	E	F	G	H
1	Month	Year	Revenues	Expenses	Materials	Rent	Electricity	Total Income
2	Jan	1993	2,543.00	2,224.45	1,023.00	1,100.00	101.45	318.55
3	Feb	1993	4,200.00	2,309.90	1,106.00	1,100.00	103.90	1,890.10
4	Mar	1993	3,245.00	2,313.65	1,115.00	1,100.00	98.65	931.35
5	Apr	1993	3,561.00	2,417.35	1,228.00	1,100.00	89.35	1,143.65
6	May	1993	3,456.00	2,430.33	1,245.00	1,100.00	85.33	1,025.67
7	Jun	1993	4,523.00	2,488.45	1,315.00	1,100.00	73.45	2,034.55
8	Jul	1993	4,120.00					
9	Aug	1993	4,321.00					
10	Sep	1993	4,216.00					
11	Oct	1993	3,145.00					
12	Nov	1993	4,902.00					
13	Dec	1993	5,685.00					
14	Jan	1994	2,864.00					
15	Feb	1994	4,533.00					
16	Mar	1994	3,599.00	2,736.65	1,515.00	1,100.00	121.65	862.35
17	Apr	1994	3,885.00	2,823.35	1,578.00	1,100.00	145.35	1,061.65
18	May	1994	3,810.00	2,745.33	1,545.00	1,100.00	100.33	1,064.67
19	Jun	1994	4,888.00	2,783.45	1,565.00	1,100.00	118.45	2,104.55
20	Jul	1994	4,505.00	2,816.45	1,598.00	1,100.00	118.45	1,688.55

PivotTable Wizard - Step 2 of 4

Type or select the worksheet range that contains the data you want to use.

Range: A1:H25   Browse...

Help   Cancel   < Back   Next >   Finish

Sheet1 Sheet1 (2)

Figure 10.2 Step 2 of the PivotTable Wizard

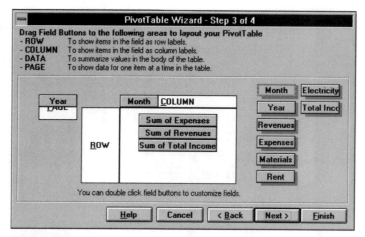

Figure 10.3   Step 3 of the PivotTable Wizard

⑨ Choose Finish (see Figure 10.6). Excel will import the pivot table you created into the range you selected and the Query and Pivot toolbar will become visible.

Step 3 of the PivotTable Wizard is the hardest step to figure out. You can always take a guess at how to arrange the labels, then return to the PivotTable Wizard if you don't like how the pivot table turns out. You can also rearrange field labels directly on the pivot table after it's created.

A page field is a column label which you assign to display the data for one item at a time. The PivotTable Wizard places a drop-down arrow

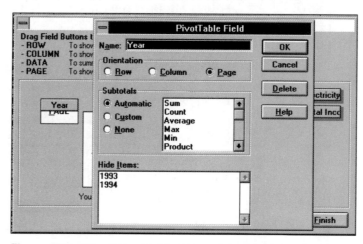

Figure 10.4   The PivotTable Wizard Field dialog box

Figure 10.5 **Step 4 of the PivotTable Wizard**

on the Page field, so you can switch between each Page field individually, or you can choose All.

A Column or Row field lines the data up beneath a column or within a row of your pivot table. You can have one or more, depending on what want to you show in the pivot table.

A summary function is a calculation function, such as SUM, COUNT, or AVERAGE, which you call when combining source data in a pivot or consolidation table or when inserting automatic subtotals in a list or database.

The data fields are summarized by the summary function you choose in the PivotTable Wizard. At least one data field is required. You can change or add summary functions to this data after the table is created. For instance, if you choose to have the data summarized with the SUM function, you can change the summary to AVERAGE or you can keep SUM and add AVERAGE.

Let Excel Propose the Range

If you are creating your pivot table from a list in an open Excel workbook and you want the pivot table based on the entire list, select a cell

1	Year	[All]												
2														
3		Month												
4	Data	Jan	Feb	Mar	Apr	May	Jun	Jul	Aug	Sep	Oct	Nov	Dec	Grand Total
5	Sum of Expenses	4948.9	5069.8	5050.3	5240.7	5175.7	5271.9	5387.9	5342.1	5406.6	5540.3	5592.6	5664.3	63691.09
6	Sum of Revenues	5407	8733	6844	7446	7266	9411	8625	8966	8827	6675	10204	11791	100195
7	Sum of Total Incom	458.1	3663.2	1793.7	2205.3	2090.3	4139.1	3237.1	3623.9	3420.4	1134.7	4611.5	6126.7	36503.91
8														
9						Query and Pivot								
10														
11														
12														

Figure 10.6 **A pivot table and the Query and Pivot toolbar**

in the list before you start the PivotTable Wizard. If you want to base it on only part of the list, select the range before you begin. Excel will propose the range in Step 2.

Don't Include Totals in Your Range

The PivotTable Wizard automatically places grand totals in the pivot table it creates. Therefore, if your list has totals, select only the row labels, column labels, and data as the range for the PivotTable Wizard to use, as shown in Figure 10.7.

Don't Save the Data with the Table Layout

One of the options in Step 4 of the PivotTable Wizard is to save the data of the pivot table. If you have a large amount of hidden data it may slow down recalculation. You may want to turn off the Save Data With Table Layout check box. The data will not be stored with the pivot table, but each time you change or refresh the pivot table it will automatically be updated from the source data.

When the Last Slick Trick Isn't So Slick

If you are going to create a second pivot table from the first, you will probably want to leave the data saved with the pivot table. The reason for this is that you may not want to refresh them both at the same time, which is what will happen automatically if you delete the hidden file.

	A	B	C	D	E	F	G	H
1	Month	Year	Revenues	Expenses	Materials	Rent	Electricity	Total Income
14	Jan	1994	2,864.00	2,724.45	1,523.00	1,100.00	101.45	139.55
15	Feb	1994	4,533.00	2,759.90	1,556.00	1,100.00	103.90	1,773.10
16	Mar	1994	3,599.00	2,736.65	1,515.00	1,100.00	121.65	862.35
17	Apr	199						1,061.65
18	May	199						1,064.67
19	Jun	199						2,104.55
20	Jul	199						1,688.55
21	Aug	199						1,887.44
22	Sep	199						1,840.68
23	Oct	199						727.35
24	Nov	199						2,496.90
25	Dec	1994	6,106.00	2,834.12	1,600.00	1,100.00	134.12	3,271.88
26	Total	47844	100195	63691.09	34750	26400	2,541.09	36,503.91

PivotTable Wizard - Step 2 of 4

Type or select the worksheet range that contains the data you want to use.

Range: $A$1:$H$25

Browse...

Help   Cancel   < Back   Next >   Finish

Figure 10.7 Selecting a pivot table range without totals

Rename Fields and Items in the Finished Pivot Table

When you create a pivot table using multiple consolidation ranges, Excel creates generic row and column field names, such as Row 1 and Column 1. Excel also creates these generic field names when you group, as described later in this chapter. You can rename these field names in the same way you enter text in any other cell on a worksheet.

1 Select the heading.

2 Type a new name and press Enter; or click on the check mark.

Update a Pivot Table

If you change data in a pivot table's source, you can update (refresh) it without recreating it. The changes which will refresh are changes in the data field, fields or items that have been deleted, and new or changed items in existing rows or fields. It will not refresh cells that have not been defined in Step 2 of the PivotTable Wizard. Therefore, if you insert rows or columns in the source range, you may need to call the wizard, go to Step 2, and change this reference to correctly update your pivot table.

To change the range in Step 2:

1 Select a cell in the pivot table.

2 Click on the PivotTable button 🖳 on the Query and Pivot Toolbar and choose Back.

3 Change the range reference in the range box (you can select the box, then select the range if the list you are using is in the same workbook), and choose Finish.

To refresh the data using the menu:

1 Select a cell within the pivot table.

2 Choose Data, Refresh Data (**Alt/**, **D**, **R**).

To refresh the data using the Refresh button:

1 Select a cell within the pivot table.

2 Click on the Refresh button 🖳 on the Query and Pivot toolbar.

To refresh the data using the pivot table shortcut menu:

1 W Right-click M Control+click on a cell within the pivot table.

2 Choose Refresh Data.

Name Ranges

If you use a named range in your source list, and you use that name when you create a pivot table, inserting rows or columns into the range in the source data will automatically be updated in the pivot table.

Refreshing Removes Formats

When you refresh the data in a pivot table, only formatting applied from AutoFormat, or from the Format Number command in the PivotTable Field dialog box (see the next trick), will stay intact. If you have added any formats, using the Format Cells commands, they will be removed.

Create Number Formats

To create number formats within a pivot table that will not be removed when you refresh, use the Number button in the PivotTable Field dialog box shown in Figure 10.8.

1 Select the cell you want to format (if the cell is part of a subtotal range, the whole range will be affected).

2 Click on the PivotTable Field button 🈂 or the shortcut menu to choose PivotTable Field.

3 Choose Number and select the number format you want, then choose OK in the Number dialog box.

4 Choose OK in the PivotTable Field dialog box.

Make a Copy of a Pivot Table

If you would like to take snapshots as you change a pivot table, or if you would like to edit the pivot table data without editing the source, you can make a copy. When you make a copy of a pivot table, it becomes data; it can no longer be changed and rearranged as a pivot table. The

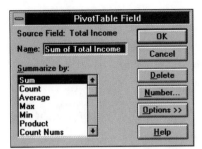

Figure 10.8 The PivotTable
Field dialog box

data within a pivot table cannot be edited because it maintains a link to the source. The way to edit it is to edit the source. However, if you make a copy, you can edit the new list or table.

1 Select the pivot table.

2 Click on the Copy button on the Standard toolbar, or
Ⓦ Right-click Ⓜ Control+click on the selection and choose Copy.

3 Ⓦ Right-click Ⓜ Control+click on the upper left cell of the target range.

4 Choose Paste Special.

5 Turn on the Values option button and choose OK.

Add Fields

1 Select a cell within the pivot table.

2 Click on the pivot table button or use the shortcut menu to choose PivotTable.

3 Drag the fields to the Row, Column, or Page areas; or double-click on them and use the PivotTable Field dialog box, and choose Finish.

Delete Fields

You can delete Page, Column, and Row fields without opening the PivotTable Wizard. For data fields, you will need to open the wizard. At least one data field is required, so you will not be able to delete all of the fields.

To remove Page, Column, and Row fields, drag them off the pivot table.

To remove a data field:

1 Select a cell within the pivot table.

2 Click on the Pivot Table button 🔲, or use the shortcut menu to choose PivotTable.

3 Drag the data field to anywhere outside of the white areas in Step 3 of the PivotTable Wizard, then choose Finish.

Hide a Row, Column, or Page Field

1 Double-click on the field or select it, and press the Pivot-Table Field button 🔲.

2 Select the items you want to hide in the Hide Items box.

Figure 10.9 shows how the pivot table from Figure 10.6 would look after hiding all items except those pertaining to the first quarter.

Move a Field or an Item

You can move a field by dragging it with the mouse. Drag a column field to a row or a row field to a column. For instance, the Page field, Year (shown in Figure 10.9) was dragged to the row field area in Figure 10.10. The pivot table example now displays annual comparison data for the first quarters of 1993 and 1994.

You can also rearrange items in rows or columns to view them in a different order. For instance, in Figure 10.11, 1994 was moved to the top of 1993.

	J	K	L	M	N
1					
2	Year	(All) ▼			
3					
4		Month			
5	Data	Jan	Feb	Mar	Grand Total
6	Sum of Expenses	4948.9	5069.8	5050.3	15069
7	Sum of Revenues	5407	8733	6844	20984
8	Sum of Total Income	458.1	3663.2	1793.7	5915

Figure 10.9 New pivot table after hiding items

			Month			
1						
2						
3						
4			Month			
5	Year	Data	Jan	Feb	Mar	Grand Total
6	1993	Sum of Expenses	2224.45	2309.9	2313.65	6848
7		Sum of Revenues	2543	4200	3245	9988
8		Sum of Total Income	318.55	1890.1	931.35	3140
9	1994	Sum of Expenses	2724.45	2759.9	2736.65	8221
10		Sum of Revenues	2864	4533	3599	10996
11		Sum of Total Income	139.55	1773.1	862.35	2775
12	Total Sum of Expenses		4948.9	5069.8	5050.3	15069
13	Total Sum of Revenues		5407	8733	6844	20984
14	Total Sum of Total Income		458.1	3663.2	1793.7	5915

Figure 10.10 Move fields by dragging with the mouse.

Automatically Create a Separate Page for Each Page Field

When you have page fields, you can click on the Show Pages button
to automatically create a separate page in your workbook for each
Page field item.

1 Select a cell in the pivot table.

2 Click on the Show Pages button , or use the shortcut menu
to choose Show Pages.

3 From the Show Pages dialog box, select the Page field you
want separated onto different worksheets and choose OK.

Excel creates a separate worksheet for each item in the page field. The
original worksheet containing the summary (All) will remain. The new
worksheets will automatically be named the same as the items in the
field. For instance, in the pivot table in Figure 10.12, the Show Pages
command would create two new worksheets named 1994 and 1993.
The existing worksheet will remain and contain the summary data.

			Month			
4			Month			
5	Year	Data	Jan	Feb	Mar	Grand Total
6	1994	Sum of Expenses	2724.45	2759.9	2736.65	8221
7		Sum of Revenues	2864	4533	3599	10996
8		Sum of Total Income	139.55	1773.1	862.35	2775
9	1993	Sum of Expenses	2224.45	2309.9	2313.65	6848
10		Sum of Revenues	2543	4200	3245	9988
11		Sum of Total Income	318.55	1890.1	931.35	3140
12	Total Sum of Expenses		4948.9	5069.8	5050.3	15069
13	Total Sum of Revenues		5407	8733	6844	20984
14	Total Sum of Total Income		458.1	3663.2	1793.7	5915

Figure 10.11 Move items by dragging with the mouse.

	A	B	C	D	E
1	Year	1993 ↓			
2		**1994**			
3		**1993**			
4	Data	[All] Jan	Feb	Mar	Grand Total
5	Sum of Expenses	2224.45	2309.9	2313.65	6848
6	Sum of Revenues	2543	4200	3245	9988
7	Sum of Total Income	318.55	1890.1	931.35	3140
8					

Figure 10.12 Page field items

Unless you tell Excel in Step 4 of the PivotTable Wizard not to create subtotals and grand totals, they will be created automatically. Values are calculated (directly from source data) on the items within the existing visible pivot table, not on hidden items.

Show the Source Data Detail of a Total

To show a list of the source rows or records which Excel used to calculate the value of a cell in your pivot table, double-click on the cell. A new worksheet will open with a complete, labeled, and formatted breakdown of the source data detail, as shown in Figure 10.13.

Use Custom Calculations

Excel automatically uses the SUM function to create subtotals and grand totals for numerical data, and the COUNT function for text. You

			Month			
4			Month			
5	Data	Year	Jan	Feb	Mar	Grand Total
6	Sum of Expenses	1994	2724.45	2759.9	2736.65	8221
7		1993	2224.45	2309.9	2313.65	6848
8	Sum of Revenues	1994	2864	4533	3599	10996
9		1993	2543	4200	3245	9988
10	Sum of Total Income	1994	139.55	1773.1	862.35	2775
11		1993	318.55	1890.1	931.35	3140
12	Total Sum of Expenses		4948.9	5069.8	5050.3	15069
13	Total Sum of Revenues		5407	8733	6844	20984
14	Total Sum of Total Income		458.1	3663.2	1793.7	5915

Double-click on this cell
to create a new worksheet
displaying detail from the source data

	A	B	C	D	E	F	G	H
1	Month	Year	Revenues	Expenses	Materials	Rent	Electricity	Total Income
2	Jan	1994	2864	2724.45	1523	1100	101.45	139.55
3	Jan	1993	2543	2224.45	1023	1100	101.45	318.55

Figure 10.13 Double-click on a subtotal or grand-total cell to show detail.

can add a custom calculation or change the existing totals in the Pivot-Table Field dialog box.

To change an existing calculation or add a custom calculation:

1 Double-click the field to display the PivotTable Field dialog box.

2 Select the Custom option button.

3 Select as many of the subtotal functions as you want displayed for the field, and choose OK.

Group Items in the Source Data

You can group items to summarize data into higher levels than they existed in your source data. Once they are grouped, they can be rearranged as any other Row, Column, or Page field. For instance in Figure 10.14, the first of the three month periods, Jan, Feb, and Mar, were grouped. This created a new column field. Excel proposed Month2 as the Column field name, but in the figure, it has been re-named Quarters. The first group name was renamed 1Q. The next obvious steps are to group the last three months, then rename Group2, Group3, and Group4 to 2Q, 3Q, and 4Q.

You can group selected items into categories, numeric items into ranges, or dates or times into larger units, such as days, months, or years.

To create a group:

1 Select the items you want to group.

2 Click on the Group button ⬆, use the shortcut menu to choose Group and Outline, then choose Group from the submenu.

To expand or collapse grouped items, double-click on the group heading.

When you double-click on a group heading, the group will toggle between expanded and collapsed. Totals will summarize or break apart into detail automatically as you expand or collapse the group.

	J	K	L	M	N	O	P	Q	R
1									
2	Year	(All)							
3									
4		Quarters	Month						
5		1Q	Group2	Group3			Oct	Nov	Dec
6	Data			Jul	Aug	Sep	Oct	Nov	Dec
7	Sum of Expenses	15069	15688.26	5387.9	5342.12	5406.64	5540.3	5592.55	5664
8	Sum of Revenues	20984	24123	8625	8966	8827	6675	10204	117
9	Sum of Total Income	$5,915	$8,435	$3,237	$3,624	$3,420	$1,135	$4,611	$6,1
10									
11									

Figure 10.14 Rearranging grouped items

To expand and show detail:

1. Select the Group Heading.

2. Click on the Show Detail button ⬛, or use the shortcut menu to choose group or outline, then choose Show Detail from the submenu.

To collapse and summarize:

1. Select the Group Heading.

2. Click on the Hide Detail button ⬛, or use the shortcut menu to choose Group or Outline, then choose Hide Detail from the submenu.

To ungroup:

1. Select the group heading.

2. Click on the Ungroup button ⬛, or use the shortcut menu to choose Group and Outline, then choose Ungroup from the submenu.

When you ungroup all items in the field, the row or column field label will disappear.

Grouping Page Fields

Page fields cannot be grouped where they are. To group them, they need to be dragged into a Column or Row field position first. After they have been grouped, they can be moved back into a Page field position.

Chapter 11

. . . .

Creating Charts

WHEN YOU CHART THE DATA ON YOUR WORKSHEETS, the data is easier to compare and more interesting. Charts can be based on outlined worksheets, subtotaled lists, filtered lists, and pivot tables. They can be embedded on the worksheet with the source data or stand alone on a chart sheet. There are 14 chart types and each chart type has a number of subtypes. All of this can be accomplished in slick ways using the Chart Wizard, Chart toolbar buttons, menu commands, and templates.

Regardless of whether charts are embedded as objects on worksheets or stored on separate chart sheets, they are linked to the original worksheet data. Changes to the data in either the chart or the worksheet will automatically reflect in both.

What Is a Chart?

. . . .

Charts are graphs. If you are used to calling the subject of this chapter *graphs*, you are not alone. Why does Excel refer to a graph as a chart?

Way back before Microsoft Excel evolved into the incredible, comprehensive product that it is today, there was a product called Microsoft Chart. When Excel and Chart eventually merged, it was too late: Microsoft was deeply entrenched in the habit of calling a graph a "chart."

Creating Charts with Templates

Far be it from me to insult a wizard, especially the ChartWizard, which I hold in the highest esteem, but it is rarely necessary to go through the ChartWizard steps each time you create a chart, as many Excel users do.

Create a New Chart Quickly

An embedded chart is one that is located on a worksheet. It is usually on the worksheet that contains the data from which it was plotted, but you can copy or cut and paste it to other worksheets as any object. A chart that is not embedded is located on a chart sheet. When a chart sheet is active or when an embedded chart is activated by double-clicking on it, the Main menu changes to contain chart specific commands.

The fastest ways to create a chart on a chart sheet are to press F11 or to click on the Create Chart Sheet button ▣. To use the Create Chart Sheet button, you will need to copy it to a toolbar from the Charting category in the Customize dialog box.

The fastest way to create an embedded chart is to click on the Embedded Chart button on the Chart toolbar ▦.

When you press F11 or click on either of these "build a chart according to the template buttons," the ChartWizard will be activated if Excel does not have enough information to understand the selection you have made.

To create a new chart on a chart sheet:

1 Select the worksheet data that you want in a chart.

2 Press F11 or click on the Create Chart Sheet button. Excel will open a new chart sheet and create a new chart, using the specifications of the current chart template.

To create a new embedded chart:

1 Select the worksheet data that you want in a chart.

2 Click on the Embedded Chart button on the Chart toolbar.

3 Drag the mouse on the worksheet to create a rectangle that will contain the chart. The embedded chart will be created, using the specifications of the current chart template.

The Embedded Chart button can also be used to format an existing, embedded chart with the selected template format in the Tools, Options dialog box on the Chart tab (see the next trick).

Use the Current Chart As a Template

You can create and AutoFormat simultaneously, using the current chart as a template.

1 Create a chart the way you like it.

2 Choose Tools, Options (**Alt/, T, O**); and select the Chart tab.

3 Click on the Use the Current Chart button, and type in a name for the AutoFormat you are creating.

4 Choose OK in the Create AutoFormat dialog box.

5 Choose OK in the Options dialog box.

You can create several AutoFormats and use them as templates. Once an AutoFormat exists, you can change it to be the default by selecting it from the Default Chart Format drop-down list (instead of choosing the Use the Current Chart in step 3 above). You can also create a chart from the current template, then apply an AutoFormat after it exists. See the section on AutoFormats later in this chapter.

To reset the default template to the original Excel format:

1 Choose Tools, Options (**Alt/, T, O**); and select the Chart tab.

2 Select Built-in from the Default Chart Format drop-down list, and choose OK.

Choosing Chart Data

Chart data can be plotted on visible rows and columns (with others hidden), or on nonadjacent selections. You can plot data that is automatically subtotaled or filtered, or plot the data of a pivot table. As long as the data makes sense to Excel, Excel will create a chart from the selection. The selection must be a rectangular shape; for instance in Figure 11.1, cell A3 would need to be selected in order for Excel to create a chart from the noncontiguous selection.

When you create a chart, you tell Excel how to plot the data—in rows or in columns. You can change the orientation in Step 4 of the ChartWizard.

Create a Chart from a Subtotaled List

You can create a chart with summary data by subtotaling the list first. Then select the subtotaled ranges, excluding the grand total (see Figures 11.2 and 11.3).

Preventing a Filtered List Chart from Being Updated

When you create a chart from a filtered list, it will be updated if you change the filter or show all the rows. To prevent this, you can click on the Select Visible Cells button ▦ before selecting the ranges on your worksheet to plot your chart. The Visible Cells button is in the Utility category of the Customize dialog box.

Create a Chart from a Pivot Table

Creating a chart from a pivot table is much like creating a chart from any other set of data, but the following restrictions apply:

	A	B	C	D	E	F	G	H
1	Beeper's Airline Ticket Sales							
2								
3		Jan	Feb	Mar	Apr	May	Jun	Jul
4	LAX	$7,530	$3,290	$4,315	$3,163	$3,526	$3,658	$3,526
5	OAK	$2,893	$3,346	$3,454	$3,792	$1,180	$1,007	$1,180
6	SFO	$5,460	$6,978	$7,272	$8,382	$6,828	$7,216	$6,828
7								

Figure 11.1 Plot a chart from a noncontiguous selection

	Total
Salary Total	$49,400
Maintenance Total	$14,120
Overhead Total	$12,000
Fuel Total	$30,300
Grand Total	$105,820

Figure 11.2 A subtotaled list

- Use a pivot table that has no more than two row fields and two column fields.

- Delete grand totals and subtotals before charting (or leave them out of your data range).

- Use only the main body of the pivot table, excluding the Page fields.

You can save and print charts for each Page field if you copy them to separate worksheets, using the show Pages button on the Query and Pivot toolbar, then chart each separately. For more about pivot tables, see Chapter 10.

The ChartWizard

The ChartWizard takes a lot of the guesswork out of creating charts. It systematically prompts you for necessary information and displays visual

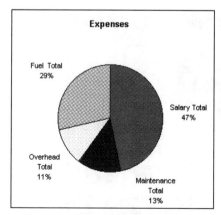

Figure 11.3 A chart displaying summary data from the subtotaled list in Figure 11.2

choices, including a preview of your actual chart. The ChartWizard dialog boxes contain a Back button that you can use to redo previous steps if you don't like what you see in the preview.

Use the ChartWizard to Create an Embedded Chart

An embedded chart does not overwrite data. It is created in a layer on top of the worksheet in the same manner as other Excel objects. It can be moved or sized, and can obscure worksheet data without affecting it.

1 Select the range that includes the column and row headings and the numbers you want to include in your chart, and click on the ChartWizard button.

2 Drag the mouse on the worksheet to create the rectangle that will contain the chart.

3 Choose Next to confirm or change the range in the Chart-Wizard Step 1. You can change the range by typing in a new one or by selecting one with the mouse.

4 Choose a chart type in Step 2 (Figure 11.4), and choose Next.

5 Choose a format for the chart type in Step 3 (Figure 11.5), and choose Next.

6 Choose either the Rows or Columns option button in Step 4 (see Figures 11.6 and 11.7). This selection can make a huge

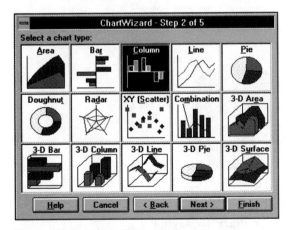

Figure 11.4 ChartWizard step 2, with Columns selected

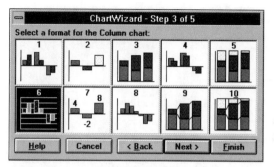

Figure 11.5 ChartWizard Step 3 of 5,
available chart formats

difference. The ChartWizard helps you make your choices by giving you a preview of the results. The sample chart is actually created from your data (I love Excel). You may also change the selection for the (X) Axis Labels or the Legend text.

7 Choose Next.

8 Type in a title for your chart and a title for each axis in Step 5 (Figure 11.8). The sample chart will display titles when you finish typing.

9 Choose Next.

If the embedded chart does not look the way you want it to look, or doesn't look like the sample chart, you may need to resize it as you would any object—by dragging the border(s). If you hold down the Shift key as you drag, it will keep its proportions.

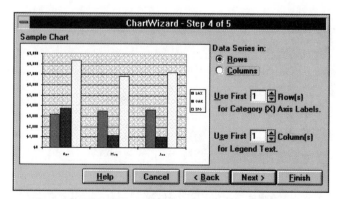

Figure 11.6 ChartWizard Step 4 of 5, showing a
sample column chart with Rows selected

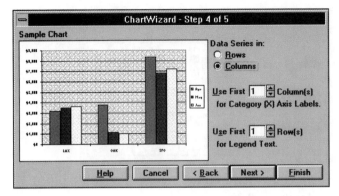

Figure 11.7 Another View of ChartWizard Step 4 of 5 with columns selected

Create a Chart on an Independent Chart Sheet

To use the ChartWizard to create a chart on an independent chart sheet, replace step 2 of the previous instructions with these two steps:

1 Choose Insert, Chart (**Alt/, I, H, A**).

2 Choose As New Sheet on the submenu.

Selecting and Activating Charts

To select an embedded chart, click on it once; to activate it, double-click on it. Select a chart sheet as you would any workbook sheet. You may also rename the chart sheet in the same way as any workbook sheet. Double-click on the tab or Ⓦ right-click Ⓜ Control+click on the tab and choose Rename from the shortcut menu.

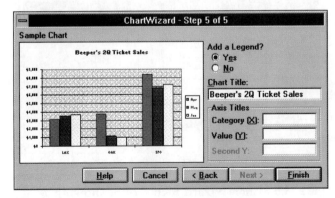

Figure 11.8 ChartWizard Step 5 of 5

Once a chart is activated, the commands on the Main menu change and you can select each item in the chart individually.

Shortcut Menus

There are several shortcut menus available on an activated chart. They customize themselves to fit all possible commands for the selected item. Ⓦ Right-click Ⓜ Control+click on the chart itself or individual chart items to display them.

Create 3-D Charts

If your data has two categories *plus* values, the ChartWizard will make the 3-D options available when you are creating a chart.

Sizing

All of the boxes, the plot area, and the legend on a chart can be sized by dragging, including the chart itself.

❶ Select the box.

❷ Place the mouse pointer over one of the handles until it turns into a two-headed arrow.

❸ Drag it to the size you want.

To keep the size proportional, hold down the Shift key as you drag.

Sizing the Plot Area

You can select the plot area of a chart in order to size or format it, but beware of sizing pie charts; you will drag the pieces apart (see Figure 11.9). A "sliced" pie could be just the special effect you are looking for, or it might be a lousy surprise. If you want the pie to be larger but stay together, size the whole chart until it becomes the size you want. You can then make other items smaller if they have become too large.

Remember, you can Undo unpleasant surprises. This includes the last edit of a chart.

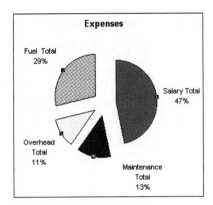

Figure 11.9 **A sliced Pie chart**

Chart Parts

You can select any item in a chart, and the menu commands will reflect the selection. For instance, the Trendline and Error Bars commands on the Insert menu are available only when a data series is selected.

Figure 11.10 shows the elements of a 2-D chart, and Figure 11.11 shows the additional elements of a 3-D chart.

Selecting Chart Items

When a chart is active, a thick, diagonally striped border surrounds it. Once it is activated, you can select the chart or individual items on the chart.

Select the chart itself by clicking anywhere in it except on an item within the chart. Select an item by clicking on it. The same is true within the legend; click on the legend anywhere except on a legend entry or key. Click on an entry or a key to select it.

When you click on one data point in a data series, you select the whole series. If you click again, you select the data point itself. For instance, in Figure 11.12 the SFO data series was selected by clicking on the first SFO column. Clicking on it again selected the first column only, shown in Figure 11.13.

Selection handles identify the selection. When an item is selected, the name of the item is displayed in the name area of the formula bar. You might not always recognize the name, however, because Excel sometimes uses codes, such as S1P1.

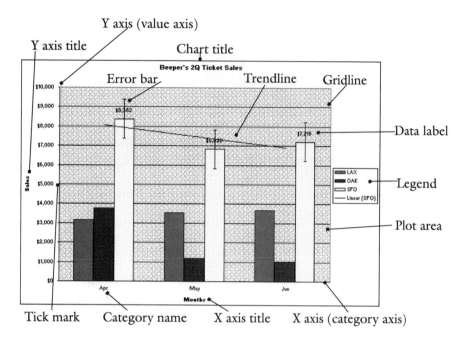

Figure 11.10 The components of a 2-D chart

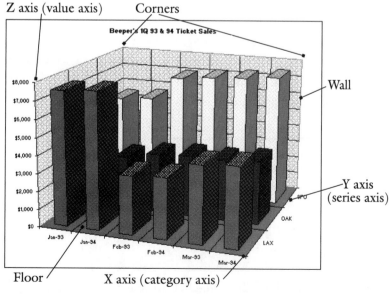

Figure 11.11 Additional elements of a 3-D chart

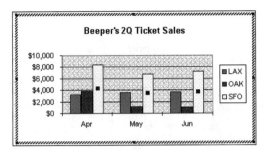

Figure 11.12 Click once on an item in a series to select the series.

Chart Types

There are 14 chart types, and each one has several subtypes or variations. Some chart types are more suited to showing relative importance of values over time. Some are preferable for comparing values against each other, and some are better at showing trends or proportions of parts to a whole. Still others are suited to specific industries, such as the high-low close charts for the stock market. Depending on the nature of your data, there is probably a chart which will display it well.

If you are not sure what kind of chart you want to use, the easiest way to find out is to create one; then try out the types, using the chart toolbar. The Chart Type button contains a palette of AutoFormat buttons that make it easy to play with your chart (see Figure 11.14). For instance, the 3-D chart shown in Figure 11.11 is not the best way to display its connected data. A preferable chart type would be one that doesn't hide a data series behind another.

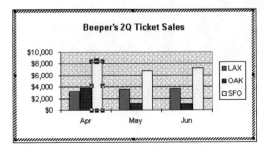

Figure 11.13 Double-click to select a data point.

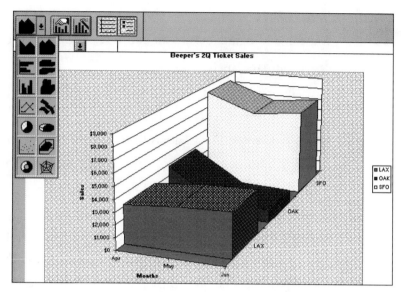

Figure 11.14 The Chart Type drop-down palette

To try out chart types:

1 Make sure the chart toolbar is visible.

2 Select the chart and click on the Chart Type drop-down list.

3 Select each chart type that you think might work for your data.

Once you decide what kind of chart type you want, you can select the subtype or change the chart type of one or more of the data series to combine two chart types together. For instance you may want most of your data represented in a bar chart, but like to see one data series as a line chart. For these slick tricks, see Chapter 12, "Editing Charts."

Adding Titles, Labels, and Other Chart Items

After you have created the essence of your chart with the ChartWizard, your creativity need not end. Excel makes it easy to add labels and special effects to accent or increase information. You can format each new item as you add it, or you can format all of the items when you have finished adding them.

Data Labels

You can add data labels to an entire series or to just one data point.

To add data labels:

1 Select the data series or data point and Ⓦ right-click Ⓜ Control+click on it.

2 Choose Data Labels from the shortcut menu.

3 Choose the kind of data labels you want from Data Labels dialog box, and choose OK.

To format a data label:

1 Double-click or Ⓦ right-click Ⓜ Control+click on the label, and choose Format Data Labels from the shortcut menu.

2 Make changes to the Patterns, Font, Number, or Alignment in the Format Data Labels dialog box, and choose OK.

Titles

To add or change a title:

1 Ⓦ Right-click Ⓜ Control+click on the chart.

2 Choose Titles from the shortcut menu.

3 Select the title you want to add from the Titles dialog box, and choose OK.

4 Type the title. It will be displayed in the Formula bar as you type.

5 Press Enter.

To format a title:

1 Double-click or Ⓦ right-click Ⓜ Control+click on the title and choose Format Title from the shortcut menu.

2 Make changes to the Patterns, Font, or Alignment in the Format Chart Title or Format Axis Title dialog box.

3 Choose OK.

Legends

The legend button on the Chart toolbar creates a legend if you do not have one and deletes it if you do.

To add or delete a legend, click on the Legend button ▣ on the Chart toolbar.

To format a legend:

1 Double-click on the legend.

2 Make any changes to Patterns, Font, or Placement in the Format Legends dialog box and choose OK.

You can also Ⓦ right-click Ⓜ Control+click on a legend to use the shortcut menu.

Gridlines

Gridlines help you see values by extending tick marks on an axis across the plot area. You can click on the Gridlines button ▦ on the Chart toolbar to add or delete major horizontal gridlines. The same is true for major vertical gridlines. The Vertical Gridline button is in the Charting category of the Customize dialog box.

To add or delete all gridlines:

1 Ⓦ Right-click Ⓜ Control+click on the active chart.

2 Choose Insert Gridlines from the shortcut menu.

3 Make selections in the Insert Gridlines dialog box, and choose OK.

To format gridlines:

1 Double-click on the gridlines or Ⓦ right-click Ⓜ Control+click on one of the lines and choose Format Gridlines from the shortcut menu.

2 Make changes to the Pattern or Scale in the Format Gridlines dialog box, and choose OK.

Axes

You normally create axes when you originally create your chart, but you can delete them or insert them again in the Insert Axis dialog box. You can also plot a secondary axis.

To add or delete axes:

1 Ⓦ Right-click Ⓜ Control+click on the chart.

2 Choose Insert Axis.

To hide or display axes:

1 Ⓦ Right-click Ⓜ Control+click on the axes.

2 Choose Hide or Unhide from the shortcut menu.

When you create a secondary axis, you may also want to have two chart types within your chart. For instance, you might want a line or area chart on top of a column chart. For slick tricks illustrating combination charts with secondary axes, see Chapter 12, "Editing Charts."

To plot one data series on a secondary axis:

1 Ⓦ Right-click Ⓜ Control+click on the series.

2 Choose Format Data Series from the shortcut menu and choose the Axis tab.

3 Turn on the Secondary Axis option button and choose OK.

To plot a group of data series along a secondary axis:

1 Ⓦ Right-click Ⓜ Control+click on the series.

2 Choose Chart Type from the shortcut menu and select the Axis tab.

3 Turn on the Secondary Axis option button and choose OK.

When you format an axis, you format the associated tick marks as well. You can format them on the scale tab to show the increments that make the most sense for your purposes.

To format axes:

1 Double-click or Ⓦ right-click Ⓜ Control+click on the axis, and choose Format Axis from the shortcut menu.

2 Make changes to the Patterns, Scale, Font, Number, or Alignment in the Format Axis dialog box, and choose OK.

Trendlines and Error Bars

One of Excel 5.0's new features is the ability to add trendlines and error bars to charts.

To add trendlines or error bars:

1 Select a data series and W right-click M Control+click on it.

2 Choose Trendlines or Error Bars from the shortcut menu.

3 Make your selections in the dialog box and choose OK.

To format trendlines or error bars:

1 Double-click on them or W right-click M Control+click, then use the shortcut menu to select Format trendlines or Format Error bars.

2 Make your selections in one of the Format dialog boxes and choose OK.

AutoFormats

· ·

You can use built-in chart AutoFormats or create your own to give your charts a consistent look. They work very much like the AutoFormats in worksheets. They include the chart type, subtype, patterns, legend gridlines, data labels, colors, patterns, and placement of additional items.

Apply a Built-In AutoFormat

1 W Right-click M Control+click on the chart and choose AutoFormat from the shortcut menu.

2 Turn on the Built-in option button and select a chart type from the Galleries list.

3 Click on the picture that contains the AutoFormat you want to apply, and choose OK.

Create a Custom (User-Defined) AutoFormat

1 W Right-click M Control+click to select the chart that has all the features you want in an AutoFormat.

2 Choose AutoFormat from the shortcut menu.

3 Turn on the User-Defined option button and choose Customize.

4 Choose Add in the User-Defined AutoFormats dialog box.

5 Type in a name and description for your AutoFormat in the Add Custom AutoFormat dialog box, and choose OK, then Close.

To apply a User-Defined AutoFormat:

1 W Right-click M Control+click on the chart and choose AutoFormat from the shortcut menu.

2 Turn on the User-Defined option button.

3 Select a chart type from the Formats list and choose OK.

You can be bold when trying out chart formats and AutoFormats; if you don't like the results, you can always use Undo.

AutoFormatting Removes Custom Formatting

Beware of overwriting all of your hard work. If you like the way a chart looks and you only want to change the chart type, don't change it using AutoFormat. For more about custom formatting, see Chapter 12, "Editing Charts."

Add Objects to Charts

Another of Excel 5.0's new features is the ability to use the drawing buttons on charts. You can emphasize or label items in your chart in the same way you do a worksheet by adding text boxes, arrows, lines, and other objects. Turn on the drawing toolbar and go for it, or turn to Chapter 13, "Graphics and Object Linking," to find out more.

Chapter 12

Editing Charts

O NCE A CHART IS CREATED, it has a great future. It can be edited to display two chart types or customized with a multitude of other slick tricks. Okay, maybe not a multitude, but there are a lot of new ways to edit a chart as described in this chapter. If you are not new to Excel, and especially if you have been using Excel a long time, you will probably find that editing and formatting a chart is now as easy as you always wished it would be.

Changing the Chart

Embed an Existing Chart from a Chart Sheet

It may be easier for you to have a chart on its own sheet most of the time, but embed it on a worksheet for comparison or printing.

1 Select the entire chart and copy or cut it.

2 Select the tab of the worksheet you want to place it on, and paste it.

It will be pasted using the active cell as the upper left corner for placement. You can control placement by selecting a cell in the worksheet

195

before pasting, but if you don't, you can move (and size) the chart after it is embedded. It will not overwrite any worksheet data.

Copy Several Charts to One Worksheet

For presentations or comparisons, you can paste more than one chart to a page. You can then place the header or footer and any other special effects you need on the worksheet. You may want to remove gridlines; but if you do this and forget where the original data resides, activate the chart and click on any data series marker. The sheet name will be displayed in the formula bar.

Edit an Existing Chart with the ChartWizard

You can use the ChartWizard to edit existing charts, as well as to create new ones. Just select the chart, then click the ChartWizard 🔳. The ChartWizard is the only way you can change:

♦ The range

♦ The column or row orientation

Other specific edits are easily accomplished by other methods, including selecting the item you want to edit, then using a shortcut menu or the chart toolbar.

Changing the Chart Type

You can change the chart type with a menu command, the Chart Type toolbar, or by applying a different AutoFormat. Remember: If you use an AutoFormat, it will overwrite all custom formatting. When you use a Chart Type button to change the chart type, the chart type changes without offering any choices to change the subtype or other attributes of the chart. When you use a menu command, you can select other options.

When a chart is active, a thick, diagonally-striped border surrounds it. Once it is activated, you can select the chart or individual items on the chart. Select the chart itself by clicking anywhere in it, except on an item within the chart. Select an item by clicking on it. The same is true within the legend: Click on the legend anywhere, except on a legend entry or key. Click on an entry or a key to select it.

To change the chart type using the Chart Type toolbar:

1 Select the chart.

2 Click on one of the Chart Type buttons in the Chart Type drop-down palette.

To change the chart type using the menu command:

1 Ⓦ Right-click Ⓜ Control+click on the chart.

2 Choose Chart Type from the shortcut menu.

3 Choose Options to change the subtype, series order, axis, or other chart-type options.

4 Choose OK, or choose Chart Type to switch back to the other dialog box.

Change the Series Order

Sometimes a chart would make more sense or just look better if one of the sets of data series markers (i.e., matching sets of columns or bars) was in a different place. For instance, in Figure 12.1, the top chart has one data series hidden by another. The bottom chart has the series in a different order showing how moving a series down or up can improve the display tremendously.

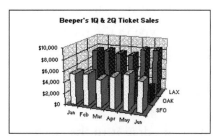

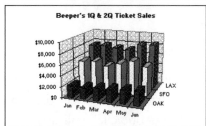

Figure 12.1 Moving data series markers

To change the series order:

1 Ⓦ Right-click Ⓜ Control+click on the chart.

2 Choose Chart Type from the shortcut menu.

3 Choose Options.

4 Select the Series Order Tab.

5 Select the series you want to move and then choose move up or move down.

6 Choose OK.

Add or Delete Data Points or a Data Series

To add data to a chart, you can use the New Data command or copy and paste the data from the worksheet to the chart. On an embedded chart, you can also drag the data from the worksheet.

If Excel is not certain how to place the data, a chart version of the Paste Special dialog box will open so that you can specify whether the new data is series or points.

To use the New Data command:

1 Select the chart.

2 Choose Insert, New Data (**Alt/, I, N**); and switch to the worksheet containing the data if necessary.

3 Select the data or type in the range in the New Data dialog box (Figure 12.2), and choose OK.

To drag the data:

1 Select the worksheet.

2 Select the data and drag it to the chart.

To copy and paste:

1 Select the worksheet.

2 Select the data and copy it.

3 Switch to the chart sheet or select the chart (you do not need to activate it—one click will do).

4 Paste the data.

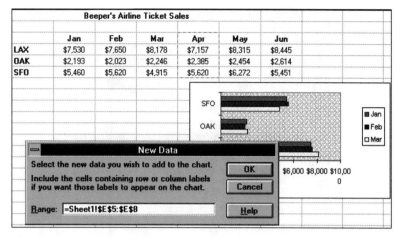

Beeper's Airline Ticket Sales

	Jan	Feb	Mar	Apr	May	Jun
LAX	$7,530	$7,650	$8,178	$7,157	$8,315	$8,445
OAK	$2,193	$2,023	$2,246	$2,385	$2,454	$2,614
SFO	$5,460	$5,620	$4,915	$5,620	$6,272	$5,451

New Data

Select the new data you wish to add to the chart.

Include the cells containing row or column labels if you want those labels to appear on the chart.

Range: =Sheet1!$E$5:$E$8

OK Cancel Help

Figure 12.2 The New Data dialog box

Figure 12.3 shows how Excel would add the selection in Figure 12.2, using any of these three methods.

To delete a series:

1 Select the series or Ⓦ right-click Ⓜ Control+click on the series.

2 Press Del or choose Clear from the shortcut menu.

Copy the Data from One Chart to Another

Another way to add data to a chart is to add one chart to another. When you do this, you can determine which format to keep. You can also copy the format from one chart to another. See the section, "Formatting Tricks," later in this chapter.

1 Activate the chart you want to copy and copy it.

2 Activate the second chart and choose Edit, Paste Special (**Alt/, E, S**).

3 Choose All if you want the format to be the same as the first chart.

4 Choose Formulas, if you want the format to be like the second chart.

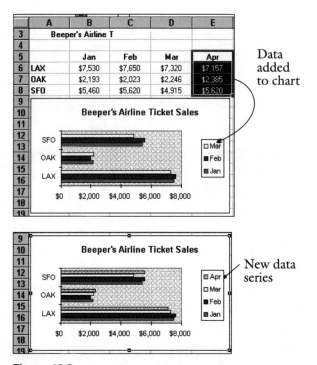

Figure 12.3 New data added to a chart

Change the Range of Plotted Data

The only way to change the range a chart was plotted from is to use the ChartWizard.

1 Select the chart sheet or activate the embedded chart.

2 Click on the ChartWizard button.

3 Change the range in Step 1 and choose Finish.

Change the Plot

You have already seen the value of changing the orientation of data from rows to columns or columns to rows (in Figure 11.6 in the previous chapter). You can change this orientation after the chart is created, using the second step of ChartWizard, as in the last trick.

To reverse the plot order using the Format Axis dialog box:

1 Double-click on the axis you want to reverse and select the Scale tab.

2 Turn on the Categories in the Reverse Order check box, or the Values in the Reverse Order check box, then choose OK.

Move and Size with Ease

It is now much easier to move everything on a chart, including the legend. For instance, in Figure 12.4, after reversing the plot, you may want to move and resize the legend, as shown in Figure 12.5. Or after creating a pie chart, you may find that some of the data series labels are scrunched together, as shown in the first chart in Figure 12.6. You can now drag a data series to anywhere you want it. You can move and size the legend as easily as any graphic object. For more about moving and sizing objects, see Chapter 13, "Graphics and Object Linking."

Zoom to Make Adjustments Easier

When you are adjusting the size or moving items around on a chart, it sometimes helps to change the magnification level to a larger view. For more about Zooming, see Chapter 6, "Views, Outlining, and Printing."

Linking Text to the Worksheet

When you create a chart, the data labels, legend entries, and axis tick-mark labels are already linked to the worksheet. If you edit them on the

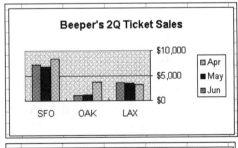

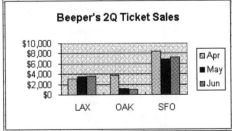

Figure 12.4 Reversing Plot Order

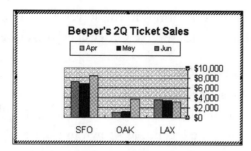

Figure 12.5 **Formatting adjustments to Figure 12.4**

chart, the link is broken, so it's preferable to change them on the worksheet. If you break the link to data labels, they can be restored. You can also link titles and text boxes to worksheet cells.

To restore data series links:

1 Double-click on a data series, or select and then double-click on a single data point; then select the Data Labels tab.

2 Turn on the Automatic Text check box and choose OK.

To link titles and text boxes to worksheet cells:

1 Select the title, click in the Formula bar, and type an equal sign (=).

2 Select the cell on the worksheet or type in the reference, then press Enter.

Check the Spelling on Charts

You can check all the spelling of chart text by clicking on the Spelling button on the Standard toolbar. All of the text which is not linked to the worksheet will be checked.

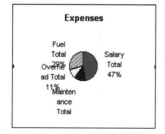 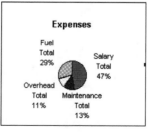

Figure 12.6 **Move chart items with the mouse**

Rotate a 3-D Chart with the Mouse

Rotating a 3-D chart can certainly make you feel like Excel is under your power. In fact, it's so much fun that I think you should try it even if you don't need to.

1 Select the plot of a 3-D chart, then place the mouse pointer at one of the handles on one of the corners of the plot.

2 Drag the ghost to a new position and then let go to see your handiwork.

If you don't like the results, you can rotate it further or Undo to regain the original perspective before trying again.

Change Chart Values

Since the data in a worksheet and a chart are linked, the usual way to change the data is to edit the worksheet. However, on 2-D bar, 2-D column, 2-D line, 2-D stacked, 2-D pie, doughnut, and xy scatter charts, you can drag the data markers in the chart to adjust the value and the worksheet will change accordingly (Figure 12.7). The mouse pointer changes to a two-headed arrow when you drag, and the exact value will change in the formula bar as you drag. If the data marker is plotted from a formula, the Goal Seek dialog box will pop up and prompt you to enter a cell reference for the value in the formula that needs to be adjusted.

Name area indicates the changing value

Mouse pointer changes to a two-headed arrow

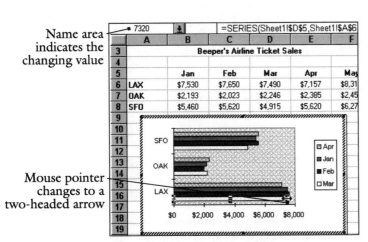

Figure 12.7 **Drag the value in a chart to adjust it.**

Omit Blanks in Worksheet Data from a Line Chart

Blank worksheet cells are not plotted in any type of chart but a line chart. If you encounter blanks and errors as you plot a line chart, you can specify that they be treated as zeros or interpolated into the chart. There are three choices on the Chart tab of the Tools, Options dialog box. If blank cells of a worksheet are not plotted on a line chart, Excel leaves blanks, making the line disconnected, as shown in the top chart of Figure 12.8. If Zeros is selected, blank lines are plotted as zeros, as shown in the middle chart of Figure 12.8. If Interpolated is selected, Excel fills in for empty cells with connecting lines, as shown in the bottom chart of Figure 12.8.

(Interpolated is one of those words you don't use every day. If you find yourself using it every day, you should probably apply for a job at Microsoft University.)

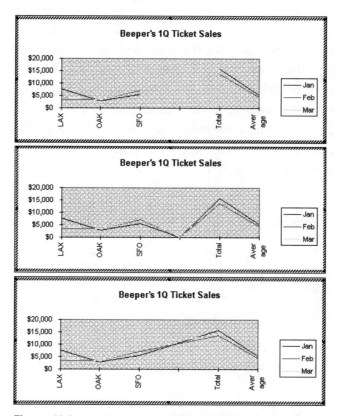

Figure 12.8 A chart with empty cells plotted as Gaps, Zeros, and Interpolating

To plot the blanks from the worksheet in a line chart:

1 Activate the chart.

2 Choose Tools, Options (**Alt/**, **T**, **O**); and select the Chart tab.

3 Turn on one of the Empty Cells Plotted as option buttons, then choose OK.

Combining Chart Types

A preferable way to display the data in Figure 12.8 would be to combine chart types, as shown in Figure 12.9. You can create a combination chart by using the ChartWizard, or by changing the chart type of one or more data series.

You cannot combine chart types when using 3-D charts. On 2-D charts, you can combine area, column, line, and xy scatter charts. Or, you can have one group assigned as a bar, pie, doughnut, or radar chart combined with an area, column, line, or xy scatter chart. A bar chart group needs a secondary axis because the value axis is horizontal. In fact, most combined charts display the data better with a secondary axis.

To create a combination chart with the ChartWizard:

1 Select the worksheet data you want to plot.

2 Use the ChartWizard in the same way as you do when plotting any other chart, but choose Combination in Step 2.

Sometimes the only kind of chart that makes sense is a combination chart with a secondary axis, such as when you have mixed types of data. For instance, in Figure 12.10, a comparison is being made between top

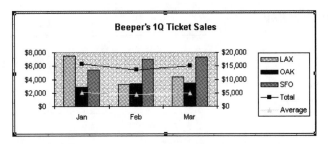

Figure 12.9 A combination chart created with the ChartWizard

installers, productivity, and overtime hours. The chart on top does not display the data accurately.

To create a combination chart by changing the chart type of a data series and create a secondary axis:

1 Activate the chart.

2 Ⓦ Right-click Ⓜ Control+click on the series you want to format with a different chart type, and choose Chart Type from the shortcut menu.

3 Select a different Chart Type (in Figure 12.10, a line chart was chosen to combine with a bar chart).

4 Choose Options and select the Axis tab.

5 Turn on the Secondary Axis option button and choose OK.

Sizing

Size a Chart on a Chart Sheet

When a chart is located on a chart sheet, you can change the size of it by dragging it with the mouse. In the Page Setup menu, you can make all of the usual page, margin, and header/footer adjustments, but when a chart is selected, a chart tab is also available.

1 Select the chart sheet and choose File, Page Setup (**Alt/, F, U**); then choose the Chart tab.

2 Turn on the Custom option button, and choose OK.

3 Drag the chart by the handles to the size you want.

No Help from the Shift Key

When you drag to size a chart on a chart sheet, the Shift key does not keep the sizing proportionate.

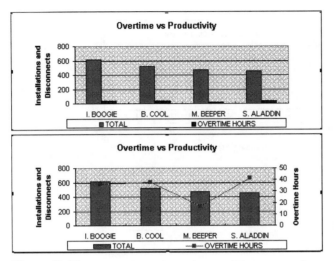

Figure 12.10 A Combination chart with a secondary axis (bottom) created from the Bar chart (top)

Formatting Tricks

. . . .

Here are a few chart formatting slick tricks to add to the others dispersed throughout this chapter and Chapter 11, "Creating Charts." Most are also located throughout the book in the sections describing how to create items that can be formatted.

Copy the Format of One Chart to Another

You can copy the format of one chart to another. To accomplish the same task, you could make a copy of a chart and then change the range. For instance, in Figure 12.11, instead of creating the chart on the bottom and then copying that format to the other, you could make a copy of the top chart and change the range to reflect the second-quarter data. You would then edit the title as well.

To copy the format of one chart to another:

1 Activate the chart whose format you want to copy, then copy it.

2 Activate the chart that needs to be formatted.

3 Choose Paste Special (**Alt/, E, S, A**).

4 Choose Formats, then choose OK.

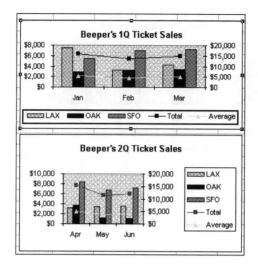

Figure 12.11 Two charts that need
the same format

To copy a chart, then change the range:

1 Activate the chart whose format you want to copy, then
copy it.

2 Select a cell where you want to place the copy, then paste it.

3 Activate the copy and click on the ChartWizard button.

4 Change the range in Step 1 and choose Finish.

Change the Pattern of a Region from the Legend

You can change the pattern of a region by selecting the key in the
legend.

1 Activate the chart and select the legend.

2 Select the key, then double-click on it.

3 Change the pattern in the dialog box, then choose OK.

Chapter 13

. . . .

Graphics and Object Linking

THIS CHAPTER IS FOR THE ARTIST, the importer, and the exporter. Actually, if you don't consider yourself artistic, you may change your mind when you see how easy it is to add pictures, lines, and shapes to Excel documents. And although you may have thought it was complicated to import, export, and link with other applications, Object Linking and Embedding (OLE) has simplified that process.

Technically, this chapter is about graphic objects, but most of the time they will be called graphics or objects. When you are working with graphics, scrolling and printing can take forever (unless you have a megamachine); so before you start creating them, you might like to have a couple of slick tricks to help you keep your sanity.

Speed Up Scrolling

Graphics can really slow you down when you are scrolling. Rather than leaving them visible on your screen, you can speed things up by hiding them or by replacing them with placeholders.

To switch between showing and hiding graphics (or replacing them with placeholders), press Ⓦ Ctrl+6 Ⓜ Command+6.

To hide graphics:

1 Choose Tools, Options (**Alt/, T, O, V**); and select the View tab.

2 Turn on the Hide All option button in the Objects box and choose OK.

To replace graphics with placeholders:

1 Choose Tools, Options (**Alt/, T, O, V**); and select the View tab.

2 Turn on the Show Placeholders option button in the Objects box, and choose OK.

Speed Up Printing

It takes time for graphics to be communicated to your printer, and for your printer to print them. It also takes longer to Print Preview a worksheet with graphics. Even placeholders can affect the amount of time it takes to print. After you have created graphics, you can hide them, which prevents them from being printed, or you can set each object individually to print or not.

To toggle between printing or hiding an object:

1 Double-click on the border of the object.

2 Select the Properties tab, and turn the Print Object check box on or off.

When an object is linked to another application, double-clicking on it opens the other application. (See more about objects linked to other applications later in this chapter.) When you double-click on the border of a nonlinked object, you open the Format Object dialog box which is also located on the Format menu.

Not for Intricate Pictures

The Excel graphics capabilities are superb for the most commonly used worksheet or chart graphics. It is easy to draw lines, arrows, boxes, circles, and text boxes. It is not intended for complex pictures, such as a graphic representation of a face complete with eyelashes and ears.

Intricate pictures should be drawn in a sophisticated drawing program and then imported using the Clipboard, or �W the Insert, Pictures command. For some slick tricks to help you import graphics, see the section, "Importing and Exporting," later in this chapter.

Creating Graphics

• •

Slick Drawing Tools

The drawing toolbar contains almost all of the drawing buttons. There are more that might be of interest to you, and one on the Drawing toolbar that deserves mention:

- ◆ The Drawing toolbar toggle button ⬛, which makes the Drawing toolbar visible, is located on the Standard toolbar.
- ◆ The Color Palette button ⬛ is used to add color to graphics.
- ◆ The Dark and Light Shade buttons ⬛⬛ are used to apply dark and light shading.
- ◆ The Shape button ⬛ contains 13 of the buttons on the drawing toolbar, one of which is used to select objects by dragging. The Shape button, with its drop-down palette, is shown in Figure 13.1 along with the Drawing toolbar.

Microsoft loves the Text Box button ⬛ so much that it shows up on the default Standard toolbar, the Drawing toolbar, and on the drop-down palette of the Shape tool. The reason is that it can be used to exceed the 255-characters-per-cell limitation and link the text to a cell, and can be formatted to stand out in style. (There is more about text boxes later in this section.)

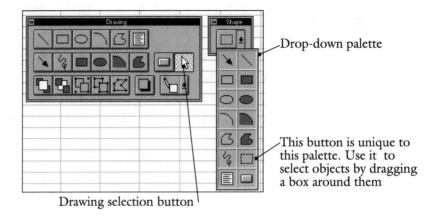

Drop-down palette

This button is unique to this palette. Use it to select objects by dragging a box around them

Drawing selection button

Figure 13.1 The Drawing Toolbar and the Shape Tool drop-down palette

Create a Concise Drawing Toolbar

Since the Shape button contains most of the drawing tools, you can economize on space by creating a toolbar that contains it and perhaps adding a few of the other drawing buttons you will use the most. For instance, if you are going to do a lot of shading or bringing objects to the front or back, you might want to create or further customize a toolbar like the one shown in Figure 13.2. This toolbar Contains the Drawing Selection button Bring to Front and Send to Back buttons, Add Dark and Light buttons, and the Shape Tool, with its drop-down palette. (For more about customizing toolbars, see Chapter 5.)

Docking a Toolbar

Don't forget that you can double-click on a toolbar to dock or undock it. It will automatically go to the last docked and undocked positions.

Figure 13.2 A customized Drawing Toolbar built around the shape button

Using the Drawing Buttons

There are two kinds of buttons on the drawing toolbar: *actual* and *auxiliary*. The actual buttons are the buttons with which you draw; the auxiliary buttons are the ones you use to select, format, and edit objects. Two of the auxiliary buttons behave differently than the rest—the Object Selection buttons. The first is the arrow, which looks like the mouse pointer most of the time 🔲. The second is the oddball, dotted rectangle 🔲, located only on the drop-down palette of the Shape button. (I think we should write to Microsoft and ask them to replace it with the Drawing Selection button in their next release, because this button only does half of what the Drawing Selection button can do.)

To use the actual drawing buttons to draw one object:

1 Click on the button.

2 Draw the object. The button will be deactivated when you are through drawing.

To use the actual drawing buttons to draw consecutive objects:

1 Double-click on the drawing button.

2 Draw as many objects as you want.

3 Click on the button again, press Esc, or click on another drawing button to deactivate the button.

To use the auxiliary drawing buttons:

1 Click on the object.

2 Click on the tool.

To use the Drawing Selection button:

1 Click on it.

2 Click on an object to select it, or drag a box around objects to select them all.

3 Click on it again, or press Esc to deactivate it. (The Drawing Selection button stays active with a single click, as other buttons do with a double-click.)

While the Drawing Selection button is active, only objects will be selected, not cells. Selecting objects with the Drawing Selection button will not run attached macros.

Use the Rectangular Selection Button on the Shape Palette

To use the Rectangular Selection button found on the Shape drop-down palette:

1 Click on it. Double-click to keep it active for more than one action.

2 Drag a box around objects to select them all.

3 Click on it again, or press Esc to deactivate it if you double-clicked on it.

The Drawing Selection Button Disables Direction Keys

If you have been drawing and press Home or an arrow key, then you press again because you can't figure out why they didn't work, it could be that the drawing selection button is still turned on. It could also be that you have hidden the toolbar so that you can't see that the Drawing Selection arrow is still depressed, indicating that it is active. Another possibility is that the graphics are being redrawn and your system has slowed down. If you wait a minute, Excel will respond to your requests.

The Freeform and Reshape Buttons

Most of the drawing buttons are logical to use, but the freeform buttons are a little different. Once you click on the Freeform or Filled Freeform buttons, you may find yourself wondering how to get the little tail to let go of your mouse pointer.

To draw a polygon:

1 Click on the Freeform or Filled Freeform button 🖊🖊.

2 Hold the mouse button to draw as you drag. (While the mouse button is held down, the pointer will look like a pen, as shown in Figure 13.3.)

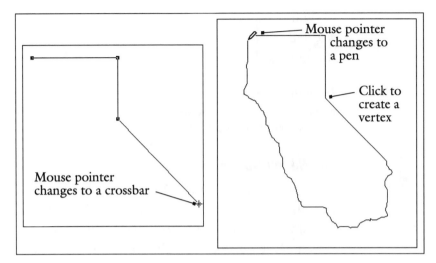

Figure 13.3 **Polygon magic**

3 Let go of the mouse button to draw lines (the pointer changes to a crossbar). This will draw a line to connect between each place you "touch down" by clicking with the mouse. The line will stay attached to the mouse pointer, but not appear to be connected to the workspace. (Note: An intersection of two lines is called a vertex. Click on a line to create a vertex.)

4 Click at your starting place or double-click anywhere else to end your artistic adventure (even Esc can't set you free).

To change the shape of a polygon:

1 Select it and click the Reshape button [K].

2 Place the mouse pointer on top of the selection handles: It will change to a crossbar, as shown in Figure 13.4.

3 Drag the shape until the dotted line indicates you are in the new location, and let go of the mouse button.

You can Undo your last edit. And if you draw freeform as well as I do, you will frequently find yourself selecting unfinished objects and pressing Del.

Figure 13.4 Selection handles
at each vertex of a polygon

The Button Button

The button button on the drawing toolbar is a convenient place to attach a macro. Yep, a button button ▣. After creating a button with it,
the Attach Macro dialog box opens. When you are through with the
Attach Macro dialog box, the button is selected (unless you need to
deselect it to record a macro), and is ready for you to choose a name
other than the proposed Button 1, Button 2, etc.

To use the button button:

1 Click on the button button. The mouse pointer changes to a
small crossbar and the status bar reads "Drag in document to
create a button."

2 Drag the button to the size you want, then let go of the
mouse button.

3 In the Assign Macro dialog box, make one of three choices:

♦ Double-click on the name of an existing macro.

♦ Choose Record, then record the macro you want assigned
to the button.

♦ Choose Esc to attach a macro later.

4 Ⓦ Ctrl+click Ⓜ Command+click on the button (or use the
drawing selection button) if it has been deselected by recording a macro.

5 Place the insertion point on top of the proposed button name,
then type a descriptive name for your button, such as the one
shown in Figure 13.5.

6 Click somewhere other than on the button to deselect it.

Exit Invoice & Subtract Inventory from Database

Figure 13.5 A button with a macro attached

Shift, Alt, and Copy Commands

Hold down the Shift key to:

- Keep the sizing constant when you are creating or sizing objects. This enables you to draw a perfect circle or square.

- Keep a line straight and horizontal, vertical, or at a 45-degree angle as you draw.

- Keep the proportions of an object constant as you drag a corner.

Hold down Ⓦ Alt Ⓜ Option to align an object with gridlines as you draw.

Hold down Ⓦ Ctrl Ⓜ Command to copy as you drag.

You can remember this as S, A, and C — Steady with Shift, Align with Ⓦ Alt or Ⓜ Apple, and Copy withT Ⓦ Ctrl Ⓜ Command.

Straight Lines without the Shift Key

If you want to draw a straight diagonal line, you can straighten a line as you draw it by adjusting it until all of the zigzags disappear before you let go of the mouse button.

Zoom to Get a Better View

If you are connecting lines and arrows or boxes, you can get a much better view if you zoom in on the object. For more about the Zoom command, see Chapter 6, "Views, Outlining, and Printing."

The Great Reversos

Many of the drawing buttons are great reversos, meaning that if you press the Shift key on one, it causes the action of the other. These include all of the filled and not filled drawing buttons, the bring to Front and Send to Back buttons, and the Group and Ungroup buttons. Figure 13.6 shows the drawing buttons and their reverses.

Figure 13.6 The great
drawing reversos

Fill It Up

When you draw an object with one of the filled drawing buttons, it will fill according to whatever pattern is selected in the pattern drop-down palette (Figure 13.7). You can also select an object, open the palette, then click on the pattern (or color) to fill it (and color it).

You can drag the palette off the Pattern button for easy access if you need to change patterns frequently.

If the Drawing Selection button is activated and you click on the pattern palette, it will not open unless an object is selected. It will instead respond with an obnoxious beep.

The Name of a Graphic

To see the name of an existing graphic object, click on it. The name will appear to the left of the formula bar. You can also name graphics in the same way you do cells. For instance, if you create or import a picture, Excel will name it something very creative, such as Drawing 1, Picture 7, or Oval 3. You can select the object, then type a more meaningful name into the name box. You cannot use Go To with graphics, as you can with cells and cell ranges; but if you are referring to the pictures in formulas, macros, or from other applications, a meaningful name is easier to identify.

This pattern will be used

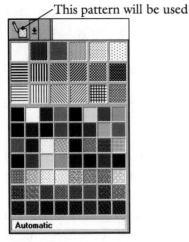

Figure 13.7 **Fill patterns**

Take a Picture with the Camera

You can take a picture of a range of cells on your worksheet with the Camera button or by using the Copy Picture command on the Edit menu. The Camera button is not on any default toolbar, so you will need to copy it from the Utility category of the Customize dialog box. (For more about customizing toolbars, see Chapter 5.)

To copy a picture using the camera:

1 Select the cell, range, graphic, or chart you want to copy, and click on the Camera button.

2 Click on the upper left cell within Excel or on the location where you want the picture placed in another application that supports Object Linking and Embedding (OLE).

To copy a picture using the menu:

1 Select the cell, range, graphic, or chart that you want to copy.

2 Hold down the Shift key and Choose Edit, Copy Picture (**Alt/, E, C**).

3 Make selections in the Copy Picture dialog box.

4 Paste the picture into Excel by pressing Shift+Insert, Ctrl+V; or clicking on the Paste button 📋. Paste the picture into other applications that support OLE, using the Clipboard (or according to the application's documentation).

For more about OLE, see the section, "Importing and Exporting," later in this chapter.

Text Boxes

A text box is a box you draw to the size you want on your sheet. After you have drawn it, the insertion point within the box is ready for you to enter text. A text box is handy for adding notes or accenting particular cells. It does not have the same 255-character limitation as a cell. Once the text box is created, you can format the font and alignment of the text, as well as edit and format the box itself. You can also link the text to a cell so that when the cell changes, the text will change accordingly.

To create a text box:

1 Click on the Text box button.

2 Drag from one diagonal corner to the other, then let go of the mouse button.

3 Type the text or link it to a cell.

To change the word or value content of the text:

1 Double-click on the text.

2 Edit as in a cell.

To format the text or the box:

1 Double-click on the border of the box.

2 Select the tab(s) you need.

3 Make your changes and choose OK.

When you double-click on the border of an object, the Format Object dialog box (Figure 13.8) will appear with three tabs: Patterns, Protection, and Properties. When you double-click on a text box, two more tabs are available: Font and Alignment. The Alignment tab has a check box for automatically sizing the box to fit the text.

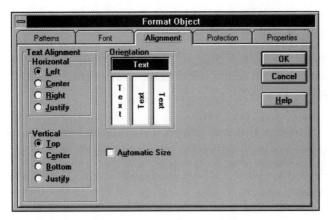

Figure 13.8 The Format Object dialog box for a text box

To automatically size a text box to fit text:

1 Double-click on the text box and select the Alignment tab.

2 Turn on the Automatic Size check box and choose OK.

To link a text box with a cell:

1 Select the text box and click in the Formula bar.

2 Type an equal sign and click on the cell or type in the reference.

Print What You See in Text Boxes

Some call it WYSIWYG, which means "What You See (on the screen) Is What You Get (from the printer)." (Who ever thought Flip Wilson would be quoted in computer books?) If you want the text in your text boxes to break in the same places when you print as they do on the screen, select a TrueType font from the font tab of the Format Object dialog box. After selecting the font, look for one of the two messages (shown in Figure 13.9) to be displayed at the bottom of the dialog box.

Editing and Formatting Graphics

You can select an object as you would any cell, unless there is a macro attached to it.

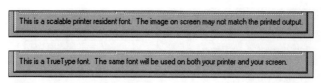

Figure 13.9   **TrueType Font Messages**

You can also use one of the object selection buttons. The Drawing Selection button on the Drawing toolbar 🔲 or the Rectangular box button 🔲 on the Shape drop-down palette will select objects without calling a macro.

Select One, Several, or All Objects

Use the following methods for selecting one, several, or all objects:

- ♦ To select one object not attached to a macro, click on it.
- ♦ To select an object attached to a macro, Ⓦ Ctrl+click Ⓜ Command+click on it.
- ♦ To select several objects using the Shift key, Shift-click on each object you want to select and Shift-click on each selected object to deselect.
- ♦ To select all objects, select at least one object and press Ⓦ Ctrl+Shift+Spacebar Ⓜ Command+Shift+Spacebar.
- ♦ To deselect objects, click anywhere on your sheet other than on an object.

Edit Objects with a Shortcut Menu

Ⓦ Right-click Ⓜ Control+click on an object to display the Object shortcut menu.

Format Objects in the Format Object Dialog Box

① Double-click on the border of the object.

② Make changes in the Format Object dialog box and choose OK.

Move Objects

To move objects:

♦ Select them and drag the ghost(s) to a new location, or

♦ Use the same cut and paste shortcut keys and buttons as for cells.

Copy Objects

To copy objects:

♦ Ⓦ Ctrl+click Ⓜ Option+click on them, drag the ghost(s) to a new location, then let go of the mouse button; or

♦ Use the same copy and paste shortcut keys as for cells.

Delete Objects

You can delete any selected objects in the same way that you delete cells. Use the Delete button ⬜, press Del, or Ⓦ right-click Ⓜ Control+click on the object and choose Delete from the shortcut menu.

Resize Objects

To resize an object:

1 Select the object.

2 Drag the ghost to the size you want and let go of the mouse.

Group and Ungroup Objects

You can group objects together that you want to edit, move, or size.

♦ Select the objects you want to group or ungroup. Click on the Group Object button ⬛ or the Ungroup Object button ⬛, or

♦ Ⓦ Right-click Ⓜ Control+click on the selected objects and choose group or ungroup from the shortcut menu.

Overlap Objects

When you move objects around, you can place them on top of one another to create special effects. When they are layered, you can select the one you want to be on top and bring it to the front, or select the one you want to be on the bottom and send it to the back.

To move objects to the front or back:

♦ Select the object. Click on the Move to Front button or Send to Back button ⊞, or

♦ Ⓦ Right-click Ⓜ Control+click on the object. Choose Move to Front or Send to Back from the shortcut menu.

Cool Shadows and Round Corners

You can create special effects, such as those shown in Figure 13.10. For instance, you can use the Shadow button to add shadows ⊡.

To round the corners of a box:

1 Double-click on the border of the box, and select the Pattern tab in the Format Object dialog box.

2 Turn on the Round Corners option button and choose OK.

Detaching Objects from Cells

You may not want an object to change size when the cells beneath it change. For instance, the objects shown in Figure 13.10 changed (as shown in Figure 13.11) when the row height of the cells beneath them was increased. To prevent this, you can detach objects from cells.

To change the way cells move or size with cells:

1 Double-click on the object and select the Properties tab.

2 Turn on the option button you want, as shown in Figure 13.12, and choose OK.

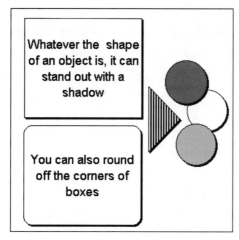

Figure 13.10 Some special effects

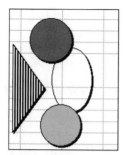

Figure 13.11 The effect of changing cells on adjacent objects

Control the Way Objects are Cut, Copied, and Sorted with Data

Use the Tools menu to control whether objects are cut, copied, or sorted with the cells beneath them. This command affects all objects on worksheets in the workbook.

1. Choose Tools, Options (**Alt/, T, O**); and select the Edit tab.

2. Set the Cut, Copy, and Sort Objects with Cells check boxes to on or off, and choose OK.

Importing and Exporting

Importing and exporting data has been greatly improved by the applications that support the latest version of Object Linking and Embedding (OLE). If you have trouble executing any of the following instructions, it could be that the other application with which you are working has not been upgraded enough to use these slick tricks.

Excel for the Macintosh needs to be running on System 7. Macintosh users can also establish Publishers and Subscribers.

When you embed an object, it is inserted from another application. When you link an object, it is inserted from another application and it

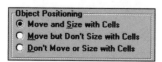

Figure 13.12 Object positioning choices on the Properties tab

retains a connection to the source document. If the source document is updated, an embedded object is not affected, but a linked document updates automatically.

Open Other Microsoft Applications with a Toolbar

If you have another Microsoft product installed, you can switch to it if it is open, or open it and switch to it if it is not. If the buttons shown in Figure 13.13 do not work, the alert box will tell you that they are not installed properly. It could be that you do not have the latest, greatest version of the application installed. After all, at least a portion of your software became obsolete—just since yesterday.

Drag OLE to Embed

If both applications support OLE 2, you can copy or cut and paste an object from one application to another by dragging.

To copy from one application to another:

1 Open both applications, then position them on the screen so that both the source and the target applications are visible.

2 Drag the data from one to the other.

3 Press the Shift key to insert the data at the cursor or into the active cell.

To cut and paste by dragging:

1 Open both applications, then position them on the screen so that both the source and the target applications are visible.

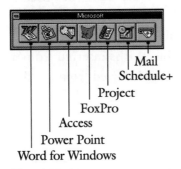

Figure 13.13 The Microsoft Toolbar

OLE and DDE To embed objects, the other application needs to support OLE. To maintain a link, the other application needs to support OLE or Dynamic Data Exchange (DDE).

2 Hold down the ⊞ Ctrl ⌥ Option key as you drag the data from one to the other.

3 Press the Shift key to insert the data at the cursor or into the active cell.

Copy from One Application to Another

You can use the Clipboard to cut or copy and paste from one application to another, just as if you are copying within Excel. If the result does not paste exactly the way you want, choose Undo, then use the Paste Special dialog box to make corrections. Use the Paste Special dialog box to link. When you are copying from another application, the Paste Special box is customized for the task, as shown in Figure 13.14.

Embed Objects or a Word 6.0 Document

When you use the Insert Object command, you embed an object or document. Click on the Link check box if you want the object to stay linked to the source application. Click on the Display As Icon check box to keep the object or document in Excel as an icon.

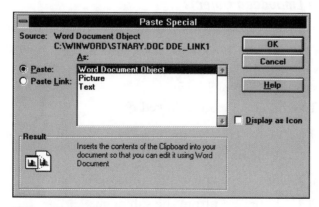

Figure 13.14 The Paste Special box when importing from another application

Pasting Text from Another Application When you are pasting text from another application into Excel, Excel will decide what format to use when a cell is the target. If the formula bar is the active target, all copied text is pasted into it. If an object is selected, text will be embedded as an object, unless the object is a text box, in which case the text will be pasted into the text box.

To insert an object or document:

1 Choose Insert, Object (**Alt/, I, O**); and select the Create New tab to open an application and create a new file.

2 Select the Create from File tab to import an existing file and choose OK.

Update Links without an Alert Box

You can tell Excel not to ask you each time a workbook is opened if you want to automatically update links.

1 Choose Tools, Options (**Alt/, T, O**); and select the Edit tab.

2 Turn off the Ask to Automatically Update Links check box and choose OK.

Edit Embedded Objects

When you embed an object that is still linked to the original application, the shortcut menu contains a command and a submenu. It lists the application and the kind of object as a command, and it has a submenu, as shown in Figure 13.15.

To edit an embedded, linked object:

1 Double-click on the object or Ⓦ right-click Ⓜ Control+click on the object.

2 Choose the application object command.

3 Choose Edit from the submenu.

Cut			
Copy			
Paste			
Clear			
Paintbrush Picture Object		**Edit**	
Format Object...		**Convert...**	
Bring to Front			
Send to Back			
Group			
Assign Macro...			

Figure 13.15 The Embedded
Object shortcut menu

Convert to a Simple Graphic

You can greatly reduce the size of a file if you no longer need to edit it in the original application. Excel keeps a lot more information about an embedded or linked document behind the scenes.

To convert an embedded object to a simple graphic:

1 Ⓦ Right-click Ⓜ Control+click on the object.

2 Choose the application object command.

3 Choose convert from the submenu.

Use the Picture Command in Excel for Windows

The insert command in Excel for Windows has a Picture command. Use this command to import a graphic saved in any of the proposed file types in the dialog box.

Chapter 14

. . . .

Visual Basic and Macros

I F THIS IS THE FIRST CHAPTER YOU TURNED TO, you may well be an aspiring nerd. Remember that this is not a tutorial. This chapter gives some tricks for recording macros, for attaching macros to objects, and some tricks to get you started using Visual Basic Application (VBA). When you opened the box that contained your Excel software, you probably noticed a whole manual dedicated to VBA. This little chapter is to help you jump into it with confidence, but not to teach you what is within.

Basic Macro Recording

. . . .

The word macro is actually a shortened version of the word *macroinstruction*. It is a single instruction which carries out a sequence of programmed instructions. A macro is a legitimate slick trick in its own right. An Excel macro can do anything that Excel can do. If there is a

Macro vs. Procedure   In VBA documentation and help screens, a macro is often called a procedure; but the Tools menu and VBA toolbar buttons status bar messages still use the term macro.

task which you find yourself repeating, that task is a candidate for a macro. Excel macros can be simple, such as the ones in this chapter, or they can be combined with others to create a complex, custom application with Excel as the environment.

A Choice of Language

You can record macros in VBA or in the Excel 4.0 macro language. Microsoft is fazing out the Excel 4.0 macro language, but they are trying to make the process as painless as possible for those of us who have code from Excel 4.0. Excel 5.0 fully supports the Excel 4.0 macro language. All Excel 4.0 macros will run in Excel 5.0 and can be called from VBA procedures. The Excel 4.0 language has been updated to support Excel 5.0's new features, and the Excel 4.0 functions are now listed in Macro Functions on-line Help. But if you can start out your Excel programming career using VBA, it is definitely to your advantage, because you will have only one language to learn.

Open the Visual Basic Toolbar

1. Ⓦ Right-click Ⓜ Control+click on a toolbar.
2. Choose Visual Basic, or if it is not available on the menu, choose Toolbars, then turn on the Visual Basic check box.
3. Choose OK.

In Excel 5.0, macros can be written and recorded on a module sheet or an Excel 4.0 macro sheet. Another new, advanced programming feature (that is out of the scope of this book) is the dialog sheet, which is used to program interactive dialog boxes that gather input from users and return values to macros or procedures.

The Run Macro button is a shortcut for:

♦ Choosing Tools, Record Macro (**Alt/**, **T**, **R**, **R**)

♦ Choosing Record New Macro from the submenu

A macro name can contain letters, numbers, and underscores, but it must begin with a letter. In VBA, a procedure name cannot contain punctuation marks. An Excel 4.0 macro name, however, can contain periods. For example, you can name a macro wrap_text, but you cannot name it wrap text. In the Excel 4.0 language you can name it wrap.text.

To record a macro:

1 Go to the sheet in your workbook where you want to start recording. For instance, if you want the macro action to start at a worksheet, go to a worksheet. If you want the macro to start its action at a chart, macro sheet, or module, go to a chart, macro sheet, or module.

2 Click on the Record Macro button █ and type a name for your macro or accept the proposed name.

3 Type a description in the Description box or accept the proposed description.

4 Choose Options, turn on the Assign To check box if you want the macro to appear on the Tools Menu, then type in the command name in the Menu Item box the way you want it to appear on the Tools menu (see Figure 14.1).

When you place an item on a menu, put an ampersand (&) in front of the command letter. For instance, to have the command letter in Wrap to be W, type **&Wrap**. To have the command letter to be R, type **W&rap**.

5 Enter a shortcut key, if you want to run your macro with one.

6 Turn on one of the option buttons to store your macro in your Personal Macro Workbook, This Workbook, or New Workbook.

7 Turn on the MS Excel 4.0 Macro option button if you want to record in the Excel 4.0 macro language.

8 Choose OK. The Stop Recorder button █ will appear on your sheet and Recording will be displayed in the Status bar.

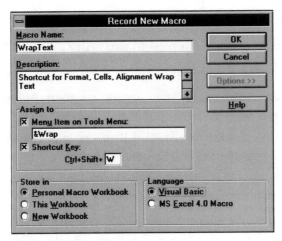

Figure 14.1 **The Record New Macro dialog box after choosing Options**

9 Carry out the actions you want recorded. When you are finished, click the Stop Recorder button ▣.

In Excel 5.0, saving your macro in the Personal Macro Workbook is like saving a macro as global in Excel 4.0. The macro will be available to you in every workbook you open.

The following example shows how to create a Macro that will format numbers as text, using a shortcut key of T.

1 Go to a worksheet and click on the Record Macro button ▣.

2 Type **NumbersAsText** in the name box

3 Type **Shortcut** for Format Cells, and **Numbers as Text** in the Description box.

4 Choose Options and select the proposed entry in the Shortcut Key box.

5 Press the Shift key and type **T**.

6 Turn on the Personal Macro Workbook option button and choose OK.

7 Press Ctrl+1 and choose the Number tab.

8 Select the Text category which has the @ format code and choose OK.

9 Click the Stop Recorder button ▣.

Set the Recorder for Relative or Absolute

If you want your macro to affect the same cells each time it runs, set the recorder to absolute. If you want your macro to affect the cells the same relative distance from the active cell, set the recorder to relative. If your macro action does not include any selection except the active cell, it doesn't matter which way the recorder is set. For instance, if you are performing an action, such as the example above, which changes the number format of the selection to text, but during the macro action you do not select any other cells before you stop the recorder, it doesn't matter how the recorder is set.

Setting the recorder to relative or absolute is a toggle between Use Relative References (or not) on the Tools, Record New Macro submenu.

To set the recorder to relative, turn on the Use Relative References check mark:

1 Choose Tools, Record New Macro (**Alt/, T, R, U**).

2 Choose Use Relative References on the submenu (unless it is already selected).

To set the recorder to absolute, turn off the Use Relative References check mark:

1 Choose Tools, Record New Macro (**Alt/, T, R, U**).

2 Choose Use Relative References on the submenu if a check mark is in front of it.

Excel Records Mistakes, Too

While you are recording a macro, everything is recorded, including mistakes. If you want to remove your mistakes, you can either overwrite your macro by rerecording it with the same name, or you can edit it to delete the unnecessary actions.

Run a Macro

You can run a macro in several ways. You can press the shortcut keys, press the Run button on the VBA toolbar, or use the Tools menu. You can also attach it to a graphic object or a button, both of which are explained later in this chapter. Finally, you can call it from another macro, which makes it a subroutine and takes it out of the scope of this book.

To run a macro with its assigned shortcut keys, press Ctrl+the shortcut key (or Ctrl+Shift+the Shortcut key if you assigned an uppercase shortcut key).

To run a macro using the Run Macro button:

1 Open to the sheet where you want to run the macro, and click on the Run Macro button ▣.

2 Double-click on a name in the Macro Name/Reference box or select one of the names, then choose Run.

To run a macro using the Tools menu:

1 Open to the sheet where you want to run the macro, and choose Tools, Macro (**Alt/, T, M**).

2 Double-click on a name in the Macro Name/Reference box or select one of the names, then choose Run.

Interrupt a Macro

To interrupt a macro in progress, press Esc or ⌘ Command+Period. Note that you can only Undo the last edit of a macro.

Display a Macro So That You Can Edit It

There are several ways to display a macro once it has been recorded—instructions for the three quickest ways will follow. After you display a macro, you can edit as you would in any word processing program. You can select characters or words, then delete, edit, copy, or move them. The contents of editing, however, need to stay within the bounds of acceptable syntax.

The first way to display a macro is to switch to the VBA module or to the Excel 4.0 macro sheet that contains the code. If the code is in your Personal Macro Workbook, you will need to unhide it, using the Window menu. Figure 14.2 shows a module with two recorded macros. The first, a macro to wrap text, will be attached to a customized toolbar button in a following example. The second is the NumbersAsText macro from the example above.

```
'
' WrapText Macro
' Shortcut for Format Cells, Alignment, Wrap Text
'
' Keyboard Shortcut: Ctrl+W
'
Sub WrapText()
    With Selection
        .HorizontalAlignment = xlGeneral
        .VerticalAlignment = xlBottom
        .WrapText = True
        .Orientation = xlHorizontal
    End With
End Sub
'
' NumbersAsText Macro
' Shortcut for Format Cells, Numbers as Text
'
' Keyboard Shortcut: Ctrl+T
'
Sub NumbersAsText()
    Selection.NumberFormat = "@"
End Sub
```

Figure 14.2 **A VBA module with two macros**

Two other ways to display a macro use the Macro dialog box or the Assign Macro dialog box.

To display a macro using the Macro dialog box:

1 Choose Tools, Macro (**Alt/, T, M**).

2 Select the name of the macro you want to display from the Macro/Name Reference Box and choose Edit.

To display a macro assigned to a worksheet button or graphic object:

1 Ⓦ Right-click Ⓜ Control+click on an object to bring up the Object Shortcut Menu, and choose Assign Macro.

2 Select the name of the macro you want to display from the Macro/Name Reference Box and choose Edit.

Change the Name of a VBA Macro

Once you have opened the text of a VBA macro, you can change its name by selecting the present name, then typing in a new one. The only tricky part is that the name appears in two places, in the remarks section and in the sub section. Of course, you will want to change it in both places, but the only one that will actually change the macro name is the one in the sub section.

Changing a Macro Name

Remember that if you change the name of a macro and you are running it from another macro, you will need to change the name there as well.

Use Find and Replace

If you change the name of a macro, rename a worksheet, or make other changes, you can use either Edit, Find (Ctrl+F) or Edit, Replace (Ctrl+H). When you call the Find or Replace dialog box from a module, the proposed choices in the Look In box are different than when they are called from a worksheet. These, shown in Figure 14.3, help you determine the scope of your search.

Change the Shortcut Key or Other Macro Options

You can change the description of a macro, the keyboard shortcut, or the way the name of a macro appears on the Tools menu in the Macro Options dialog box. You can also change the status bar and Help information connected to it.

To change the options of a macro:

1 Choose Tools, Macro (**Alt/, T, M**) and select the name of the macro from the Macro Name/Reference box.

2 Choose Options to display the Macro Options dialog box shown in Figure 14.4, change any of the Options, then choose OK.

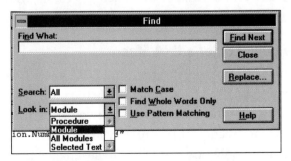

Figure 14.3 The Find dialog box called from a VBA module

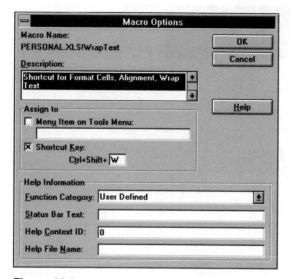

Figure 14.4 The Macro Options dialog box

Capture Detailed Code with the Macro Recorder

The macro recorder has definite limitations for programming, but it can be a valuable tool to help you write your own programs. Recording actions gives you the opportunity to examine code or copy portions of it into your written code. For instance, rather than write a page or two of code to set the values in the Page Setup dialog box, you could record a simple macro that opens it and records the Page Setup settings. You could either insert the recorded macro into the existing code, as described in the next trick, or examine it first, edit it if necessary, then import it into your written code to save valuable time and energy.

Insert a Recorded Macro or Code into Existing Code

You can insert a recorded macro or additional code, in the form of text, into existing code. Code, in the form of text, might come from a downloaded or backup file.

To record and insert a new macro into code:

1 Place the insertion point into the code at the place where you want to add the macro and choose Tools, Record Macro (**Alt/, T, R, M**).

2 Choose Mark Position For Recording from the submenu.

Attach a Macro to a Button Button One of the most common graphic objects to attach a macro to is the button button on the drawing toolbar. That's right—a button button ⬜. When you click on the button button, the mouse pointer changes to a small cross-bar and the status bar reads "Drag in document to create a button." After you drag a button to the size you want it and let go, the Assign Macro dialog box opens. You can then assign an existing macro, press Record, or press Esc to attach a macro later. For more about the button button, see Chapter 13, "Graphics and Object Linking."

3 Switch to the sheet where you want the macro action to begin recording and choose Tools, Record Macro (**Alt/, T, R, E**).

4 Choose Record at Mark from the submenu and carry out the actions you want recorded.

5 Click on the Stop Recorder button ⬜ when you are done.

To insert text from a file into a macro:

1 Place the insertion point into the code at the place where you want to add the text and choose Insert, File (**Alt/, I, F**).

2 Double-click on the filename of the file you want to insert; or select it, then choose OK.

Turn Code into Comments with an Apostrophe

Just as an apostrophe causes Excel to read numbers as text, an apostrophe causes VBA to read code as a comment. You can deactivate macro code in this way, and keep it in place to be reinstated as code at a later date by removing the apostrophe.

Attached Macros

. . . .

Attaching Macros to Objects

You can attach macros to graphic objects. Once they are attached, you can run the macro by clicking the object. For instance, you could have several labeled graphic objects, such as those shown in Figure 14.5,

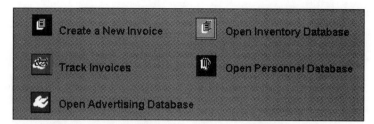

Figure 14.5 Labeled graphic objects attached to macros

which run macros that automatically perform some of your daily tasks, such as opening a template to create an invoice, or opening a database.

Attach an Existing Macro to a Graphic Object

If a macro is already attached to a graphic object, you can attach a different macro, using the same steps for attaching a macro the first time.

1 W Right-click M Control+click on the graphic object, and choose Assign Macro from the shortcut menu.

2 Double-click on the name of the macro you want to assign in the Macro Name/Reference box.

Attach and Record a Macro

To attach a macro to an object and record the macro simultaneously:

1 W Right-click M Control+click on the graphic object, and choose Assign Macro from the shortcut menu.

2 Choose Record and carry out the actions you want recorded.

3 Click on the Stop Recorder button ▨.

Attach Macros to a Toolbar Button

With all the toolbar buttons available, you may still find that you would like to have more buttons available to automate the tasks you perform most often. Assigning a macro to a toolbar button is very much like assigning a macro to any other graphic object, but you need to add a couple of steps to the process. Open the Customize dialog box to move the toolbar button (if necessary) and to make it possible to W right-click M Control+click on the toolbar button to call the Button shortcut menu. You will also need to close the Customize dialog box when you are through.

The following example adds a custom button to the formatting toolbar that aligns text to wrap.

1 Ⓦ Right-click Ⓜ Control+click on a toolbar.

2 Choose Formatting to make the Formatting toolbar visible if it isn't already.

3 Ⓦ Right-click Ⓜ Control+click on a toolbar again and choose Customize.

4 Select the Custom Category and drag a button to the formatting toolbar, such as the one shown in Figure 14.6, and choose Record.

5 In the Macro Name box of New Macro dialog box type WrapText.

6 Choose Options, select the Personal Macro Workbook option button, and choose OK.

7 Press Ctrl+1 and select the Alignment tab.

8 Turn on the Wrap Text check box and choose OK.

9 Click on the Stop Recorder button and choose Close in the Customize dialog box.

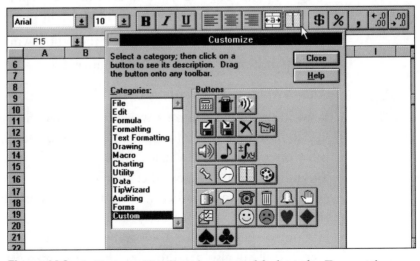

Figure 14.6 A Custom Toolbar button added to the Formatting toolbar

When you use a custom toolbar button, you can also edit it with the Button Editor. (For more about the Button Editor, see Chapter 5, "Toolbars and Workspace Options.")

Customize the Formatting Toolbar to Accommodate a New Button

When you add a button to a toolbar, as in the Wrap Text example above, you might want to rearrange the existing toolbar. For instance, you might want to scrunch the number formatting and palette boxes to the right a bit, after shrinking the Font Style Box. Follow the instructions below. (For more about customizing toolbars, see Chapter 5, "Toolbars and Workspace Options.")

1 Open the Customize dialog box, and place the mouse pointer at the right side of the drop-down arrow of the Font Style box until it turns into a black cross with two horizontal arrows.

2 Drag the outline of the box to the left to make it smaller.

3 Click on the buttons to the left of your new button and drag each of them to the right a bit, grouping them logically.

4 Choose Close.

VBA Help

• •

The VBA Shortcut Menus

When you Ⓦ right-click Ⓜ Control+click on a Visual Basic sheet or on a Dialog sheet, you call the shortcut menus.

Use Excel 5.0 Examples to Get Acclimated

To delve deeper into writing procedures with VBA, open the Code Samples workbook in the directory or folder in which you installed Excel. These examples are not only educational, you may find sections of prewritten code that you would like to copy into your programs.

Use Help

VBA is fully supported by on-line Help. When you are in a VBA module, you can select a property, statement, or other key word, then press

Ⓦ Fl Ⓜ Command+Shift+? (question mark) to get context-sensitive Help. Remember also that all dialog boxes have a Help button which brings up context-sensitive Help.

Help Transition for 4.0 Users

Buried within the layers of on-line Help is one of the greatest boons to experienced Excel 4.0 developers. If you are in transition from the Excel 4.0 macro language to VBA:

1. Press Ⓦ Fl Ⓜ Command+Shift+Question Mark on any open sheet to bring up Help, Contents.

2. Choose Reference Information.

3. Choose Microsoft Excel Macro Functions Contents.

4. Choose Visual Basic Equivalents for Macro Functions and Commands.

Chapter 15

Top-Ten Slick Tricks

T HIS CHAPTER LISTS THE TOP TEN SLICK TRICKS in this book, in the author's humble opinion. It is here to inspire you to challenge the author's opinion (maybe you think one is better that's not on the list), or to try something new that you might have overlooked. The top ten are not ranked from top to bottom, nor in Letterman-style, but I must confess that the first three are my favorite.

This chapter also contains a list of the shortcut keys used most often by the author and a genius, Excel consultant in Tulsa, Oklahoma, who specializes in Pivot Table consulting and Excel Application development. All shortcut keys are listed in the appendix, but there are so many Excel 5.0 features, so many convenient ways to use them, and so many shortcuts, this chapter was written to help you find some of the best.

Figure 15.1 A Customized
Standard toolbar

Top-Ten Slick Trick 1:   *Customize the Standard Toolbar*

Toolbars are so easy to use and customize, but there are a lot of buttons. You can customize the Standard toolbar to contain the buttons you use most and get rid of one half of each "great reverso" and any other buttons you seldom use. Then, use Ctrl+7 to toggle the Standard toolbar between visible and invisible.

A great reverso is a button that has a partner. You can press the Shift key when you click on one of them, and cause the action of the other.

Figure 15.1 shows how I have customized my Standard toolbar. Following are my personal reasons for customizing it the way I have. You, of course, would need to customize yours to suit your needs, but I thought the best way to get you thinking would be to give you an example.

Customized by:	Reason:
Large buttons	I'm a baby boomer on my first set of bifocals.
Undocked	I keep it invisible most of the time and bring it up with Ctrl+7. I prefer not having the screen redraw each time I bring it up. Besides, with large buttons you can't see the last few buttons at the right side when it is docked.

Removed:	**Reason:**
Repeat ⟳, Print Preview 🔍, and Descending Sort ⬇	I seldom use Repeat, and all three are great reversos.
Text box ▣	It's located on the Drawing toolbar which is brought up by the Drawing toolbar button ✏.
TipWizard 💡	Used, and was amused for about a week.
Cut ✂, Copy ▥, and Paste 📋	I use Ctrl+X, Ctrl+C, and Ctrl+V.

Added because I use them:

Create New Worksheet ▦	Center Across Selection ▤
Delete ✎	Embedded Chart 📊
Freeze pane ⊞	Chart Sheet ▣
A custom button attached to a macro which wraps text ▥	

Customizing toolbars is described in Chapter 5, "Toolbars and Workspace Options." The great reversos are mentioned throughout the book; use the index to find lists of them, or if you think you have found a logical opposite, give it a reverso try. Ctrl+7 is listed with the other keyboard shortcuts in the appendix, as well as in Chapter 5.

Top-Ten Slick Trick 2: *Format Painter* 🖌

Certainly, the new feature that has saved me the most time is Format Painter. It is previewed in Chapter 1, "New Features," and is described fully in Chapter 4, "Worksheet Formatting." Basically, you click on a cell that has the format you want, click on the Format Painter button, then click on another cell or range to copy the format. What a tool.

Top-Ten Slick Trick 3: *Format Best Fit Rows and Columns*

I love this feature, though it is not new. When you enter (or import) data into a cell, it is often too long. Sometimes a whole column will contain extra space within each cell, which makes the worksheet wider than it needs to be. If you wrap text, the row height often becomes too short. You can tell Excel to make the entire row or column of cells the right size to fit your entries.

1 Select a row, column, or several rows or columns.

2 Place the mouse pointer on top of one of the header boundaries, and double-click.

Top-Ten Slick Trick 4: *Make Edits to More than One Worksheet*

I love computers because they do repetitive tasks automatically. One repetitive task that was left up to me on way too many occasions was to copy the same changes to multiple, similar worksheets. No more. With the new workbook and tab layout, you can select all worksheets, then simultaneously make the corrections to all worksheets. For more about selecting worksheets within a workbook, see Chapter 2, "Basic Slick Tricks." For more about editing multiple worksheets, see Chapter 3, "Worksheet Editing."

Top-Ten Slick Trick 5: *Analyze with Pivot Tables*

With Pivot Tables, you can change and rearrange data by dragging field labels with the mouse. If you skipped them because you were somewhat overwhelmed, I suggest that you go back and give them a try. They are sophisticated, very high-tech, and actually a lot of fun. See Chapter 10, "Pivot Tables." Remember that in each dialog box there is a Help button which calls topic-specific help.

Top-Ten Slick Trick 6: *Filtering Lists*

Filter a list to show a subset of the data in a list. Filtering hides all the rows that do not contain the criteria you specify. You can use AutoFilter for most filtering, but there is also an Advanced Filter command. These are both located on the Data, Filter submenu (**Alt/, D, F**). (See Chapter 8, "Lists, Tables, and Databases.")

Top-Ten Slick Trick 7: *Consolidate a List*

One feature that can save you hours of time is the Consolidation command on the Data menu. With it, you can bring in data from past reports to create new ones. For instance, you can consolidate monthly reports into quarterly, then into annual reports. The source documents can be in the same workbook, in a different workbook, or saved in a different document in a different subdirectory. They can be saved in different applications or on the Excel platform. (See Chapter 8, "Lists, Tables, and Databases.")

Top-Ten Slick Trick 8: *Create Formulas with the Function Wizard* f_x

The Function Wizard helps you step through the process of writing formulas in a worksheet. You can also turn Function Wizard into an edit wizard to display the references of each function and help you edit and debug formulas. (See Chapter 7, "Slick Tricks with Formulas.")

Top-Ten Slick Trick 9: *Rotate a 3-D Chart*

Rotating a 3-D chart may not be the chart trick you will use most, but it certainly makes me feel powerful. It's really a high-tech, fun trick. Try it. Just click on the corner of a wall in a 3-D chart and drag. (See Chapter 12, "Editing Charts.")

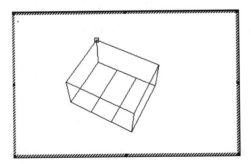

Figure 15.2 The Ghost of a Rotating Chart

Top-Ten Slick Trick 10: *The Macro Recorder*

You can record macros in VBA or in the Excel 4.0 macro language. An Excel macro can do anything that Excel can do. If there is a task which you find yourself repeating, that task is a candidate for a macro. You can attach them to buttons or to objects. You can also use the recorder to help you write your own macros or create full applications in the Excel Environment. (See Chapter 14, "Macros and Programming.")

Most Frequently Used General Shortcuts

Be sure to check out these if you are not familiar with them.

Undo—Press Ⓦ Alt+Backspace or Ⓦ Ctrl+Z Ⓜ Command+Z or click on ⤺.

Sum—Click on Σ. (See Chapter 7.)

Select all graphics—Press Ctrl+Shift+Spacebar.

To switch between showing graphics, hiding graphics, and replacing them with placeholders—Press Ⓦ Ctrl+6 Ⓜ Command+6.

Dock and undock a toolbar—Double-click on it.

Replace—Press Ctrl+H.

Apply box border—Press Ctrl+Shift+& (ampersand).

Remove all borders— Press Ctrl+Shift+_ (underscore).

Insert a range—Press Ⓦ Ctrl++ Ⓜ Command++ to insert.

Delete a range—Press Ⓦ Ctrl+- Ⓜ Command+- to delete.

Most Frequently Used Shortcuts When Writing Formulas

Function Wizard—Press Shift+F3 or click on ƒₓ.

Copy a formula from the cell above without changing the reference—Press Ctrl+ʹ.

Paste Name—Press F3, or click on 🔳.

Create Names— Press Ⓦ Ctrl+Shift+F3 Ⓜ Command+Shift+F3.

To calculate a single value in a formula—Double-click on the reference or press F9 (set calculation to manual on large worksheets/workbooks).

To calculate the workbook—press F9, or click on 🔳.

To calculate the current worksheet—press Shift+F9.

To select direct dependents— Ⓦ Press Ctrl+[Ⓜ Command+[. Or tab to Go To all selected cells if the formula is long and there are several dependents.

Go To the direct dependents, then return to original formula:

1 Turn off Edit Directly in Cell check box in Tools, Options, Edit Tab (**Alt/, T, O, E**).

2 Double-click on formulas to Go To direct dependents.

3 Press F5, Enter to Go To last location.

Appendix

Keystroke Shortcut Tables

A.1 Function Keys 254
A.2 Numbers and Characters 256
A.3 Letters 258
A.4 Scroll Lock Exceptions 259
A.5 End Mode Exceptions 259
A.6 [W] Transition Navigation Keys 260
A.7 Keys 261

Table A.1 Function Keys

Function Keys	Alone	Shift	Ctrl	Alt	Alt+Shift	Ctrl+Shift
F1	[W] Help—contents [M] Undo	Help—context sensitive		New Chart	New Worksheet	
F2	[W] Edit active cell [M] Cut	Note	Displays Info window			
F3	[W] Paste Name [M] Copy	Function Wizard	Define name			Create names
F4	[W] Repeat last action. When editing a formula, converts from relative to absolute, from absolute to mixed, from mixed to relative. [M] Paste.	Find the next occurrence of a number or text string	Close active window	Exit Excel		Find the previous occurrence of a number or text string
F5	Go To	Find	Restore window size			
F6	Next pane	Previous pane	Next window			Previous window
F7	Spell Check		Move window with arrow keys			Move window with arrow keys
F8	Extend Mode toggle	Add Mode toggle	Size window with arrow keys			Size window with arrow keys
F9	Calculate all sheets in all open windows	Calculate active sheet	Minimize Workbook with arrows			

Table A.1 *(continued)* **Function Keys**

Function Keys	Alone	Shift	Ctrl	Alt	Alt+Shift	Ctrl+Shift
F10	Activate menu bar (deactivated when Transition Navigation Keys check box is activated) (Alt,T,O)	Activates edit/formatting shortcut menu	Maximize/restore window toggle			
F11	New Chart	New Worksheet	New 4.0 macro sheet			
F12	Save As	Save	Open			Print

Table A.2 Numbers and Characters

Key	Ctrl+	Ctrl+Shift+	Function	Alt+
1	Format dialog box	Exclamation point (!)	Two decimal place format with commas	
2	Bold font **B**	At sign (@)	Time format with the hour and minute and indicate A.M. or P.M.	
3	Italic font *I*	Pound sign (#)	Date format with day, month, and year	
4	Underline	Dollar sign ($)	Currency format with two decimal places—negative numbers appear in parentheses	
5	Strikethrough	Percent sign (%)	Percentage format with no decimal places	
6	Switch between hiding objects, displaying objects, and displaying placeholders for objects	Caret (^)	Apply the exponential number format with two decimal places	
7	Show or hide the Standard toolbar	Ampersand (&)	Format outline border	
8	Show outline symbols	Asterisk (*) on main keyboard	Select current region	
9	Hide rows	Open parenthesis (	Unhide rows	

Table A.2 *(continued)* **Numbers and Characters**

Key	Ctrl+	Ctrl+Shift+	Function	Alt+
0 (zero)	Hide columns	Close parenthesis)	Unhide columns	
Plus sign (+) on numeric keypad	Insert blank cells the size of the selection 🖼️			
Minus sign (-)	Delete the selection 🖼️	Underscore (_)	Remove all borders	
Period (.)	Move clockwise to the next corner of a selection			
Apostrophe (')	Copy formula from cell above into the active cell without adjusting the reference	Quotation marks (")	Copy formula value from cell above into the active cell	Style dialog box
Single quotation mark (') (beneath the tilde ~)	Switch between formulas/values	Tilde (~)	General number format	
Colon (:)	Enters the time			
Semicolon (;)	Enters the date			
		Question mark (?)	Select next cell with cell note	
Left bracket ([)	Select direct dependents	Left upper bracket ({)	Select all dependents	
Right bracket (])	Select direct precedents	Right upper bracket (})	Select all precedents	
Backslash (\)	Select row differences	Straight slash (|)	Select column differences	

Table A.3 Letters

Key	W Ctrl+ M Command+	W Ctrl+Shift+ M Command+Shift+
A	Select the entire Worksheet	Enters function arguments if you have entered an equal sign and a valid argument.
B	Bold font [B]	
C	Copy	
D	Fill down	
F	Find	Calls Format Cells at Font tab unless Formatting toolbar is visible. If Formatting toolbar is visible, press once to jump to the Format Font Name box on the Formatting toolbar. Press a second time to call Format Cells at Font tab.
H	Replace	
I	Italic [I]	
N	New Workbook [ ]	
O	Open file [ ]	
P	Print [ ]	Jumps to Point drop-down list box on the Formatting toolbar if it is visible. If it is not visible, it opens Format Cells at Font tab.
R	Fill right	
S	Save [ ]	
V	Paste [ ]	
U	Underline [U]	
X	Cut [ ]	
Y	M Repeat last edit [ ]	
Z	Undo [ ]	

Tabel A.4 Scroll Lock Exceptions

Key	Alone	Shift+
Up/down arrows	Screen scrolls up or down one row	Becomes inoperable
Right/left arrows	Screen scrolls right or left one column	Becomes inoperable
Home	Moves to the upper left cell in a window	Selects to the upper left cell in a window
End	Moves to the lower right cell in a window	Selects to the lower right cell in a window

Tabel A.5 End Mode Exceptions

Key	Alone	Shift+
End	Turns End mode on/off	
Enter	Moves to the last cell in the current row (unavailable with Transition Navigation Keys turned on)	Extends a selection to the last cell in the current row (unavailable with Transition Navigation Keys turned on)
Arrow key	Moves by one data block within a row or column	Extends a selection to the end of the data region in the direction of the arrow
Home	Moves to the lower right corner of the worksheet	Extends a selection to the lower right corner of the worksheet

Table A.6 Ⓦ Transition Navigation Keys

Shortcuts initiated by turning on the check box in the Tools, Options (Alt, T, O) Transition Tab

Navigation Keys	Function
Ctrl+left Arrow	Left one page
Ctrl+right arrow	Right one page
Ctrl+Page Up	Next worksheet in a workbook
Ctrl+Page Down	Previous worksheet in a workbook
Tab	Right one page
Shift+Tab	Left one page
Home	Selects the cell in the upper left corner of a sheet
Function Keys	**Function**
F5	Positions the entered cell or range in the upper left corner of the window
F6	Next window of the same workbook
Shift+F6	Previous pane of the same window
In Data Find Mode	**Function**
Left arrow	Moves to the previous field of the current record
Right arrow	Moves to the next field of the current record
Home	Moves to the first record
End	Moves to the last record
Text-Alignment Prefix Characters	
Apostrophe (')	Aligns data to the left
Quotation mark (")	Aligns data to the right
Caret (^)	Centers data in the cell
Backslash (\)	Repeats characters across the cell

Table A.7 Keys

Key	Alone	Shift	Ctrl	Alt	Ctrl+Shift	Ctrl+Alt	Alt+Shift
Enter	Moves down	Moves up. (See also End+Shift+Enter on End Table.	Fills a selection of cells with the current entry	W When cell is activated—inserts a return.*	Enters a formula as an array		
Esc	Cancel a selection. When a cell is activated—cancels entry.*		W Task List dialog box from the Control menu	W Next application			W Previous application
Home	Moves to the beginning of a row. When a cell is activated—moves to the beginning of a line.*	Selects to the beginning of a row. When cell is activated—selects to the beginning of a line.*	Moves to cell A1		Extends the selection to cell A1		
End	End mode on/off (see End Table)		Goes to last (lower right) cell in worksheet				
Del	Worksheet—Clear contents. When a cell is activated —deletes the character to right.* Chart—clear series, treadlines, error bars.		When cell is activated—cuts text to the end of the line.*				

Table A.7 *(continued)* **Keys**

Key	Alone	Shift	Ctrl	Alt	Ctrl+Shift	Ctrl+Alt	Alt+Shift
Tab	Moves right	Moves left	Next Workbook window	[W] Cycles through open Windows applications—let go to switch applications	Previous workbook window	[W] When a cell is activated—inserts a tab in the cell.*	
[W] Backspace	Clears cell contents. When a cell is activated—deletes the character to the left.*			Undo—same as Ctrl+Z [↺]			
Page Up/ Page Down	Moves up or down one screen	Extends a selection up or down one screen	Moves to previous (up) or next (down) sheet in a workbook	Left (up) or right (down) one screen			
Arrows	Moves one cell in direction of arrow	Extends a selection by one cell in the direction of the arrow		Moves to the edge of current data region in direction of the arrow	Extends a selection to the edge of current data region in the direction of the arrow		Right arrow groups; left arrow ungroups
Spacebar		Selects row	Selects column	Control menu	Selects the whole Worksheet. When an object is selected, selects all objects.		

Table A.7 *(continued)* **Keys**

Key	Alone	Shift	Ctrl	Alt	Ctrl+Shift	Ctrl+Alt	Alt+Shift
Equal sign (=)	Starts a formula		Calculates all sheets in all open workbooks	Inserts AutoSum formula		[W] Displays Function Wizard after a valid function name is typed [fx]	
Num Lock	Switches numeric key pad between numbers or direction keys						

* Activate a cell by double-clicking it or [W] by selecting it and pressing F2.

Note: See Exception Tables in this appendix for the effects of Scroll Lock, End key, and Transition Navigation Keys.

Index

error, 43
@ format code, 42
3-D references, 8, 115

A

absolute references, 104
accessing menus and commands, 21
accounting number formats, 67
activate a cell,
active cell, 36, 46
    comparing to range, 127
active sheet, 14
add copied data as you paste, 50
adding with AutoSum, 119
adding buttons to toolbars, 80
additional formatting buttons, 61
adjust column width, 101
Advanced AutoFiltering, 143–147
align
    data in cells, 63
    with grid, 217
alphanumeric combinations, 42
alternate toolbar file, 83
annotations, 122
apostrophe in code, 240
arguments
    calling into a formula, 118
    defined, 116
    example, 116
    separated by commas, 116

arranging lists by sorting, 133
array formulas, 119
arrow
    on charts, 194
    on drawing toolbar, 213
auditing, 8, 120
    double names, 113
    toolbar, 123
AutoFill, 5
    formats, 70
    with a custom list, 40
    shortcut menu, 40
AutoFilter, 141
    advanced (custom criteria), 143
    new feature, 11
AutoFormats, 70
    a subtotaled list, 140
    changing chart with, 196
    chart, 179, 193
automatic,
    calculation, 122
    subtotals, 137
    styles for an outline, 93
    totals, new feature, 8
    totals within pivot tables, 174
automatically
    create names, 110
    enter decimal points, 67
    fill, 39
    filter, 141
    outline, 93
    size a text box to fit text, 221

summarize a list, 137
    total, 119
    update values in references, 104
AutoSum, 119
    on a filtered list, 147
    total the subtotals, 8
axes, 192

B

best fit
    printing, 98
    rows and columns, 62, 248
blanks
    in a filtered a list, 141
    in sorting, 133
    on a line chart, 204
borders, 58, 64–65, 250
brackets, used in formulas, 114
breaking pages, 99
    at subtotals, 140
button button, 216
Button Editor, 85
button image, 83
    adding from TipWizard, 30
    descriptions, 31
    editing, 85
    information about, 31
    new 5.0 term, 9
    removing color, 11
    shortcut menu, 84

button image (*continued*)
    with drop-down arrows, 9
buttons, *see also* toolbar buttons
    AutoSum, 119
    built-in and custom, 78
    camera, 219
    description, 80–81
    drawing, 211
    drawing selection, 214
    formatting, 58
    Format Painter, 60
    freeform and reshape, 214
    large and color, 80
    magnifying, 90
    not on built-in toolbars, 80
    not on toolbars, 61
    rearranging, reversing action, 81
    text box, 211
    used for formulas, 111

C

calculate, 251
    a formula, 121
    automatic or manual, 122
    before sorting, 134
    button, 121
    complex what-if, Solver, 159
    format vs stored value, 69
    subtotal, grand total values, 137
    options, 76
    tab, 69
    unknown value, 151
    within pivot tables, 174
camera button, 219
carriage return within a cell, 47
case sensitive
    in sorting, 136
    passwords, 26
category consolidation, 149
cell
    alignment of data within, 63
    cut, copy or paste within, 47
    deleting contents of, 52
    editing, 36, 46
    fill with same entry, 38
    getting information about, 125
    input, variable, 152–155
    limitation of characters, 211
    link with text box, 221
    naming, 107
    notes, 122
    place a tab, carriage return in, 47
    protecting, 26, 28
    references, 104
    select a work within, 47

size to precise measurement, 62
center across columns, 64
change
    a style, 73
    chart plot, 196, 200
    chart range, 208
    chart series order, 197
    chart type, 189, 196
    chart values, 203
    default chart format, 179
    default font format, 62
    defaults, editing attributes,
        75–76
    default number of sheets, 18
    Enter key action, 36
    font, point size, 59
    formats with a style, 71
    macro options or name, 237, 238
    menus with the Shift key, 22
    scenarios, 156
    view, 76, 91
changing cells, 156–161
characters
    formatting, 63
    limit within a cell, 47, 211
chart
    3-D, 185, 187, 203
    add items to, 189
    AutoFormats, 193
    axes, 192
    blanks on a line chart, 204
    changing, 196–208
    combining types, 192, 205
    copy data between, 199
    copy format between, 207
    copying, 196
    creating, 178
    custom formatting, drawing on,
        194
    data labels, 190
    default format, 179
    defined, 177
    embed an existing, 195
    embedded, 182
    filtered list, pivot table, 180
    formatting, 207
    gridlines and legend, 191
    move and size items, 185, 201
    options, 76
    parts, and figure, 186–187
    secondary axis, 192
    selecting, 184, 186, 196
    sheet, 178
    sizing on a sheet, 206
    templates, 178
    titles, 190
    treadlines and error bars, 193

types and subtypes, 177, 188
    spelling, 202
ChartWizard, 178, 181
    used for editing, 196
clear, defined, 53
    all formats, 69
    the contents of a cell, 53
clock, 43
cloned worksheet, 15, 55
code
    capture with macro recorder, 239
    changing into comments, 240
    inserting text, 239
    new date or time, 43
    samples, 243
color
    apply, 64, 218
    on toolbar buttons, 80
    options, 76
column
    best fit to contents, 62
    centering text across, 64
    differences, 127
    entering a reference to, 107
    field within a pivot table, 167
    fill by double-clicking, 39
    formatting contents, 66
    grouping, 92
    headings, printing, 98
    hiding, 62, 91, 140
    insert or delete, 54
    named, used in formula, 109
    records in a database, 129
    selecting, 33
    shortcut menu, 92
    size to precise measurement, 62
    sorting, 136
    used as titles on pages, 140
    width, 61
combining chart types, 205
combining formats with a style, 71
commas to separate arguments, 116
comparing ranges, 127
consolidating data, 148–149, 249
constraint value, 159
converting
    imported graphic to simple,
        229
    imported text into a table, 147
copy, 50
    a format with Format Painter, 9
    and link, 50
    and paste data onto a chart, 198
    between applications, 12,
        226–227
    button image, 83
    charts, 196

data and objects, 223, 225
data between charts, 199
data table, within, 156
drag and drop, 48–49
filtered data, 145
format between charts, 207
formula, 250
formula without adjusting, 107
pivot table, 170
relative references, 105
sheets, 17
shortcuts, 49
toolbar buttons, 81
value of a formula, 105
within a cell, 47
Copy Picture command, 219
create
  new workbook, 18
  formulas, 104
  names, 110, 251
  new toolbar, 80–82
  scenario, 157
  view, 88
custom
  AutoFiltering, 143
  calculations within pivot table, 174
  chart AutoFormats, 194
  criteria filtering with, 142
  date or time format, 43
  formatting on charts, 194
  lists, 5, 40–41, 76
  number formats, 68
  sort order, 135
  toolbars, 80, 83, 86
Customize dialog box, 84
cut, 50
  between applications, 12
  data and objects, 225
  relative references, 105
  within a cell, 47
cycle through tabs, 16

D

data
  aligning in cells, 63
  analyze with pivot table, 163
  between applications, 227
  consolidating, 148
  copy between charts, 199
  entering, 5
  entering and deleting, 36
  formatting numbers, 66
  importing and exporting, 225
  parse, 147

restore chart/worksheet links, 202
  used for chart, 180
data labels, chart, 190
data point selecting, 186
data series, adding or changing, 198
data table, 152–155
database
  naming a list as, 130
  setting up (list), 129
  used in pivot tables, 163
dataform, 130–132
dates
  entering automatically, 42
  entering in formulas, 44
  filling with, 38
  instead of a fraction, 69
DDE, 227
decimal places, 67, 69
decision variables, 159
default
  changing, 75
  changing number of sheets, 18
  chart format, 179
  font format, 62
  number of sheets in a workbook, 14
  toolbar settings, 83
Define Name dialog box, 108, 110
delete
  button, 5
  custom toolbars, 83
  data, 36
  defined, 53
  formats, 69
  key action, 5
  objects, 223
  outlining, 94
  range, 250
  record with a dataform, 132
  scenario, 158
  sheets, 18
  sheets with shortcut menu, 17
  shortcuts, 52–54
  style, 73
  view, 88
  with the fill handle, 39
delimited column, 147
dependents, 8, 123
  defined, 123
  finding with Go To Special, 127
  formulas, 157
  select all, 127
  selecting direct, 251
dialog sheets, 12, 232
disappearing tabs, 24
display
  changing, 76
  formulas instead of values, 121

macro, 237
distribute data, 147
docking toolbars, 78–79, 250
documents, in Find File, 21
dollar signs, 104
double names, 113
double-click
  not in Go To box, 7
  to fill a column, 39
draft quality, 98
drawing
  on charts, 194
  selection button, 218, 222
  text boxes, 220
  tools, 211
duplicate records, filtering, 146
Dynamic Data Exchange (DDE), 227

E

edit
  button image, 85
  cell, 36
  changing attributes, 76
  charts, 196
  data table, 155
  embedded objects, 12, 228
  macro, 236
  multiple sheets, 15, 55
  objects, 222
  pivot table, 170
  shortcut menu, 48, 53
  within cells, 46
Editing Function dialog box, 119
embed
  chart, 178, 182
  existing chart, 195
  objects or a Word 6.0 document, 227
Enter key action, 4, 9, 36, 132
entering
  array formulas, 119
  data, 5, 36–38
  date in a formula, 44
  dates and times, 42
  decimal points automatically, 67
  formulas and error alert, 120
  mixed fractions, 69
  numbers as text, 42
  reference to row or column, 107
equal sign
  used for AutoSum, 119
  used in formulas, 103
error bars on charts, 193
error codes in Help, 103

error in formula alert, 120
error tracers, 8, 123
Excel 4.0 macro language, 232
Excel 4.0 menu format, 3
Excel startup folder, 21
exchanging data, 227
exclamation point in formulas, 114
existing files, opening, 19
exporting, 12, 225
external precedents, dependents, 124

F

fields, 129–131
file format comparisons, 19
file
    open multiple, 21
    opening, 19–20
fill cells, fill handle, 38–39
fill patterns, 218
filter
    blanks and non-blanks, 141
    duplicate records, 146
    subtotaled list, 147
    with AutoFilter, 141, 248
    with custom criteria, 142
filtered list
    adding subtotals to, 139
    charting from, 180
    printing, 147
    using AutoSum, 147
Find, 35, 238
fit cell to size of contents, 62
fit screen to size of selection, 89
fixed decimals, entering, 67
floating toolbar, 78
font
    changing, 59
    changing default format, 62
    name box, 57
    tab (Format dialog box), 57
    True Type, 221
footers and headers, 98
format
    accounting, 67
    AutoFill, 70
    AutoFormats, 70
    charts, 207
    dates and times, 42
    default chart, 179
    default font, 62
    dialog box, 57
    individual characters, 8
    multiple sheets simultaneously, 15
    numbers, 66, 68

numbers macro, 234
numbers as scientific, 42
objects, 222
pasting, 50, 114
pivot table, 170
remove all, 69
styles, 71
text, 63
text boxes, 220
toolbar, 58–60
value vs stored value, 69
with a toolbar button, 59
with the mouse, 60
Format Painter, 9, 60, 247
formula, 117
    affected by deleting, 52
    array, 119
    auditing, 120
    AutoSum, 119
    brackets used in, 114
    calculate all or part, 121
    defined, 103
    dependent, 157
    displayed instead of values, 121
    entering dates, 44
    exclamation point in, 114
    external references, 114
    frequent shortcuts, 250
    intersected named references, 109
    linking, 119
    paste the value of, 50, 113
    pasting a name, 112
    point to cells, 104
    toolbar buttons, 111
Formula bar, 37
    and formulas, 103
    auditing clues in, 120
    check mark, 36
    name and Go To box, 34
    typing in, 37
fractions, entering as mixed, 69
freeform button, 214
freeze panes, 23
Function Wizard, 7, 117, 249, 118
functions
    defined, 116
    uppercase, type in lowercase, 117
    listed on-line, 12

G

Goal Seek, 151–152
global
    formatting with a style, 71
    macros, 234

Go To, 7, 34–35
    a named range, 108
    dialog box, 35, 108
Go To Special, 35
    precedents and dependents, 127
graphics, 209
    name, 218
    selecting, 221
    sorting, or excluding from, 136
    text boxes, 220
graphs, 177
great reversos, 51, 81, 90, 114, 126, 135, 217, 246
gridlines
    chart, 191
    printing, 98
    removing, 66
group and ungroup
    objects, 223
    rows or columns, 92
    within pivot tables, 175

H

headers and footers, 98
headings, keeping on the screen, 23
height of row, 61
hide
    by filtering, 141
    formulas, 28
    graphics, 210
    outlining, 94
    ranges, 122
    rows or columns, 62, 91, 149
    within a pivot table, 172
horizontal scroll bar, 16

I

importing, 12, 225
    text, convert to a table, 147
increase decimal places, 69
independent chart sheet, 184
Info window, 113, 124–125
information about a cell, 125
information about button images, 31
input cell, 152
insert
    4.0 macro sheet, 17
    chart sheet, 17
    object command, 227
    one or more worksheets, 17
    page breaks, 99
    picture, 229
    range, 250

sheets with shortcut menu, 17
shortcuts, 53
subtotals, 138
text into code, 239
using the shortcut menu, 54
Insert Cells button, 54
interactive worksheet, 163
interrupt a macro, 236
invisible tabs, 24
invisible toolbars, 78

J

jump
through name list, 112
to font and point lists, 59
justifying text, 63

K

keys, disabled, 214

L

languages, macro, 232
large toolbar buttons, 11, 80
legend, 191, 201, 208
line chart, omit blanks, 204
lines, on charts, 194
link
chart text to the worksheet, 201
object, 225
formulas and workbooks, 119
text box, 220–221
to chart, restoring, 202
to copied data, 50
updating, 228
list
adding subtotals to a filtered, 139
automatically summarizing, 137
charting from a filtered, 180
defined, 129
filling with, 38
filtering, 141
naming, 130
naming it database, 130
of names in workbook, 112
of variable values, 152
pivot table, 163
setting up, 129
sort by custom, 135
sorting, 133
using AutoSum on a filtered, 147

long distances, scrolling, 19
Lotus 1-2-3 transition, 76
lowercase when typing formulas, 117

M

macro
4.0 language, 232, 244
attach to button, 85, 216
attach to toolbar button, 241
changing shortcut key, 238
defined, 231
displaying, 237
editing, 236
interrupt, 236
name, 233, 237
recorder, relative or absolute, 235
recording, 12, 231, 233, 250
running, 235
saving, 233
to enter numbers as text, 42
to wrap text, 242
magnify the view, 88
magnifying buttons, 90
manual page breaks, 99
margins, 100
mathematical operation, paste, 50
mathematical operators, formulas, 103
measurement of row or column, 62
merging styles, 72
mixed fractions, 69
mixed references, 104
modifying a style, 73
mouse
and formulas, 104, 111, 114
change values on a chart, 203
draw with, 214
hide or unhide, 91
moving pivot table fields, 172
scrolling, 18
move
among unlocked cells, 28
between applications, 226
between tabs, 2
by drag and drop, 46, 48
chart data series, 198
chart items, 201
field within a pivot table, 172
from sheet to sheet, 16
from tab to tab, 16
objects, 223
sheets, 17
shortcuts, 49

toolbar buttons, 81
toolbars, 78, 79
within workbooks, 2
multiple sheets
edit, 55
formatting, 15
in pivot tables, 163
moving or copying, 18
printing, 100

N

name
apply, 109
area, 7, 19, 34
cell and range, 14, 107
created with worksheet titles, 110
creating and pasting, 251
display a list of, 34
double, 113
example of using, 154
in a pivot table, 170
in the workbook displayed
graphic, 218
macro and procedure, 233
pasting, 112
reference, 104, 107, 109
sheet, 14
using, 117
within a workbook, 2
without a home, 110
nested subtotals, 138
New Data command, 198
nonadjacent cells selecting, 34
nonadjacent range, filling, 37
NonBlanks in a filtered list, 141
noncontiguous data for chart, 180
noncontiguous sheets, selecting 15, 55
notes, 122
printing, 98
text boxes, 220
number
accounting format, 67
as text, 42
custom formats, 68
format vs stored value, 69
formatting, 66
macro to format as text, 234
of characters in a cell, 47
of default sheets, changing, 18
scientific format, 42
tab, 58
within formulas, 103

O

objective cells, 159
objects, 209, 223
    attaching macros, 240
    converting from embedded, 229
    copying, deleting and resizing, 223
    cut, copy and sort with data, 225
    editing embedded, 228
    formatting, 222
    moving, 223
    OLE, 225–227
    on charts, 194
    overlapping, 223
    round corners and shadows, 224
    selecting, 34, 221–222
    size change with worksheet, 224
outline
    and automatic totals, 137
    removing with subtotals, 141
optional passwords, 27
Options, quick reference, 75
ordinal, filling with, 38
outlines, 93–96
overlapping margins and data, 100

P

page breaks, 99
    at subtotals, 140
    within a pivot table, 173
Page Setup, 96–97
pages, printing selected, 99
painting formats, 60
palettes, tear-off, 9, 65
panes, 22–23
panoramic views, 91
parentheses, in formulas, 120
parse, defined, 147
passwords, 26
paste, 83
    between applications, 12
    formats, 50, 114
    link, 50
    mathematical operation, 50
    name, 111–112, 251
    relative references, 105
    value of formulas, 50, 113–114
    within a cell, 47
Paste Special, 50, 155
    linking with, 227
    on a chart, 198
patterns
    apply, 64

changing chart legend, 208
    fill with, 218
    making more vivid, 66
Personal Macro Workbook, 234
phone numbers, 42
picture
    inserting, 229
    taken with camera button, 219
pie charts, sizing plot area, 185
pivot table, 163
    automatic subtotals, 174
    chart, 180
    defined, 163
    editing, 170
    moving a field within, 172
    updating, 169
PivotTable Wizard, 12, 164
placeholders, 210, 126
plotting a chart, 180
    changing, 196
    area, sizing, 185
point size, changing, 59
point to cells, create formulas, 104
pointing to external references, 114
polygon, 214
position consolidation, 149
pound signs (#), 43
precedents, 8, 123
    defined, 123
    finding with Go To Special, 127
    select all, 127
Precision As Displayed, 69
preparing a list for subtotals, 137
preparing to sort, 133
prevent workbook from saved, 26
preview a document in Find file, 21
previewing before you print, 25
previous version, 58
print, 25, 95
    area, 96
    best fit, 98
    borders, 66
    faster, sharper, 98
    filtered list, 147
    headers and footers, headings, 98
    in text boxes, 221
    report, 102
    screen attributes, 98
    subtotaled list, 140
    speed up, 210
    view or scenario, 102
    workbooks, multiple sheets, 99–100
Print Preview, 25
    adjustments to margins, 101
problems in formulas, 123
procedure, defined, 232

procedure name, 233
programming, 12, 231–244
prompt for Summary Info, 77
proportional sizing, 217
protect a workbook, 26
protect a worksheet, 27
protect individual cells, 28

R

range
    changing plot of chart, 200
    entering data into, 37
    insert or delete, 250
    naming, 107
    references, 104
rearrange
    data within a pivot table, 163
    items in a pivot table, 172
    toolbar buttons, 81
    margins in Print Preview, 100
recording macros, 231–241
    attach a macro, 241
    capture detailed code, 239
    relative or absolute, 235
records
    using a dataform, 131–132
    filtering duplicate, 146
redefining a style, 72
references
    3-D, 115
    copy without adjusting, 107
    defined, 104
    intersected named, 109
    linking, 119
    list of names, 112
    named, 107
    named using titles, 110
    relative, 104–105
    remote, 122
    to entire row or column, 107
    to other sheets and workbooks, 114
    with double names, 113
    within formulas, 103, 104
rename
    chart sheet, 184
    fields in a pivot table, 169
    sheets, 15
repeat, 45
    AutoFormats, 70
    formats with a style, 71
    tasks with macros, 232
replace, 238
    subtotals, 141
report, creating, printing, 102
    scenario summary, 158, 159

required arguments, 116
resetting built-in toolbars, 83
resize objects, 223
restore toolbars, 83
reverse fill action, 39
reversos, *see* great reversos
rotate 3-D charts, 203, 249
round object corners, 224
row
    as records in a database, 129
    best fit to contents, 62
    differences, 127
    entering reference to, 107
    field within a pivot table, 167
    formatting contents, 66
    grouping, 92
    headings, printing, 98
    height, 61, 91
    hidden, 62
    insert or delete, 54
    named, used in formula, 109
    selecting, 33
    shortcut menu, 92
    sorting, 136
    used as titles on pages, 140
run a macro, 235

S

samples of code, 243
save
    custom toolbar settings, 83
    files, 26
    macro, 234
    workspace, 29
scenario
    deleting, 158
    printing, 102
Scenario Manager, 156
scientific format of numbers, 42
screen
    full, 9
    printing attributes, 98
scroll bar making more visible, 16
scrolling
    long distances, to end, 5, 19
    tools, figure, 20
    with the mouse, 18
scrolling buttons, tab, 16
secondary Axis, 192
select, 33, 55
    all, 17, 97
    a word within a cell, 47
    all sheets or tabs, 55
    chart and chart items, 184, 186,
        196

contiguous sheets, 15, 55
    direct dependents, 251
    large area, 34
    nonadjacent cells, 34
    noncontiguous sheets, 15
    objects, 221
    when sorting, 137
Select Special command, 35
selected pages, printing, 99
set a print area, 96
shading, 64, 211
shadows on objects, 224
Shape button, shapes, 211, 212
sheet
    active, 14
    chart, 178
    shortcut menu, 17
    tabs disappeared, 24
sheets, 14
    changing number of default, 18
    compared to files, 13
    contained in workbooks, 13
    deleting, 18
    edit and format multiple, 15, 55
    insert, copy and delete, 17
    moving and copying, 16–18
    renaming, 15
    selecting, 15, 55
Shift key, change menus with, 4, 22
Shift key when sizing, 217
shortcut menu
    Edit, 53–54
    Edit/Format, 48
shortcut key, macro, 236, 238
shortcut menus
    button image, 84
    chart, 185
    object, 222
    rows and columns, 92
    tab sheet, 17
    title, 22
    toolbar, 30, 78
    workbook, 89
    VBA, 243
shortcuts
    for inserting and deleting, 53
    frequently used, 250
    moving and copying, 49
size
    and holding down keys, 217
    cell to precise measurement, 62
    charts, 185
    chart items, 201
    chart sheet chart, 206
    objects affected by worksheet,
        224
    of print, font, 57

Solver, 159
sort, 133–137
    data and objects, 225
spelling check, 55
    on charts, 202
split, window, 16, 23–24
spreadsheet
    calculate, 122
    opening a former version, 20
    protect, 27
spreadsheets
    edit multiple, 55
    opening from other programs,
        19
    referring to other in formulas,
        114
Standard toolbar, 9, 78, 211, 246
startup folder or directory, 21
status bar
    calculate, 122
    descriptions of buttons, 80
    recording message, 233
stored value vs formatted value, 69
straight lines, 217
structure, protecting, 27
styles, 71
subtotals, automatic, 137–141
    within pivot tables, 174
summary function
    defined, 167
    more than one, 139
    within a pivot table, 167
Summary Info, 21, 29
summary report, 158
suspended operation, 82

T

tab, place within a cell, 47
table
    and lists, 129
    converting imported text into,
        147
    dialog box, 153
    data, 152
    pivot, 163
tear-off palettes, 9, 65
template
    chart, 178
    open when you start Excel, 21
text
    aligning, 63
    centering across columns, 64
    entering, 5
    entering numbers as, 42
    formatting, 63

text (*continued*)
over 255 characters, 47
wrapping and justifying, 63
text box, 211
defined, 220
used to write notes, 123
link with cell, 221
on charts, 194
printing, 221
TextWizard, 12, 147
tick marks, 191
time
entering automatically, 42
new code, 43
TipWizard, 6, 29–30
titles
adding, 98
chart, 190
used as names, 110
toolbar
buttons used for formulas, 111
creating a new, 82
positions and attributes, 79
shortcut menu, 78
toolbar buttons, 9, 80–85
attach a macro, 85, 241
copying, 83
descriptions, 81
drawing, 211
editing, 85
formatting with, 58–59
larger, 11
used for formulas, 111
toolbars
chart type, 197
customizing, 80–83
customized example, 246
docking, 78–79, 250
drawing, 211
formatting, 58
Microsoft applications, 226
moving, 78
shortcut menu, 30
Standard, 78, 211
visible at a new session, 31
Visual Basic, 232
Workgroup, 157
toolface, tools, *see* button image or
toolbar buttons

ToolTips, 6, 31, 59, 80
totals
automatic, 137
within a pivot table, 168
transition from 4.0 macros, 244
from other spreadsheets, 76
tracer arrows, 8, 123–126
transpose, 51
trendlines on charts, 193
True Type Fonts, 221
tutorial helpers, 6, 29

U

Undo, 45, 50, 250
chart AutoFormats, 194
rotation of a chart, 203
subtotals, 141
update pivot table, 169
update links, 228

V

variables, 151, 155, 157
decision, 159
views, 87
changing, 76, 91
creating, 88
deleting, 88
magnifying, 89
printing, 102
switching to, 88
Visual Basic (VBA), 12, 231–232

W

what-if, 152–159
wildcard characters, 45
wizard, *see* specific
Word 6.0 document, embedding,
227
word, select within a cell, 47
workbook, 13
attaching custom toolbars, 86
closing, 24
concept introduced, 1

creating by dragging a tab, 18
figure, 2
filename extensions, 19
Find and Replace throughout, 44
linking formulas, 119
list of names, 112
open when you start Excel, 21
opening a new, 19
opening two of the same, 23
options, 76
preventing without a password, 26
printing all, 100
protecting, 26
referring to other in formulas,
114
shortcut menu, 89
windows, switching between, 23
Workgroup toolbar, 157
worksheet
calculate, 122
edit multiple, 55
getting around quickly on, 35
linking text to chart, 201
opening, 19–20
options, 76
outlining, 93
printing all or part, 97
protecting, 26–27
saved within a workbook, 1
selecting, 33
splitting on the screen, 23
titles used for naming, 110
workspace attributes, 75
workspace, saving, 29
wrapping text, 63, 236, 242
WYSIWIG, 221

X

XLSTART subdirectory, 21

Z

zoom, 89–90
on a chart, 201
when drawing, 217